THOMAS WILLIAM HEYCK

D0914630

THE DIMENSIONS
OF BRITISH RADICALISM
The Case of Ireland
1874-95

UNIVERSITY OF ILLINOIS PRESS

Urbana   Chicago   London

©1974 by the Board of Trustees of the University of Illinois
Manufactured in the United States of America

LIBRARY OF CONGRESS CATALOGING IN PUBLICATION DATA

Heyck, Thomas William, 1938–
    The dimensions of British Radicalism; the case of
Ireland, 1874–95.

    A revision of the author's thesis, University of
Texas at Austin, 1969.
    Bibliography: p.
    1. Irish question.   2. Radicalism—Great Britain—
History.   I. Title.
DA957.H4   1974   320.9'42'081   74-11247
ISBN 0-252-00423-X

Acknowledgments

I am deeply indebted to a number of people who assisted me in the preparation of this work. First on the list must be Professors Stanford Lehmberg and Standish Meacham, who were my thesis supervisors at the University of Texas. Surely no Ph.D. student has had more cordial, cooperative attention than those two men gave me. Professors James C. Curtis, Anthony Esler, and James J. Sheehan also read the work in its earliest, most unpalatable form; their suggestions were crucial to the revision which followed. Professors Lacey Baldwin Smith, Walter Arnstein, John R. McLane, Lawrence McCaffrey, and Emmet Larkin gave the revised manuscript typically shrewd and helpful critiques. Professor Bill Klecka helped immeasurably with the quantitative analyses. Of course, I can blame only myself for the inaccuracies and blemishes that remain.

To the University of Texas and Northwestern University are due thanks for financial support for my research, and to Northwestern again for support of publication. My father and mother, Mr. and Mrs. Joseph G. Heyck, greatly helped finance the research, and generally assisted me in ways far beyond the call of parental duty. Flt. Lt. and Mrs. Mike Findlay helped by being splendid friends, hosts, and teachers of English ways. Dr. and Mrs. Marshal Levine encouraged me to begin the final lap when the course looked very gloomy. But greatest thanks go to my wife, Denis, who put up with this project and delayed her own work with remarkably good humor, and who edited, typed, and listened to more readings of the manuscript than she would like to remember. My son, Hunter, aged three and one-half, graciously restrained himself from tearing up my notes.

Evanston, Illinois

May 1973

Introduction

This book was written to shed light on the history of British Radicalism. Indeed, it is essentially an extended essay in definition of the late-Victorian Radical movement in its historical context. The book has contributions to make in a number of areas—the history of Anglo-Irish relations, the formation of British policy toward Ireland, and the history of the Liberal party. The reader, however, should bear in mind that the central intent of this work is to explain what kind of people the late-Victorian Radicals were, and to understand the movement they formed. The argument proceeds first by defining and analyzing briefly the personnel, structure, and ideas of Radicalism in the 1870's and early 1880's; then it explores further, to the limits of Radicalism, by testing the movement in action against the various aspects of the Irish Question.

An understanding of Radicalism is appropriate because Radicals were extremely important to the social and political history of the nineteenth century, but they have not yet been the subject of thorough analytical treatment by historians. Radicalism could be regarded as the irresistible force in nineteenth-century Britain, for the constitution of state and society seemed inexorably to move in the Radical direction. Much of the political history of the century can be interpreted as the attempts by Radicals to move the kingdom toward political democracy and the rationalization of state and society, against the efforts by conservatives to stop, delay, or moderate them. However, the major work on the Radicals, a six-volume compendium by S. Maccoby, is anything but analytical. Maccoby's thick tomes present mountains of largely undigested facts, yet never define Radicalism itself. The latest comprehensive work, John W.

Derry's *The Radical Tradition*, raises the question of defining Radicalism, but fails to come to grips with it; the reader learns only that Radicals intended to get at the root of things, and is then left with a highly selective set of biographical sketches. Recently, a few good monographs have appeared on the early history of the movement—such as those by George Rudé, Gwyn Williams, and Joel Wiener —but there is nothing comparable for the late-Victorian period, for which one must resort to biographies.

This volume tries to remedy the deficiency by reconstructing the personnel, structure, values, and ideas of late-Victorian Radicalism. A computer analysis of voting in the House of Commons is used to pick out the Radical Members of Parliament as a gateway into the movement as a whole. The result shows the Radicals to have been a very diverse and often idiosyncratic group of people; their policies and organizations lacked unity and often conflicted with each other. The late-Victorian Radicals did not make up a party, in the sense of a centralized organization with acknowledged leaders, whips, and registered members. Indeed, several attempts by Radicals to form a party, as in the past, came to nothing. Few Radicals could agree on the priority they would assign to various parts of the Radical program, and they frequently competed among themselves to gain primacy for their particular policies. These factors go a long way toward explaining the characteristic ineffectiveness of the late-Victorian Radicals, even after the number and influence of Radical M.P.'s increased within the Liberal party in the 1880's.

Yet the disorganization of Radicalism does not mean that there was no central area of agreement, no common denominator to the movement. There was, after all, a definable something called Radicalism, of which the touchstones were not so much bills and resolutions presented in parliament, as a family of ideas about British society as it existed and as it ought to exist. Radicals agreed that Britain was still dominated by certain types of privilege left from the past, and they agreed that vested interests in church, state, and society ought to be destroyed. They agreed on the identity of the enemy—Anglican, landowning society. Further, the Radicals held in common a set of values, and they shared an essentially utilitarian habit of thought. Thus their values, ideas, and behavior distinguished them not only from Whigs and Conservatives but also from the more moderate Liberals, though to a decreasing degree as Liberalism in the 1880's and 1890's came to resemble Radicalism. In other words the Radicals made up, not a party, but a *persuasion* of considerable distinctiveness and significance.

To leave the analysis of Radicalism at that point would be to define the movement in its own terms and leave too much unsaid. It would forget the limitations of assumptions and prejudices which were as much a part of Radicalism as the more positive programs. And it would miss the wealth of interactions between social forces, ideas, and actual situations which constitute the full meaning of any political movement. Here is where the Irish Question contributes, not only to the history of Radicalism, but also to its definition. The Irish Question acted as a kind of surgical knife on Radicalism, cutting through the rhetoric of professed ideals and laying bare the nerve system and bone structure of the entire movement. It established the limits, the dimensions, of Radicalism.

Why did Ireland, of all issues, most effectively cut into Radicalism? Other issues could be offered as analytical tools—the social problem, for one. But Ireland seems most appropriate, partly because the Irish Question was the biggest issue in late-Victorian politics, as perhaps it had been for most of the century. If Radicalism was the irresistible force of British politics, Ireland was the immovable object. Dealing with it inevitably made up a major part of Radical history. The Irish Question was crucial also because Ireland—an agrarian, Catholic society—was nicely calculated to test the heavy burden of preconceptions, prejudices, and principles developed by Radicals in their essentially middle-class, industrial environment.

The Irish Question worked as an analytical tool mainly because of the form it took in the late nineteenth century. In the years from 1874 to 1895, which spanned the rise and fall of the Parnellite party, Irishmen presented their demands in two different modes: confrontation and cooperation. The response of the Radicals to these different strategies tells much about them. Confrontation with the Irish, which lasted through 1885, caused most Englishmen to stiffen their resistance to Irish aspirations, but not the Radicals. Despite a great deal of revealing argument within the movement, Radicals ultimately reacted more favorably to confrontation than to cooperation. This raises crucial questions about the Radicals: why were they more vulnerable (or amenable, according to one's point of view) than other politicians to the confrontation strategy? Why were they not amenable to persuasion by the Irish, when Radical political principles logically should have led them to the Irish position? What were the inner dynamics of the Radical movement which produced Radical attitudes and policies toward Irish issues? To what extent was the Radical response to confrontation and cooperation the product on the one hand of something essential to the nature of Radicalism and on the other of situational factors? The answers to such questions will help establish the boundaries of Radicalism and illustrate the functioning of the Radical movement and mind.

The study of Radical behavior during the long Irish crisis ultimately shows the "stuff" of Radicalism—what the Radical personnel were really like, how their organizational structure worked and changed in a real situation, and what the Radicals meant by Radical programs and policies. The concept of what a program or set of principles means *in action* to a political movement is an important defining point. George Eliot, in *Middlemarch*, brilliantly contrasts an individual's ideas and self-image with the way they lie in the minds of others. The study of Radicalism in action with Irish nationalism reveals something of the same category: how ideas and self-conceptions functioned in the minds of the Radicals—how they were interpreted, applied, restricted, and limited. A persuasion, after all, is more than articulated objectives and rationales; it is also the psychological and cultural element in which all the parts of a movement operate.

Joseph Chamberlain's powerful and ubiquitous presence in these pages should cause no surprise. He was the kind of man who could crystallize issues, who never hesitated to propose solutions, and who pushed himself to the center of attention. Obviously, he was vitally important to the formation of the Radical response to the Irish crisis, and his reactions to a point expressed the feelings of many Radicals. But his actions in splitting both the Liberal party and its Radical faction over Home Rule can be overestimated. This book tries to correct some misconceptions about his role in these matters. The Irish crisis did not spell the demise of the Liberal party by stripping it of its Radical elements, nor in the end did Chamberlain's behavior symbolize the attitudes of most Radicals. When the moment of truth came, Chamberlain was revealed as a man quite different from the bulk of the Radicals: their dimensions and his did not coincide.

Contents

THE DIMENSIONS OF BRITISH RADICALISM

CHAPTER ONE

The Nature of
Late-Victorian Radicalism

In 1878 the Whig G. C. Brodrick warned that the proposal for Home Rule would win a popular vote in Ireland and that "on strictly Radical principles no sufficient answer [i.e., refutation] can be given to the demand for a *plebiscite* in Ireland, whereas the Whigs, having defended constitutional liberty against a Tory populace in one country, are in a position to defend it against a Fenian populace in another."[1] Besides giving a particularly striking statement of the Whig view of history, this remark reveals an assumption common among politically orthodox Victorians—that the principles of Radicalism inevitably led to support for the demands of Irish nationalists. The truth of the matter, however, was far more complex. This fact was recognized by the Duke of Marlborough in 1886; he argued that the British Radicals and Irish Home Rulers differed on many fundamental issues: "The only point of contact between the Irish Parliamentary groups and the Radicals, exists in the desire, which is common to both, of spoliating the classes in the interest of the proletariat: to effect a general redistribution of capital, either of land or of other forms of wealth, is the first object of both these sections."[2]

Despite some differences, these two observations bear similar inferences about late-Victorian politics. One is that Irish nationalism and British Radicalism were movements to be feared by the traditional rulers of Britain. Another is that the relations and connections between the two would be of grave consequence to British

1. "Liberals and Whigs," *Fortnightly Review* 137 (May 1878), 734. (*Fortnightly Review* is hereafter abbreviated *F.R.*)
2. "Political Crossroads," *F.R.* 40 (August 1886), 147.

politics and society. Further, the two remarks suggest that essential, vital characteristics of Radicalism determined the response of Radicals to the Irish Question. Finally, they show by their different views of Radicalism that these central features were a matter of confusion and misunderstanding.

Here in microcosm is the problem for this study. In the late Victorian years, the paths of British Radicalism and the Irish Question met at the crossroads. Ireland had provided for Britain an unwelcome series of difficulties for centuries, and especially since the act of union. In the 1870's, with the formation of the Home Rule party, the Irish Question demanded attention from every part of the British political spectrum; and in the 1880's, with the rise of the highly disciplined Parnellite faction, it dominated British politics. The Radical movement, meanwhile, seemed about to reach maturity and bear fruit in legislation designed to achieve long-standing Radical goals. The Radical response to the Irish Question would be of great importance to the events of Radical history, and it would be equally important in revealing the full nature of Radicalism. How would Radicals react to the various aspects of the Irish Question? How would they be changed, if at all, by confronting this major political and constitutional problem? What characteristics of the movement would stand out under the pressure applied by Irishmen?

To begin answering these questions, one must first understand the meaning of Radicalism in the 1870's, and how Radicals had reacted to Ireland before this vital period. The problem of defining Radicalism is not easy. One might think that the solution is to name the policies in the Radical program and call them Radicalism, but as R. K. Webb has written, this method is "plagued by difficulties" arising from the perplexing variety of Radical programs, which tend to "make a meaningless hodge-podge of Radicalism."[3] While it is important to notice specific Radical policies, it is important also to define the Radical turn of mind and approach to problems. In this regard, it is helpful to recall that Gladstone once said Radicals were people who were in earnest.[4] But there must have been something

3. R. K. Webb, *Harriet Martineau: A Radical Victorian* (New York, 1960), 363.

4. John Morrison Davidson, *Eminent Radicals in Parliament* (London, 1879), 1.

else—for it would be wrong to regard him as a Radical, yet he was at least as earnest as anyone else. Matthew Arnold singled out their doctrinaire attributes: "Violent indignation with the past, abstract systems of renovation applied wholesale, a new doctrine drawn up in black and white for elaborating down to the very smallest details a rational society for the future. . . ."[5] This unfriendly description accurately catches something of the forceful spirit of Radicals, the tendency to apply principles rigidly whatever the situation, but it distorts the portrait by making Radicals too intellectual and rational. Like all political movements, Victorian Radicalism conveyed a meaning implicitly tied to historical circumstances; it was a core of historically evolved characteristics shared by all Radicals. Elusive as it was, that central family of attributes constituted the meaning of Radicalism.

By the 1870's the meaning of British Radicalism had been established through a process of historical accretion. Having descended from the seventeenth-century Levellers through the Wilkite movement, English Jacobinism, Philosophic Radicalism, Chartism, the Anti–Corn Law League, and militant Nonconformity, the Radical program—admittedly in various formulations—aimed at establishing political democracy (for men), and at breaking the privileges and power of Anglicanism and the landed orders. The Radical habit of thought was both utilitarian and moralistic, inclined toward simplistic application of principles. The structure of the Radical movement, faulted at its very base by a potentially wide chasm between middle- and working-class elements, was held together by an essentially middle-class Nonconformist ideal accepted by politically active workingmen during the mid-Victorian years: a society entirely free from traditional privilege, open to the rise of prudent, self-made men, and operating in every aspect by competition. Radicals differed from Conservatives and Whigs in their hostility to the landed orders, their dislike of tradition, and their ardent impatience with existing institutions. They differed from moderate Liberals in their analysis of society and in their perception of what must be done to bring it to the ideal state. Liberals believed in preserving a balance

5. Matthew Arnold, *Culture and Anarchy*, ed. J. D. Wilson (Cambridge, 1960), 65–66.

of interests and forces in society, and in providing opportunities for individual development, but they thought that by the 1870's only relatively minor reforms needed to be made to achieve these ends. Radicals, however, characteristically saw British society as still dominated by the traditional landed elite. Cobden, for instance, once complained that "we are the only nation where feudalism with its twin monopolies, landed and ecclesiastical, is still in power."[6] Such an analysis, unrestrained by reverence for tradition and custom, demanded immediate and extensive legislation, not to establish a balance of social forces, but to bring about a predominance of middle-class values, styles, and institutions.[7]

I

After 1867 the number of men in parliament who behaved according to the Radical persuasion grew to serious proportions. The number of Radical M.P.'s fluctuated over the years from the late eighteenth century, but in the parliament of 1868–74 it probably stood at between 100 and 125, most of them being, as John Vincent calls them, "Dissenter-capitalists."[8] These men did not constitute a separate party, but cooperated with the Liberals, mainly because of their deep affection and respect for the piety and sincerity of Gladstone. By 1874, however, their tacit union with Liberalism splintered, for Gladstone's relative moderation on a number of issues—the ballot, the 1870 education act, disestablishment of the Church, the trades union act, and the land laws—caused them to become disenchanted with him. As a result, many Nonconformists and trade unionists, which were two of the main sources of Radicalism, took a much

6. Quoted in T. Wemyss Reid, *Life of the Right Honourable William Edward Forster*, 2 vols. (London, 1888), I, 367.

7. Harold Perkin, *The Origins of Modern English Society, 1780–1880* (Toronto, 1969), is enormously helpful to understanding social ideals and values. For a more complete discussion of the historical development of Radicalism, see the unpublished dissertation by T. W. Heyck, "English Radicals and the Irish Question," (Austin, Texas, 1969).

8. John Vincent, *The Formation of the Liberal Party, 1857–68* (London, 1966), 28–30.

less favorable attitude toward the Liberals in the general election of 1874 than in 1868. The disenchantment of Radicals with Gladstone was an important factor in his decision in 1875 to retire from the party leadership and in the rise of a more militant, independent Radicalism. It was this aggressive Radicalism, struggling to recover from a poor electoral showing in 1874, then reaching for real power after a substantial improvement in the election of 1880, which came face to face with the Irish Question.

After 1874, as before, the Radical movement had two wings, middle class and working class, but the parliamentary elite came almost exclusively from the middle-class section. With the help of a statistical procedure called multiple discriminant analysis, one can set the number of M.P.'s who voted as Radicals at any one time at about 80 for the 1874–80 parliament and about 120 for that of 1880–85. (Appendix A explains the method of selecting Radical M.P.'s, and Appendix B lists the names of Radical M.P.'s for both parliaments.) In both cases the Radicals amounted to approximately one-third of the Liberal parliamentary party. Most of the Radical M.P.'s were big businessmen and wealthy lawyers; over 80 percent in both parliaments earned their incomes from middle-class occupations. (Appendix B, Table 1.) Unlike both the Conservative parliamentary party and even the Liberal parliamentary party as a whole, only about 8 percent of the Radical M.P.'s derived their incomes from the traditional aristocratic sources, land and the armed services. But this fact should not suggest that the Radical M.P.'s were from the ranks of the common man. Like Josiah Bounderby, they were among the men who made things go in the commercial and industrial centers of Britain—a role of which they were very conscious. Very few had struggled to prominence from working-class origins. At the same time, they were men of wealth but not of leisure, for they prided themselves in being self-made men who, regardless of wealth, felt morally bound to work in some productive enterprise.

These observations raise the question of why such men would enter active politics. Only a few of them were raised in circles which expected as a matter of course that their ablest young men would take a part in ruling the country. Nor do the Radical M.P.'s appear to have expected their political careers to open magic doors to wealth or social prestige, even though relatively few had received the public honors to which their economic success entitled them (see Appendix B, Table 3). Rather, most of them sought parliamentary seats in order to correct some specific grievance imposed on them by existing political and social arrangements, or more generally to give political expression to a stridently middle-class perspective of British life. Of course, not all middle-class men in late-Victorian Britain were Radicals; nor were all Radicals throughout the country middle-class. But it does seem true that most Radical M.P.'s were middle-class men who for some reason—family influence, intellectual training, or particular social position—felt that one or another oppressive privilege needed reforming, and had the money to do something about it.

The factor that generated the strongest discontent among them was religion: of the Radical M.P.'s in these two parliaments whose religion is known, about 70 percent were Nonconformists. Including Jews, Roman Catholics, and nonbelievers, more than 75 percent stood outside the established Church. (See Appendix B, Table 2.) Precise figures for the religious affiliation for all members of the House are not available, but it is clear that there was a high correlation between Radicalism and Nonconformity, even though there was also a significant number of Nonconformists who were Gladstonians.[9] The latter were interested in alleviating specific Nonconformist grievances, but not as much in disestablishing the Church or in pressing on with democratic measures as their Radical colleagues. The number of Radical M.P.'s who were Anglicans may seem surprisingly large. This group was made up of men whose evangelical piety and ideas about religious equality matched those of the Nonconformists, plus a small number whose constituents led them to take a more Radical stance, which was sometimes the case in Wales

---

9. For estimates of the number of Nonconformist M.P.'s, see: Herbert S. Skeats and Charles S. Miall, *History of the Free Churches of England, 1688–1891* (London, 1891), 599, 669; H. J. Hanham, *Elections and Party Management: Politics in the Time of Disraeli and Gladstone* (London, 1959), 124; *The Liberator*, March 2, 1874; May 1, 1880.

and Scotland, where religious feelings ran very hot, as well as in some of the predominantly Nonconformist areas of England—the North, Northwest, Midlands, East Anglia, and the Southwest from Bristol to Cornwall.[10]

Religion, however, was not the only social determinant of Radicalism. An analysis of the constituencies returning Radicals to parliament from 1874 to 1885 suggests that a whole set of variables usually went together to produce Radicalism. The Radical movement tended to be strong in any area in rough proportion to that region's social and geographic distance from traditional, rural, Anglican England. Where Nonconformity, industrialism, or Celtic culture was strong—as in the major provincial centers of industry and trade, the Scottish highlands, and the rural areas of Wales—so was Radicalism; where they were weak, so also was Radicalism. (See Appendix B, Tables 4 and 5.)

A Radical prototype emerges from the statistical data. The late-Victorian Radical M.P. was a businessman, most likely a coal owner or iron founder, and of the second generation of the family firm. He had received education beyond that of most Englishmen—perhaps even a university degree, but not from Oxford or Cambridge. As a young man he devoted himself completely to his business, and after accumulating a large fortune, he won various civic honors such as a town councilorship or office in the chamber of commerce. He was a strong Nonconformist, active in his congregation, regularly pious in his home life. He belonged to the local Liberal association, but first became politically active through the local school board or the agitation on the Eastern Question. He was acutely conscious of Nonconformist disabilities and of the political and social privileges of the landed aristocracy. His belief that the social and political systems did not express his own pious and work-oriented values, or respond to his grievances, made him a Radical; his money and local influence made him a parliamentary candidate. Entering parliament

---

10. The best sources for the geographic distribution of Nonconformity are Henry Pelling, *Social Geography of British Elections, 1885–1910* (New York, 1967); and Michael Kinnear, *The British Voter: An Atlas and Survey since 1885* (London, 1968), esp. pp. 122–29.

at the age of forty-five, he devoted himself to one or two of the numerous political and religious causes that constituted Radicalism. Due to his limited experience and outlook, he depended on a few simplistic principles and the advice of a few Liberal and Radical leaders—Gladstone, John Bright, Joseph Chamberlain, Samuel Morley, Duncan McLaren, and Henry Richard—to guide him on questions beyond his special interests. He identified first with the small circle of colleagues who had the same special concerns, then more generally with other Radicals, sharing with them a set of bourgeois values, a utilitarian habit of thought, and a keen awareness of the enemy—privilege. He was loyal to Gladstone but hated the Whigs, and often felt that the Liberal party, his ideological and institutional home, was corrupted by Whig influence.

The man who perhaps best typified parliamentary Radicalism was Henry Joseph Wilson, M.P. for a division of Sheffield. Wilson was born in Nottinghamshire in 1833, the son of a prosperous cotton spinner. Austere Nonconformity dominated his early life. His mother and father, strong Congregationalists, actively supported anti-slavery and foreign missionary work. They did not smoke, drink, or dance. Wilson attended a Dissenters' school in Taunton and, briefly, University College, London. He joined a Sheffield smelting business, which he built into a large operation. According to the standards of the day, he was a good employer. He cut the weekly hours of labor in his factory to forty-eight and even provided a bath-house for the workers. Bentham's utilitarianism and Samuel Smiles's *Self Help* were his intellectual guides, but Puritanism remained the most important influence in his life. Being fervent Dissenters, Wilson and his wife became interested in Josephine Butler's crusade to abolish the contagious (venereal) diseases acts, which they regarded as laws sanctioning prostitution. In 1870 Wilson was powerfully upset by Forster's education act, and shortly afterward he and a few other men founded the Sheffield Nonconformist Committee, with the objects of reforming the act and controlling the local school board. By 1874 Wilson had plunged completely into Radical politics in Sheffield. He became secretary of the Sheffield Liberal Association, a campaign worker for Joseph Chamberlain, and in 1885 M.P. from Holmfirth, eager to enact purity into law. He never won great prominence, but the Radicals in parliament consisted of row upon row of men just like him; for Ireland, the consequences of their personal nature would be crucial.[11]

II

The nature of Victorian Radicalism can also be seen in the organizational structure of the movement. Paradoxically, the Radicals organized too much and too little. This was always one of their primary characteristics: they had local organizations, societies, leagues, and clubs, but no national agency to coordinate their activities. Further, as both the debate over the French Revolution and the dispute between Chartism and the Anti-Corn Law League showed, the middle- and working-class wings of the movement were never welded into a single institution. Since the early nineteenth century there had been attempts to form a Radical party; but all had failed, and by the 1870's and early 1880's Radical M.P.'s usually attached themselves to the Liberal parliamentary party. But they felt that the Liberal party all too often was too moderate, and as a result there was no single institution inside parliament or out that could speak for, much less mobilize, Radical sentiment.

Middle-class Radicals from 1874 to 1885 had little influence in the central circles of the Liberal party and no effective parliamentary organization of their own. Joseph Chamberlain, a successful industrialist with a genius for organization and an impatience with ineffectiveness, tried to organize the Radical M.P.'s as soon as he entered the House of Commons, but even his attempts failed.[12] Radical M.P.'s dissipated their strength in a kaleidoscope of special interest groups and temporary alliances. The same was true outside the House. The Reform League and the National Reform Union were important national pressure groups in the 1860's, but they de-

11. W. S. Fowler, *A Study in Radicalism and Dissent: The Life and Times of Henry Joseph Wilson, 1833–1914* (London, 1961).

12. His most notable attempt was the "new party," which included for a time in 1876 Dilke, Joseph Cowen, Thomas Burt, L. L. Dillwyn, E. D. Gray, and John Morley, in addition to Chamberlain. Dilke Memoirs, 43,932, ff. 248–49; J. L. Garvin anl Julian Amery, *The Life of Joseph Chamberlain*, 6 vols. (London, 1932–69), I, 241–46.

clined after 1867. Until the founding of the National Liberal Federation in 1877, various Nonconformist societies were the main Radical extra-parliamentary organizations—the Peace Society, the Liberation Society, the United Kingdom Alliance, the National Education League, and the Central Nonconformist Committee.[13] Each of these had a specific goal and did not attempt to unify all Radicals in support of a comprehensive program. Chamberlain wanted to unite the power of these societies in the National Liberal Federation and use it to make Radical opinion dominant in the Liberal party, destroying Whig influence in the process. However, only the Education League was dissolved into the Federation; the other Nonconformist societies retained their independence.[14] Down to 1886 the Federation did not exert the power that Chamberlain wanted and the Whigs feared. It proved unable to force any Radical policy on the parliamentary Liberal party, and as late as 1884 more Liberal borough constituency associations, even those of the post-1867 democratic kind, remained independent than affiliated.[15] The Radical movement, therefore, continued to diffuse its efforts in a variety of panaceas.

Perhaps an even more serious feature of the Radical structure was that Radical workingmen were not integrated into the main Radical organizations. This ultimately had an important influence on Radical history, and particularly on the Radical response to Ireland. The local Liberal associations dominated by Radicals were theoretically open to all, regardless of social class. In practice, however, they were under the thumb of the bourgeois leaders who paid the bills, set the policies, and selected the candidates. Workingmen were called upon for electoral support but only very rarely consulted on matters of policy.[16] There were numerous working-class Radical clubs

13. For the Peace Society: A. C. F. Beales, *The History of Peace* (New York, 1931), esp. Ch. 8; the United Kingdom Alliance: Hanham, *Elections and Party Management*, 120, 413–19; and Brian Harrison, *Drink and the Victorians* (London, 1971), esp. Ch. 13. There is no history of the Liberation Society, so one must turn to J. Guinness Rogers, *An Autobiography* (London, 1903), 214–15, and the Society's paper, *The Liberator*.

14. F. H. Herrick, "The Origins of the National Liberal Federation," *Journal of Modern History* 17 (June 1945), 116–29.

15. Hanham, *Elections and Party Management*, 139.

16. G. D. H. Cole, *British Working Class Politics, 1832–1914* (London, 1941),

throughout the country, but these were neither attached to the middle-class structure nor regarded by the middle-class leadership as recruiting grounds for the movement's elite. In London, where the Radical clubs were especially numerous, working-class Radicals reacted by asserting their independence from middle-class leaders.[17] Throughout the 1870's and 1880's there were national organizations of trade unionist Radicals—the Labour Representation League and the Parliamentary Committee of the Trades Union Congress—which acted on values identical to those of the middle-class societies. They were connected to middle-class Radicals through a few labor organizers like George Howell and the small circle of British positivists who had worked for trades union rights in the 1860's. Yet these working-class organizations were used but not absorbed by the middle-class elite, and the main elements of Radicalism remained separate.[18]

Among all the Nonconformist societies, leagues to reform certain laws and institutions, trade unions and Radical clubs, the materials existed for a unified Radical movement. Frequently the various organizations were connected by interlocking directorates and memberships, though not between groups of different social classes. Chamberlain did more to unite them than anyone else, but the diversity of the Radical organizations frustrated even his efforts. It is hard to escape the conclusion that organizational diffusion was a fundamental, essential element in the Radical movement. This is understandable when viewed in the light of what kind of people the Radicals were. What made Radicals of men was their individual sense of grievance at the hands of some aspect of privilege. Intensely dedicated to the removal of that grievance, Radicals inevitably struggled among themselves for priority in public attention. Their sense of mutual identification in the face of the common enemy, privilege,

Chs. 5, 6, 8; B. C. Roberts, *The Trades Union Congress, 1868–1921* (London, 1958), 109–90.

17. Charles Booth, *Life and Labour of the People in London*, final vol. (London, .903), 77; Paul Thompson, "Liberals, Radicals, and Labour in London, 1880–1900," *Past and Present* 27 (April 1964), 73–101.

18. For a fuller discussion of this point, see T. W. Heyck, "British Radicals and Radicalism, 1874–1895: A Social Analysis," in *Modern European Social History*, ed. R. J. Bezucha (Lexington, Mass., 1972), 28–58.

was real, but only occasionally adequate to overcome the structural diversity. This would help make their reaction to Irish issues exceptionally confused, because Irish affairs would have to compete with their special grievances, and because the Irish would find no central Radical agency with which to deal.

III

Despite their difficulty in achieving organizational unity and in settling on the emphasis to be given various policies, the Radicals of the 1870's and 1880's did agree on basic political and religious principles and on the general objectives for a Radical program. This program reflected, therefore, the implicit social ideal of the Radical movement. It would have replaced the traditional, particularist, and ascriptive elements in British society with rational, equalitarian, and achievement-oriented institutions. To do this, Radicals would first have destroyed privilege in political arrangements. This involved the extension of the franchise to county laborers, equalization of electoral districts, and, especially after 1884, reduction of the power of a hereditary House of Lords.[19] As T. H. S. Escott, editor of the *Fortnightly Review*, put it, if there was a common denominator to Radicalism, it was a "belief in the right and ability of the people as a whole to govern themselves."[20]

The Radicals would also have abolished privilege in the religious arrangements of the country. This meant disestablishment of the churches of England, Wales, and Scotland, and the removal from the state school system of any vestige of state support of denominational education—all in the name of complete religious equality.[21]

19. *Dod's Parliamentary Companion* gives a fairly good summary of the important features of election addresses, which included many references to these political measures. Also: T. H. S. Escott, "The Radical Programme. II.-Measures," *F.R.* 201 (September 1883), 433-47; J. E. T. Rogers, "The House of Lords," *F.R.* 212 (August 1884), 257-70; and Henry Labouchere, "People and Peers," *F.R.* 213 (September 1884), 321-31. (The articles entitled "The Radical Programme" were unsigned. The authors are supplied here from Joseph Chamberlain, *A Political Memoir, 1880-92,* ed. C. H. D. Howard [London, 1953], 108.)

20. "The Future of the Radical Party," *F.R.* 199 (July 1883), 6.

21. Joseph Chamberlain, "The Liberal Party and Its Leaders," *F.R.* 81 (September 1873), 287-302; R. W. Dale, "The Disestablishment Movement," *F.R.* 111 (March

They would open burial grounds attached to parish churches to Nonconformist burials with Nonconformist ceremonies. Finally, though it was not so much a matter of religious equality as of moral purity, they would establish one or another kind of strong temperance reform: publicans would go the way of the Establishment.[22] What they thought they would have accomplished by all these enterprises was the construction of a nation in which no ecclesiastical authority interfered with the right of an individual to find his own religious truth, and in which no brewer impeded the self-development of a prudent individual.

Finally, the Radicals would have attacked privilege in the ownership of land. Working-class Radicals thought that a monopoly in land, and the consequent high food prices and the crowded misery of urban life, were the sources of most of their difficulties. In this belief they drew upon a long tradition of hostility to landlords and industrial society, and a nostalgia for the rural past: the good life would be that of a small proprietor or secure tenant farmer. Middle-class Radicals saw the land laws as the symbol and substance of the old England dominated by a social order from which they were excluded, and whose paternalistic social ideal they found repugnant; the land laws were the anachronistic, unbusinesslike, and irrational bulwarks of the landed classes. The Radical solution was to abolish what they called primogeniture and entail, and to make free trade in land prevail.[23]

This was essentially a middle-class program, arising from a middle-class Nonconformist perspective of British society. To a remarkable degree, the politically active workingman shared the perspective.[24]

1876), 311–39; John Morley, "The Radical Programme. VI.-Religious Equality," *F.R.* 209 (May 1884), 569–92; *The Congregationalist* (January 1874); Francis Adams, "The Radical Programme. V.-Free Schools," *F.R.* 205 (January 1884), 1–20.

22. *Sir Wilfrid Lawson: A Memoir*, ed. G. W. E. Russell (London, 1909); *Hansard* 220 (June 17, 1884), 2; 253 (June 14, 1881), 340.

23. G. O. Morgan, "Land Law Reform," *F.R.* 156 (December 1879), 805; G. J. Shaw Lefevre, *English and Irish Land Questions*, 2nd ed. (London, 1881); F. M. L. Thompson, "Land and Politics in England in the Nineteenth Century," *Transactions of the Royal Historical Society*, 5th ser., 15 (London, 1965), 23–44.

24. Henry Pelling, *The Origins of the Labour Party* (Oxford, 1965), 6; Trygve Tholfsen, "The Transition to Democracy in Victorian England," *International Review of Social History* 6 (1961), 226–48.

Even in the famous Radical Programme put together by Joseph Chamberlain in 1883–85, in which urban social problems were addressed, the Radical solutions conformed to a competitive ideal. Rights of property were to be abbreviated only in the sense that landowners and urban landlords would have to pay for their privileges, for their "unearned increment."[25] The ideas of Henry George became very popular in Radical circles in the 1880's because they articulated the long-standing Radical antipathy to landlords; but Radicals consistently rejected the cooperative ideal underlying socialism. The novelist George Gissing, like the Duke of Marlborough, believed that late-Victorian Radicalism was tantamount to socialism, but in fact Radicals stuck to Manchester School economics inherited from the Philosophic Radicals and the Anti–Corn Law Leaguers.[26] Of course, they claimed that they spoke for the working class, and they advocated what Chamberlain called "Free Labour"; but this slogan meant providing a legal framework to allow the growth of effective trade unions, institutions clearly within the existing capitalist system.[27] Essentially, Radicals would limit the rights of landed property owners, not because they opposed property rights, but because they considered that their ancient enemies, the landowners, enjoyed abusive privileges to which they were not entitled by virtue of productive work.

In all of their policies or programs, whether political, ecclesiastical, or social, the Radicals meant to add a moral dimension to politics. They wanted to abolish privileges not simply because they were inefficient, but also because they were immoral. Puritan tradition taught them that no one should get rewards except as he had earned them. Wealth, status, and power should accrue to those who had performed a service for society, that service defined normally as production of tangible goods. Even the Radical intellectuals of the

25. Frank Harris, "Housing of the Poor in Towns," *F.R.* 202 (October 1883), 599–600 (included also in *The Radical Programme*, ed. Joseph Chamberlain [London, 1885], Ch. 4). See also Joseph Chamberlain, "Labourers' and Artisans' Dwellings," *F.R.* 204 (December 1883), 761–62.

26. For example, see George Gissing's *Demos* (1886).

27. Joseph Chamberlain, "The Liberal Party and Its Leaders," 287–302; also Royden Harrison, *Before the Socialists: Studies in Labour and Politics, 1861–1881* (London, 1965).

1870's, most of whom—like Henry Fawcett, Leonard Courtney, Frederic Harrison, and John Morley—were disciples of J. S. Mill and aggressive freethinkers, shared this moralistic orientation. This attitude is what the Radicals had in common with Gladstone—a moral earnestness that crossed sectarian lines.

IV

Obviously, all these aspects of Radical ideology, like Radical social origins and organizational inclinations, had important implications for the Irish Question. Ireland provided a set of issues that was external to the defining core of the Radical movement. Throughout the nineteenth century, Ireland had played an extremely important part in British politics, but it did not have a decisive role in shaping the essentials of Radicalism. In his *Irish Nationalism and British Democracy*, Eric Strauss argues the opposite point—that the Irish Question was crucial in forming British democracy.[28] But his evidence shows only a simultaneous development: as British politics became progressively more democratic, they were continually involved with Irish issues. All during their history in the nineteenth century, Radicals brought to Irish problems a formidable set of preconceptions, principles, and prejudices.

The most important impact of Ireland on the Radicals before the 1870's came from Irish working-class immigrants in Britain. The political history of these people has never been written, but it seems clear that they provided thousands of recruits to Radical organizations ranging from the British Jacobins to the London Working Men's Association of William Lovett and the Chartists of Feargus O'Connor. They added a revolutionary element to the more disciplined and orderly working class of England.[29] They undoubtedly caused Radical groups to worry more about Irish issues than they otherwise would have. English historians commonly assume that wherever Irish immigrants were most numerous, British workers

28. Eric Strauss, *Irish Nationalism and British Democracy* (London, 1951), Ch. 8.

29. E. P. Thompson, *Making of the English Working Class* (New York, 1964), 432–40.

reacted out of fearful self-interest by supporting anti-Irish candidates and policies. However, this assumption does not seem true, at least for Radical workingmen. In general, Radical groups in the working class, among whom most of the politically active Irish immigrants could be found, consistently showed more sympathy to Irish nationalism than did middle-class Radicals.[30] At the same time, the abuses which middle-class Radicals most frequently and fervently attacked—the power of the aristocracy, the injustice of the established Church, and the economic privileges of the landlord—were most flagrantly displayed in Ireland; thus the Radicals often were more friendly toward the amelioration of Irish misery than were other British political elements.

Yet Radicalism and Irish nationalism were never identical. Radicals and Irish nationalists alike, particularly the middle-class elite of both, judged Irish issues according to their own preconceptions and interests. In the early years of Radicalism, for example, the Bill of Rights Society made redress of Irish grievances part of its basic program, but in 1778 Sir Cecil Wray, a member of the Society, led the opposition to the Irish free trade bills, all while professing the best intentions for the Irish.[31] Similarly, William Cobbett strongly supported Catholic Emancipation, but was furious with Daniel O'Connell when the Irish leader accepted disfranchisement of the Irish forty-shilling freeholders as the price of getting it.[32] Indeed, regarding religious issues in general, British Radicals were sympathetic to the plight of the Irish masses—but in spite of, and not because of, Roman Catholicism. Anti-Catholicism was very strong among "the people" during the late eighteenth and early nineteenth centuries.[33] Radicals supported Gladstone's disestablishment of the Irish Church in 1869, but one should recall that the Irish nationalists opposed the particular Church that had been established, while Radicals opposed the principle of establishment itself. On a number of

30. *Ibid.*, 123–26, 167–74, 440; G. D. H. Cole, *The Life of William Cobbett* (London, 1947), 351; Strauss, *Irish Nationalism and British Democracy*, 127.

31. Simon Maccoby, *English Radicalism, 1762–85* (London, 1955), 170, 269–70.

32. John W. Osborne, *William Cobbett: His Thought and His Times* (New Brunswick, N.J., 1966), 211–13.

33. Walter L. Arnstein, "Victorian Prejudice Reexamined," *Victorian Studies* 12 (June 1969), 452–57, briefly reviews recent literature on the subject.

other religious issues, especially pertaining to education in Ireland, the Radicals had, and would continue to have, strong differences with Irish reformers.[34]

The same was true in connection with Irish economic problems. Land tenure was central to Irish difficulties. Being hostile to landlords, British Radicals considered the Irish landlord the worst kind of social parasite. David Ricardo, for instance, believed that the oppressor of Ireland was not England, but the aristocrat, who was interested only in squeezing the last farthing out of his land, regardless of the consequences. However, down to the Famine, the Radicals found their solution in their own economic principles, derived as they were from the English industrial situation. They sought to establish free trade in Irish land; they believed this would hand over Irish agriculture to businesslike farmers of the best English model, who would consolidate holdings, clear the land of uneconomic tenants, and introduce modern farming methods. It was not until the Famine that some Radicals, principally John Stuart Mill, recognized that the real problem was to improve Ireland for its present inhabitants—the tenants.[35] Over the next twenty years he developed a program of fixity of tenure, fair rents established through a public commission, and tenant right of sale of his share in the holding.[36] Others, like John Bright, advocated schemes to enable thrifty tenants to purchase their holdings.[37] On this subject, if not other economic issues, the Radicals by the 1870's had, on the basis of their antipathy to landlords, moved a long way toward the Irish position. The problem was that they would be required after 1874 to go even further on the land question and to respond positively to other economic issues as well.

---

34. For example, Gladstone's Irish university bill of 1873, which would have prohibited teaching "controversial" subjects such as philosophy and modern history, succeeded in rousing vehement opposition from rationalist Radicals like Henry Fawcett, while splitting the Irish nationalist party.

35. R. D. Collison Black, *Economic Thought and the Irish Question, 1817–70* (Cambridge, 1960), provides a thorough analysis of both the Irish agrarian problem and English thought about it. John Stuart Mill's early thoughts on tenant security can be seen in the *Morning Chronicle* (1846–47) and in the *Principles of Political Economy* (London, 1848).

36. J. S. Mill, *England and Ireland* (London, 1868).

37. G. M. Trevelyan, *The Life of John Bright* (London, 1913), 410.

Another problem was that Radicals, because of their tendency to interpret all Irish grievances in terms of the evilness of landlords, liked to think that land reform settled even the political demands of Irish nationalism. This would prove to be a false assumption. Further, while Radicals supported the idea of elective local government in Ireland and the opening of Dublin Castle to Irish opinion, the fact remains that over the years most Radicals had opposed national self-government in Ireland and separation of Ireland from England. For the most part they felt that the problem was one of bringing better, more efficient, and reasonable—but not necessarily Irish—government to Ireland. By the 1870's most Radicals shared the English habit of regarding England and Ireland as permanently united; they believed positively that the interests of Ireland as well as England depended on the union.[38] They did not like or trust the leaders of Irish nationalism. Cobden, for example, wrote of O'Connell: "I never shook hands with him or faced his smile without a feeling of insecurity; and as for trusting him on any public question where his vanity or passions might interpose, I should have as soon thought of an alliance with an Ashantee chief."[39] Plainly, political principles alone did not determine Radical responses to Irish political demands.

By the early 1870's the meaning and structure of British Radicalism had solidified, and in the years just prior to 1885 the influence of the Radical persuasion was growing. From the latter 1870's on, Radicals exuded an air of confidence, of eager anticipation for a climatic struggle with Whigs in the Liberal party and traditional institutions in the country. But they failed to anticipate that the Irish Question would erupt in the middle of their road. From 1874 to 1895, the vital years of the Home Rule movement, Irish Home Rulers provided a seemingly endless series of difficulties for Radicals as for all British politicians. Radicals stood for democracy in the constitution and for the abolition of privilege in the church and land; but they were also a grievance-oriented, organizationally splintered, English-bred movement whose policies were tightly connected to their own im-

---

38. For instance: Mill, *England and Ireland*, 31–35; Charles Bradlaugh, *The Irish Question: What It Has Been, What It Is, and How to Deal with It* (London, 1868), 7.

39. John Morley, *Life of Richard Cobden*, 2 vols. (London, 1881), II, 27.

mediate needs. The Irish Question would compete with Radical demands for priority in the parliamentary agenda, severely test Radical principles, and require of Radicals an unwonted flexibility and intuitive understanding. The Irish Question, in other words, not only dominated the next two decades of Radical history, but also provided an extremely revealing test case for the nature of late-Victorian Radicalism.

CHAPTER TWO

Radicals and the Growth of
Irish Militancy
1874-80

In 1880 Disraeli commented that two topics seemed to monopolize public opinion: "one was the government of Ireland, and the other the principles upon which the landed property of this country should continue to be established."[1] His remark provides a good indication of how important Irish nationalism on the one hand and British Radicalism on the other became in the 1870's. The growth of the Irish Question was certainly not viewed with pleasure by the great majority of Radicals. Indeed, after 1874 Radicals, like most Englishmen, would have liked to ignore Ireland. They were quite satisfied with the Irish reforms passed during the previous Gladstone government—namely, the disestablishment of the Irish Church, which removed Anglicanism from its official privileged position in Ireland but did nothing to raise up Roman Catholicism; and the land act of 1870, which attempted to protect Irish tenants from arbitrary eviction and to provide means for tenants to purchase their holdings. Radicals, naturally interested in other things, believed that these reforms would settle all legitimate Irish grievances if only they were given a chance to work. By the same token, they were inclined to think that continued Irish demands could not be substantial, but only frivolous—the products of a minority of Irishmen who were indulging themselves in allegedly well-known Irish irresponsibility and self-interested politics. Most Radicals, in other words, simply did not take Irish nationalism seriously in 1874.

The problem for the Home Rule party, which was the latest variant of Irish nationalism, was to disabuse all Englishmen of such thinking. There was enough truth to the image of irresponsibility in

1. *Hansard* 256 (August 30, 1880), 619.

the earlier history of the Irish parliamentary representation to make establishing credibility an important task for the Home Rulers. Under Isaac Butt, the Home Rulers tried to do this and secure Home Rule through persuasion; under Parnell they turned to confrontation. The Parnellite strategy worked remarkably well; by the late 1870's the Radicals, like all Britons, faced grave difficulties arising from increased Irish militancy. What they had to respond to was not simply the substance of Irish issues but the strategy and style of the Parnellites. Together these problems caused interesting and revealing behavior within the Radical movement.

I. THE RADICALS AND ISAAC BUTT, 1874–77

Isaac Butt, the re-founder of constitutional Irish nationalism, was a conservative. He believed that he could convince the English by logical argument that his plan for Home Rule would simultaneously give Ireland justice and reduce the workload of the House of Commons. He would appeal to the English on English principles. Butt also was an imperialist; he rejected "separation" of Ireland from Britain, and did not even seek an Irish legislature equal in status to parliament at Westminster. Ireland would have in his scheme a legislature subordinate to the imperial parliament within a federal system for all of Great Britain. Scotland and Wales would also have subordinate legislatures if they desired. Irish representation at Westminster would be retained for all imperial affairs—foreign policy, defense, and imperial taxation, for example.[2]

Not all of the Home Rulers liked Butt's design for a federal system; in fact, they did not agree among themselves on many Irish issues. Their party was an ill-disciplined assortment of men, ranging in political orientation from Protestant conservatives to Fenian revolutionaries. It was fundamentally divided between genuine Home Rulers and Irish Liberals, who adhered only nominally to Home Rule and concerned themselves mainly with Catholic issues. Butt could not enforce party discipline even on the crucial matter of Home Rule. While the Home Rule party supposedly included

2. J. C. Beckett, *The Making of Modern Ireland, 1603–1923* (London, 1966), Ch. 19; David Thornley, *Isaac Butt and Home Rule* (London, 1964).

fifty-nine M.P.'s, in practice Butt could command the votes of only about twenty.[3]

Butt's attitude toward the English Radicals was ambiguous. Unlike Daniel O'Connell, who was something of a Benthamite, Butt was not a Radical and did not share Radical political principles. One of the main reasons why he and other conservatives had adopted Home Rule in 1870 was that they feared the growth of Radicalism in England, symbolized to them by the disestablishment of the Irish Church. Butt argued that Ireland should seek Home Rule because England might be "broken up by an outbreak of the infidelity and socialism that are spreading through our land."[4] Yet he did not carry this notion on to a consistent political strategy. By 1874 he had decided that, among the English, Ireland's best friends were the Radicals, apparently because the anti-deferential stance of Irish nationalists and British Radicals often put them, quite coincidentally, on the same side in various issues.

During the general election of 1874 Butt emphasized the need to "conciliate" British democrats and spent most of his own efforts in campaigning to this effect in English industrial centers.[5] His tactics combined persuasion and force. He tried to talk Radical candidates into accepting Home Rule; at the same time, groups of Irishmen living in England tried to exact from them pledges of support for Home Rule. These tactics demanded steady pressure. Instead, Butt decided that where no candidate gave a satisfactory pledge to Home Rule, the Radical should receive Irish votes simply because he would be more likely to support Irish proposals.[6] This approach to electoral affairs failed to take full advantage of the electoral power of Irishmen in England. While the Irish nationalists claimed that twenty-nine British M.P.'s during the campaign had pledged to support at least an inquiry into Home Rule, the actual number stood between fifteen and twenty, of whom all but one were Radicals. About ten to fifteen other Radical candidates had supported Home Rule but lost.[7]

3. Thornley, *Butt*, 194–95, 202.

4. Quoted in Beckett, *Making of Modern Ireland*, 377.

5. Thornley, *Butt*, 228.

6. *The Times*, January 31, 1874.

7. Thornley, *Butt*, 228. Radicals who pledged to support at least an inquiry into

Inside the House of Commons, Butt had even less success. The great mass of Liberal and Conservative M.P.'s solidly opposed Home Rule, and the Radicals were only slightly more favorable. Between 1874 and 1878 Butt and the Home Rule party on four occasions offered resolutions or motions calling for parliamentary consideration of the Irish demand for Home Rule.[8] Each of these attempts by the Home Rulers inspired a full-scale debate and attracted much attention throughout Great Britain. Yet only twice in those four years did Radicals rise to speak for the Irish request; Jacob Bright (brother of John Bright) in 1876, and Sir Wilfrid Lawson in 1877. On no occasion did Home Rule win more than ten Radical votes. In June 1874, for example, Butt asked the House to resolve itself into committee to consider the parliamentary relations between Great Britain and Ireland. No Radical spoke for the Irish; eight Radicals voted with them; and more than thirty voted in the government lobby against them.[9]

There is no evidence that Radical opinion in the country at large —apart from Irishmen living in Great Britain—differed significantly from that of the Radicals in the House of Commons. Most of the Radical M.P.'s who did vote for Home Rule seem to have done so because of the pressure from their Irish constituents and not because of any broad sympathy within British Radicalism for Irish nationalism.[10] The only exception to this point arose in some working-class

---

Home Rule and won in 1874: Burt, Carter, Cowen, Cross, Eyton, Gourley, Harrison, Havelock, James (Gateshead), Jenkins (Dundee), Macdonald, McLaren, Shaw (Burnley), and Simon. A Liberal, Stewart (Cardiff), also pledged. Dilke and Lawson supported Home Rule but made no pledges to Irish groups. Hamond, a Conservative, pledged to support the Home Rule inquiry and won. Jacob Bright pledged, but lost. He stood again at Manchester in 1876 and won, again having pledged. Barran and Hibbert pledged and won in 1876 and 1877, respectively. Losing candidates who had pledged: Charles Bradlaugh, George Odger, Benjamin Lucraft (of the Labour Representation League), and Admiral Maxse.

8. *Hansard* 218 (March 20, 1874), 110–71; 220 (June 30, 1874), 700–709, 874–969; 230 (June 30, 1876), 738–822; 233 (April 24, 1877), 1742–1846.

9. *Hansard* 220 (June 30, 1874), 700–791, 874–969.

10. For samples of Radical opinion toward Home Rule, see: *Reynolds's Newspaper*, January 4, 1874 (for Home Rule); Mundella to Leader, July 4, 1874, Mundella-Leader Letters, Mundella Papers; *Daily News*, June 30, 1874; *The Echo*, July 1, 1876.

circles. Though it is difficult to say precisely how far support for Home Rule extended in the British working class, the evidence suggests that working-class Radicals more readily agreed with Irish nationalism than did middle-class Radicals. While it is true that the *Bee-Hive*, the leading working-class newspaper, showed little patience with the Irish, the only two working-class M.P.'s, Thomas Burt and Alexander Macdonald, both supported the Irish nationalists. *Reynolds's Newspaper*, an influential working-class Radical paper, strongly advocated Home Rule. And *The Times* noticed, albeit with disapproval, that workingmen supported Home Rule.[11] Although *The Times* offered the simple explanation for such a difference as existed between middle- and working-class views that the workers favored Home Rule because they did not understand what it meant, the most plausible interpretation lies in precisely the opposite direction. Because of their close contact with the Irish immigrants, many working-class Radicals felt the Irish problem was more real and urgent than did most men of the middle class. Further, as working-class Radicals already identified landowners as their enemy, they found it easy to sympathize with their fellow workers from Ireland. *Reynolds's Newspaper* expressed this identification of interests when it argued that the problem of the English "people" was the same as that of the Irish: "a contest with all the accumulated selfishness of past generations, and which takes the form of adverse possession of the land by an aristocracy."[12]

The fact remains that the great majority of the Radicals in and out of parliament opposed or ignored the Irish demand for Home Rule; this is the point that must be explained. Here one sees the same factors which had operated before 1874, for Butt had not done much to stop them. One major cause of Radical opposition to Home Rule was inertia. Like all Englishmen, Radicals assumed that the union of England and Ireland was the natural condition; any proposal for breaking the union would bear the burden of proving that change was necessary, and that the new political arrangement would be better for both countries. For all his reasonableness and eloquence,

11. *The Times*, April 26, 1877. Also: *Bee-Hive*, August 1, 1874; July 15, 1876.
12. July 5, 1874.

Butt was not able to convince many Radicals that conditions in Ireland were not already improving markedly. As enthusiastic proponents of Irish church and land reforms enacted during the first Gladstone administration, Radicals believed that parliament not only had corrected the most outstanding Irish grievances but also had demonstrated its capacity to deal with Irish problems in general. In the light of these reforms, said *The Nonconformist*, it is difficult to treat Butt's demand for Home Rule as real: "The crave for Home Rule is, to a great degree, artificial and even fictitious. It is not what the Irish people really want."[13]

Because Britain had shown the ability to rule Ireland well, the interests of both countries lay in maintaining the union. In this belief, the Radicals shared a widespread British assumption that unity and centralization were good for a nation; diversity and decentralization were bad, both in their practical effects and as principles in themselves. Indeed, the tendency toward centralization was an important theme in the Radical reform tradition inherited from the Benthamites. The response to Home Rule of several Radicals who were more receptive than most to proposals of decentralization is enlightening. E. A. Freeman, the well-known historian and polemicist, asserted that even as an advocate of federalism he found Butt's design for Home Rule "altogether wild and impracticable." Federalism was good when it was a step toward closer union, but Home Rule meant federalism tending toward disunion.[14] In 1875, defending his failure to keep a pledge to support an inquiry into Home Rule, Sir Henry Havelock stressed the centrifugal tendency of Butt's plan. He could accept local Irish control over such matters as railway, gas, and water bills, but not Home Rule as Butt defined it. Home Rule would lead to separation of Ireland from England; separation would end in "misery, misgovernment, discord, and political extinction" for both countries.[15] Even Joseph Chamberlain, who professed to be "not at all afraid of the consequences" of Home Rule, campaigned in Sheffield in 1874 on the declaration that he

13. July 8, 1874.
14. "Federalism and Home Rule," *F.R.* 92 (August 1874), 204–15.
15. *The Times*, July 1, 1875.

could not support a scheme that would "separate the imperial relations which at present exist between the two countries."[16]

In the minds of the Nonconformist Radicals, religion was a very strong reason to oppose Home Rule. Most militant Nonconformists had a conspiratorial view of Catholicism that caused them to doubt the ability of the Irish to govern themselves. Even John Bright, long one of the Englishmen most sympathetic to Ireland, deeply and irrationally distrusted the influence of the papacy and its "gang of priests" in Ireland. He wrote Gladstone in 1875: "In Great Britain we have twenty Romish Bishops—in Ireland quite as many—every one of them more powerful than the greatest of our nobles, & every one appointed by & dependent upon a Foreign potentate, who has no sympathy with the interests & policy of this Kingdom. This is a terrible evil."[17] The *British Quarterly Review*, a relatively moderate Nonconformist journal, went so far as to group Irish Catholics with English Anglicans as the enemies of Nonconformity. It complained in 1874 that two bad influences in the leadership of the Liberal party, W. E. Forster and Chichester Fortescue, had "pledged themselves to content—the former the English clerical party, the latter the Irish Ultramontanes...." One must see the Irish Home Rule party for what they really are: "sincere fanatics" who use Butt's federalist plan "as a decent disguise for...wild separatist ambitions."[18]

All of these preconceptions combined to develop in most middle-class Radicals a blatantly patronizing—perhaps even racist—dismissal of Butt's efforts for Home Rule. Such Radicals usually praised Butt for his eloquence and expressed considerable self-satisfaction for their own readiness to give him a hearing, then rejected Home Rule as beyond the talents of the Irish people. The *Daily News*, by far the leading Radical daily newspaper, reacted to Butt's appeal of 1876 by calling it an absurdity. According to the leader-writer, the "light and entertaining qualities of the Irish genius" have to be restrained by "the more sober and shrewd judgment of Englishmen and Scotch-

16. Chamberlain to H. J. Wilson, January 17, 1874, Wilson Papers, Sheffield University, Box VI; Garvin, *Chamberlain*, I, 166.
17. January 17, 1875, Gladstone Papers, 44,113.
18. "The New Parliament," *British Quarterly Review* (April 1874), 473-85.

men."[19] *The Nonconformist and Independent* summed up the prevailing Radical attitude by declaring that the *real* Irish problem was the child-like nature of Irishmen. No matter what concessions Britain made, the Irish would always cry for more. In the end, "a grave cause of Irish discontent and distress is the easy-going temper, the indomitable good-humour, and light-heartedness of the Irish people."[20]

Throughout the period of Butt's ascendency in the Home Rule movement, Radicals continued to interpret Irish measures according to their own preconceptions. The economic measures proposed by Butt's party exposed this persistent Radical attitude. The Home Rulers, for example, wanted to revive Irish fisheries in order to remove some of the economic pressure from the agrarian sector. This relatively harmless idea met only Radical unconcern and even hostility. In 1874 a Home Rule M.P. moved a resolution in the House of Commons calling for governmental assistance to Irish fisheries. About twenty Radicals voted with the Irish, and only three against. Yet about fifty neglected to vote at all, and the only Radical to speak in the debate strongly opposed the resolution. This was Duncan McLaren, a prominent merchant and the leader of Scottish Radicalism, who argued that if the Irish fisheries did not thrive, it was their own fault. Scottish fisheries did well without assistance. Furthermore, he said, in Scotland descendants of Danish and Norwegian immigrants throve in fishing, while the Irish "Celtic race" living there did not.[21] In 1876 another prominent Radical businessman, W. E. Baxter, spoke against an Irish fisheries bill. He agreed that the British had long treated Ireland badly, but he could not approve of governmental assistance to the fisheries, for it "would be altogether opposed to all true principles of political economy."[22]

19. July 1, 1876.

20. February 26, 1880. It should be added that such views were not entirely restricted to the upper classes. In 1881 a member of the Aberdeen Trades Council remarked that the "chief obstacles" to the progress of the Irish people "lay in certain natural defects incident to their race." Quoted in Kenneth D. Buckley, *Trade Unionism in Aberdeen, 1878 to 1900* (Edinburgh, 1955), 95. For a good statement of the problem of racism in Anglo-Irish relations, see L. P. Curtis, Jr., *Anglo-Saxons and Celts* (Bridgeport, Conn., 1968).

21. *Hansard* 218 (May 1, 1874), 1504–9.

22. *Hansard* 228 (March 22, 1876), 438–40.

The economic issue most important to Butt was land tenure reform. Here, too, his proposal met Radical recalcitrance. The land
act of 1870 provided for compensation of the tenant in case of "disturbance"—that is, when the tenant was arbitrarily evicted. By pe-
nalizing the landlord for evicting, Gladstone had intended to win
greater security for the tenant. But the land act also stipulated that
there would be no compensation in case of eviction for failure to pay
rent, and it did not prohibit landlords from arbitrarily raising rents.
In practice many landlords simply increased rents and evicted the
tenants who could not pay. Butt wanted to improve tenant security
by fixing tenure for a specified period, dependent only on payment
of a fair rent, with periodic revaluation of rents by a public commission. Even though Radicals were deeply committed to land reform in England and Scotland, and even though the land problem
in Ireland was more acute than in the rest of Britain, they did not
take much interest in Butt's proposals. When Butt in June 1875
asked for a royal commission to inquire into the 1870 land act, no
Radical spoke in the House of Commons to support him.[23] A year
later, Butt proposed a land tenure bill. One Radical spoke in favor of
the measure, but only eight voted for it.[24] Though Butt's proposal
largely resembled the ideas already developed by J. S. Mill, most
Radicals ignored it. They did not know the necessary details of
Irish land tenure, for they appear to have grown weary with constant debate on Irish problems; they simply hoped that Gladstone's
land act could provide a final settlement of the Irish land question.

Radical M.P.'s took much more interest in some of the Home Rule
party's proposals for political reform in Ireland. The Irish suffered
from a number of political disabilities that plainly violated Radical
principles. Neither the Irish parliamentary borough franchise nor
the municipal franchise was as extensive as that in England. And the
finances of Irish county government were controlled by appointed
grand juries, which were notoriously unresponsive to public opinion.
Although the Radicals did not initiate efforts to reform these anom-
alies, usually they supported the Irish when the Irish themselves
proposed corrective measures. From 1874 to 1877, for example,

23. *Hansard* 224 (June 11, 1875), 1716–40.
24. *Hansard* 230 (June 29, 1876), 624–713.

Radical M.P.'s normally cast some fifty votes (about two-thirds of their strength) for extension of Irish voting rights.[25] They could do so because the Irish proposals cost them little energy, conformed to Radical precepts, and did not conflict with Radical interests. Indeed, they frequently argued that to support the Irish in such demands would help bind the nationalists more closely to the union and reduce the appeal of Home Rule.[26]

The most urgent Irish political issue of all was coercion. Here the Radicals generally failed to support Butt's nationalist party. During the 1870's, as throughout most of the nineteenth century, the English ruled Ireland almost continuously by "exceptional legislation"—coercive acts designed to control agitation through the restriction of normal legal liberties like habeas corpus and freedom from general warrants. Because of their own tradition of, and commitment to, popular agitation, Radicals had every reason to oppose coercion in Ireland. Yet their response in the mid-1870's was ambiguous at best. In July 1874 a number of Radicals spoke against coercive sections of the government's bill to continue expiring laws, and more than twenty voted against it. But their opposition was aroused as much by the government's inclusion of these important clauses in a routine annual bill as by their opposition to coercion.[27] In April 1875 a few Radicals created a considerable stir by joining the Irish M.P.'s in full-scale parliamentary resistance to a new coercion bill. One of them, Henry Fawcett, the well-known blind political economist and disciple of Mill, even earned the praise of one of the most militant Home Rulers, Joseph Biggar. In an unwonted burst of gratitude, Biggar urged Irishmen in England to "adopt the programme of the English Radicals, who by their representatives in the House of Commons had supported the Irish

25. The Irish political issues as reported in *Hansard*: Elective county boards: 225 (June 30, 1875), 746–61; and 227 (February 23, 1876), 765–88. Municipal franchise: 228 (March 1, 1876), 1164; 218 (April 24, 1874), 784; 238 (March 6, 1878), 796. Borough franchise: 228 (March 28, 1876), 703; 234 (June 15, 1877), 1882; 237 (February 19, 1878), 1925.

26. Speech by John Bright, *Hansard* 228 (March 28, 1876), 758–63; John Morley, "Home and Foreign Affairs," *F.R.* 112 (April 1876), 620. "Home and Foreign Affairs" was a monthly article by Morley. It will be cited hereafter: "Affairs."

27. *Hansard* 221 (July 30, 1874), 979–1010.

party."[28] But for all this enthusiasm, only fourteen Radical M.P.'s voted against the second reading of the bill, and seven voted for it; forty-eight acquiesced to the government's policy by neglecting to vote.[29] There was no extraparliamentary Radical agitation against coercion. Most seem to have accepted repression in Ireland as a necessary, if unpleasant, evil.

Butt liked to claim that British M.P.'s increasingly supported the Home Rulers on a variety of Irish reform measures.[30] To further this claim, he attempted on occasion to conciliate Radical opinion in the House. In 1876, for instance, he persuaded the Irish to abstain on the imperial titles bill, which some of the Home Rulers would have supported, because he knew that the Radicals opposed it. He also promised Dilke to support expansion of the county franchise in Britain.[31] Nevertheless, Butt's strategy did not win Radical converts to the Irish side. Radicals liked Butt personally; they gave him their support when he could get their attention and at the same time offer a proposal that coincided with some prior Radical principle. Essentially, however, he worked no change in their attitude toward Ireland.

II. RADICALS AND THE RISE OF IRISH MILITANCY, 1877–78

Butt's ineffectiveness finally aroused among Irishmen a strong reaction against his leadership. His inability to win significant concessions from parliament, his reputation for personal dissipation, and the evident lack of cohesion and vigor in the parliamentary Home Rule party turned many nationalists against him. After the parliamentary session of 1876 Irish frustration erupted in a new call for aggressiveness, and by 1879 a strategy of confrontation had replaced Butt's policy of persuasion. This militancy manifested itself in two ways: in parliamentary obstruction, and in an increasingly tough attitude among Irishmen in Britain toward their British

28. *The Times*, July 22, 1875.

29. Speeches by Radicals: *Hansard* 223 (April 26, 1875), 1661–62, 1667–68; (May 3, 1875), 1965–67, 1997–99; 224 (May 4, 1875), 36–41; division on second reading: 223 (March 23, 1875), 292–95.

30. Butt to Father Joseph Murphy, quoted in *The Times*, September 7, 1877.

31. Thornley, *Butt*, 299; Dilke Memoirs, 43,933, ff. 113–14.

M.P.'s. Both aspects deeply involved Radicals—obstruction, because it threatened cherished parliamentary principles; and electoral militancy, because the Irish in Britain mostly lived in large industrial towns, which often were Radical constituencies.

The essence of the new Irish obstruction was alarmingly simple: if the British would not let the Irish govern Ireland, then the Irish M.P.'s would not let the British govern Britain. The obstructives would impede the progress of all bills without regard to their content. The first Irishman to stage an obstruction was Joseph Biggar, until 1877 a Fenian, always an extreme nationalist, and to the English a personification of the worst in the Irish character: he was a gnome-like figure, partially hunch-backed, short, rude, disrespectful, and a poor speaker. But he was willing to talk for hours to stop the operation of parliament. At first he got little support from other Home Rulers, but by 1877 he was joined by a young Protestant landlord, Charles Stewart Parnell, who had only taken a seat in the House in 1875. Though relatively quiet in his first months in parliament, Parnell harbored a single-minded hatred for the English. A tall, handsome man with a drawn, solemn face, Parnell was extremely tough-minded—not brilliant, but diligent, disciplined, and direct. He always professed admiration for Isaac Butt; however, in reality he despised Butt's easy-going attitude and respect for English forms. By 1877 Parnell was convinced that Butt's strategy would never win Home Rule. He agreed with Butt's constitutional approach to politics, but he believed that pressure, not persuasion, would pry Home Rule from parliament. While the Home Rule party under Butt decided to continue their conventional tactics in the 1877 session, Parnell and Biggar gave notice that they would oppose every important English and Scottish bill in the House.[32] They obstructed the government's prisons bill, its annual mutiny bill, and in July 1877—at the peak of their obstructive effort—the South Africa Confederation bill.

The growth of Irish militancy in British constituencies was closely related to the obstructive policy in the House. Like obstruction, Irish electoral militancy in Britain was not new in 1877. Since the early 1870's Irishmen in England had been particularly enthusiastic

32. Thornley, *Butt*, 305.

for Home Rule. After 1870 the Fenians had more influence in England than in Ireland. By 1872 Irishmen, usually led by Fenians, had founded Home Rule associations in most of the large British industrial cities, primarily in the North, but also in the working-class districts of London.[33] In January 1873 the Home Rule associations in England and Scotland established the Home Rule Confederation of Great Britain, with Isaac Butt as president and John Barry (a Fenian) as secretary. The Confederation was not sufficiently well organized or led to follow a uniformly militant policy in the election of 1874, but the Confederation's executive in subsequent years increasingly urged militancy. The official organ of the Confederation, *United Ireland*, advocated obstruction as early as 1875, and it strongly supported Parnell and Biggar against Butt in their struggle over strategy.[34] In 1876 militant Home Rulers began to replace the moderates as officers of the Confederation, and in August 1877 Parnell supplanted Butt as president.

The advent of the strategists of confrontation meant nothing but trouble for Radicals. Since 1874 the Confederation had harassed the British M.P.'s who, in its opinion, had failed to honor pledges to support Home Rule. Because Radical and Irish strength coincided in many industrial constituencies, Radicals had to bear most of the Irish pressure.[35] From 1876 the Confederation renewed its organizational activities in Britain, and pressed candidates hard for Home Rule pledges. In that year, for instance, the Confederation received pledges from two men, both Radicals (Jacob Bright and John Barran), and helped them win by-elections. Unlike Butt, the new leaders of the Confederation saw no inherent advantage in electing Radicals and Liberals. They openly advocated a stalemate between the major British parties, on the theory that once the Home Rulers

33. Cities where Home Rule associations had been founded: Blackburn, Bolton, Bristol, Glasgow, Liverpool, Manchester, Newcastle, and Preston. London boroughs with associations: Chelsea, Finsbury, Fulham, Southwark, and Tower Hamlets.

34. Thornley, *Butt*, 141, 157, 291–92; John Denvir, *The Irish in Britain* (London, 1892), 262–67.

35. At the annual meeting of the Home Rule Confederation in Leeds, Carter, Harrison, Havelock, W. H. James, and C. H. Wilson, all Radicals, were criticized for their failure to support Home Rule, as was the Liberal James Stewart. *The Times*, June 29, 1875.

held the political balance, they could exact concessions from any party that tried to form a government.

Confrontation politics accomplished something that Butt had not been able to do: it forced Ireland on the attention of the Radicals. Although Radicals did not by any means respond by adopting outright the Irish nationalist program, at least they began to think seriously about Irish problems faced by parliament. Few did so happily. Most of them opposed obstruction, for one thing. To them absolute majority rule was the heart of representative government; no minority had the right to impede the will of the majority—indeed, this was one of the attitudes that distinguished most of them as Radicals. The editor of *The Echo* complained that Biggar and Parnell were forgetting the rights of the British people at large.[36] Goldwin Smith, the staunch individualist historian, warned that Home Rulers were "damaging and discrediting the House of Commons."[37] Butt himself argued that obstruction "would alienate from us the sympathies of the English democracy, who would see in an attempt to lower the House of Commons an attack upon England and themselves."[38] Nevertheless, a few Radical M.P.'s were prepared to assist in obstructing on some non-Irish issues like prison abuses and imperialism. The Irish obstructives tried to choose issues on which they could attract at least some Radical support. For this reason they made their strongest obstruction against the confederation of the South African states, a policy that many anti-imperialist Radicals opposed.[39]

Like most aspects of the confrontation strategy, Irish obstruction aroused disputes within the Radical movement. It set off, for example, an argument between Chamberlain and his intimate friend John Morley. Though brief, this disagreement was important in that it revealed conflicting tendencies in the Radical mind and foreshadowed later, crucial battles between the most outstanding Radical politician and the leading Radical intellectual. Morley, at that time editor of the *Fortnightly Review*, had developed his journal

36. April 6, 1877.
37. "Indignation Meetings," *F.R.* 139 (July 1878), 101.
38. Butt to Father Joseph Murphy, quoted in *The Times*, September 7, 1877.
39. F. Hugh O'Donnell, *A History of the Irish Parliamentary Party*, 2 vols. (London, 1910), I, 189, 196, 232–33.

into one of the most influential forces in British political thought. A small, nervous man of great sensitivity, Morley had long taken a deep and sympathetic interest in Ireland. In one of his two books on Edmund Burke, he had written that real union with Ireland had never been achieved because Ireland had not been made an equal partner with England.[40] Following a visit to America in 1867, during which he was impressed by the prosperity and respectability of the American Irish, Morley concluded that it was English misrule, not the Irish character, that made the Irish seem incorrigible. Ireland ought to be governed solely for the happiness of the Irish people; therefore it ought to be governed by Irish ideas.[41]

Now some other Radicals mouthed similar words about governing Ireland by Irish ideas, but few operated in practice according to them. Morley did; consequently, he hesitated to blame the Irish M.P.'s for obstruction. He thought that the Conservative government had contributed to the parliamentary problem by refusing to listen to what the Irish had to say or to "discuss their arguments on their merits."[42] In the August and September issues of the *Fortnightly*, Morley defended the obstructives' "severe and searching examination" of the mutiny and prison bills. While the prospect of all legislation being stopped was serious, obstruction so far had been beneficial. In October Morley criticized Parnell and Biggar for boasting that they intended to stop all the workings of parliament, but still he argued that the House could not punish them. He agreed with Leonard Courtney, who said that punishment and expulsion of the obstructives would in fact mean punishment and disfranchisement of their constituencies. This, Courtney had declared, "is really the groundwork of the demand of Home Rule."[43]

Morley's ideas about the basis of the Irish problem set him apart from Chamberlain. The great Birmingham Radical, a clean-shaven, hard-faced man who in earlier years had distinguished himself as a particularly ruthless industrialist, never troubled himself with the

40. F. W. Hirst, *Early Life and Letters of John Morley*, 2 vols. (London, 1927), I, 101.
41. *Ibid.*, 129–32.
42. Morley, "Affairs," *F.R.* 127 (July 1877), 145.
43. "Affairs," 296–99; "Affairs," 429–34; "Affairs," 591–92.

theoretical implications of a political problem. He saw that obstruction caused difficulties for Englishmen, and he came down decisively against it. He wrote to Morley: "I see you have been defending Courtney again and I fear you have a half kindness for those rascally Irishmen who are destined to give us a great deal of trouble yet, and perhaps to force on the English Parliament that 'Iron Hand' or system of cloture which has been found necessary in almost every other deliberative assembly."[44] Morley submitted to Chamberlain's opinion, as he usually did. For all his intelligence, Morley showed marked deference to men of action, especially Chamberlain:

> How many times shall I protest to you that I utterly dislike and contemn the Obstructives; they are tiresome, insolent, insincere, obstinate, without well considered aims of a respectable kind; in short they have not one single spark of quality that attracts or in any way whatever interests me.
>
> All I urge is that it will be a grievous thing if in order to crush such a brute as O'Donnell and such a very poor creature as Parnell, you forge a weapon that will most assuredly be used against yourself by the rowdy section of the Tories. Do you think that when the Church question comes seriously into the House, they will stick at a trifle?[45]

The difference between Morley's sympathetic understanding of the Irish and Chamberlain's tendency to treat them as obstacles would one day drive a wedge into both their friendship and Radicalism. But for the moment, obstruction primarily concerned the Home Rulers and the Tory government; Radicals were content to leave them to their struggle. In the constituencies, however, Irish pressure on Radicals was increasing, and at just the time when the Radical recovery from 1874 was making real headway. The Home Rule Confederation submitted to candidates in every constituency where the Irish vote was large a pledge to vote for the appointment of a select committee to inquire into the basis for the demand for Home Rule.[46]

44. October 3, 1877, Chamberlain Papers, JC 5/54/182.
45. Morley to Chamberlain, October 10, 1877, Chamberlain Papers, JC 5/54/183.
46. R. Barry O'Brien, *The Life of Charles Stewart Parnell* 2 vols. (London, 1899), I, 123.

In April 1877 the electoral activity of Irishmen in Salford brought about serious tension between Radicals and Home Rulers. There a noted advocate of land reform, Joseph Kay, stood for a seat in the House of Commons with the blessings of Radical leaders, including John Bright. When the local Home Rule association approached Kay to negotiate for the Irish vote, he agreed to support an inquiry into Home Rule. This pledge upset many Liberals who detested the idea of "buying" Irish votes. Kay got the Irish support but lost Liberal votes, and with them the election. A number of Liberals and Radicals blamed the Home Rulers for the loss.

The incident in Salford quickly ballooned into general antagonism between Irish nationalists and Radicals. One angry M.P., undoubtedly a Radical, wrote *The Times* to assert that Kay had lost because of his coquetting with the Home Rulers, and to recommend that both "Tories and Radicals" in the future agree to reject Irish electoral claims.[47] This letter, signed only "M.P.," drew a hot response from F. H. O'Donnell, vice-president and honorary secretary of the Home Rule Confederation, and one of the chief obstructive M.P.'s. O'Donnell reminded "M.P." that the Confederation wanted *neither* English party to become dominant in the House. In any British constituency the Irish vote would go to the highest bidder. In fact, he wrote, because of their very liberalism, Liberal candidates who rejected Irish demands would receive the brunt of Irish electoral vengeance. "The Liberal party [he concluded] may wait till the crack of doom, but until they have accepted Home Rule for Ireland, they will be allowed, whether most worthy or 'most unworthy,' to bear no part in the government of the British Empire."[48]

O'Donnell's challenge and the strategy it symbolized evoked an angry response from Radicals. It threatened their electoral plans and it insulted their righteous perception of themselves. In the House of Commons, Henry Fawcett gave voice to Radical anger in declaring that neither he nor other Liberals could be intimidated into voting for Home Rule; he was confident that the Liberals would prefer to remain in opposition "until the youngest Member of the Party had grown grey with age" than to submit to intimidation by

47. *The Times*, April 20, 1877.
48. F. H. O'Donnell to *The Times*, April 23, 1877.

the Irish.[49] Though in a calmer tone, John Bright also expressed the Radical attitude toward the Home Rule strategy. In a telegram to an Irish group, he wrote: "I do not see any chance for a better Government so long as the Irish members refuse to unite with English and Scotch Liberal members. An Irish party hostile to the Liberal Party of Great Britain insures the perpetual reign of the Tories."[50]

III. Radicals and Parnell, 1879

Bright believed the Irish nationalists should abandon the parts of their program that Liberals could not accept, while supporting the Liberals on liberal measures. But not all Radicals shared his one-sided concept of the problem. Three interrelated things began to turn some politically aware Radicals toward accommodation with the Home Rulers: the recovery of Radicalism, which was by now feeding on the moral power of the agitation on the Eastern Question; the anticipation of an imminent general election; and the prospect of increasing Radical influence in the House of Commons at the expense of moderate Liberals and Whigs. The most important of this group of Radicals were Chamberlain, Morley, and Dilke, each of whom characteristically had a broader perspective and a keener sensitivity to political reality than the average Radical. By mid-1878, with the political stakes mounting, they were beginning to think that Radicalism could not afford to ignore Parnell's potential power. During the next year and a half, they tried to construct an *entente* between Radicalism and the Parnellite movement, but from its start it would be an alliance of political convenience, not love.

Chamberlain, Morley, and Dilke began their policy of conciliating the Home Rulers in May and June of 1878. Morley took the occasion of the assassination of an Irish landlord, Lord Leitrim, to urge an understanding of the Irish. While not condoning the atrocity, he adopted a tone far different from the outrage expressed by most Englishmen. Morley even suggested in the *Fortnightly* that Englishmen should learn from the murder "that there are other processes of reasoning besides our own, and other codes of morality

49. *Hansard* 233 (April 24, 1877), 1800–1806.
50. Quoted in *The Times*, April 11, 1878.

and points of honor." The failure to understand Ireland had long led Englishmen to assume that what was right for England was right for Ireland. Now, he wrote, England needed a new approach to Irish problems, and Butt's retirement from the leadership of the Home Rule party provided an excellent opportunity.[51] In the House of Commons, Chamberlain and Dilke tried to demonstrate their spirit of conciliation by voting for an Irish resolution to sanction a Roman Catholic university in Ireland, which, of course, ran counter to every Radical principle.[52] Heretofore the Radicals in parliament had solidly opposed denominational education, including Catholic university education in Ireland; thus the significance of their votes was widely recognized. Matthew Arnold, no friend of Nonconformity, praised their behavior in the *Fortnightly*: "... few things in politics have ever given me more pleasure than to see the aid courageously afforded to Irish Catholics by this little band of advanced English Liberals."[53]

Meanwhile, developments within the nationalist party also tended toward *rapprochement* with the Radicals. The strong anti-imperialism of the Parnellites was replacing the imperialism of Isaac Butt. One of the issues that had separated the Home Rulers from the Radicals was the support some Irish M.P.'s gave to Disraeli's forward policy, particularly in regard to the Eastern Question.[54] But anti-imperialism gained great popularity in Ireland during 1877: the obstruction by Parnell and Biggar of the South African Confederation bill was popular in Ireland as much for its anti-imperialism as for its militancy. In 1878 most Irish nationalists reacted strongly against the pro-Disraeli Eastern policy of Butt and O'Donnell, which they associated with Butt's failure to provide aggressive leadership on Home Rule. One Parnellite wrote: "The Address in answer to the Royal Speech, which calls upon us to sanction the blood-stained acts of the Royal butchers who have invaded Afghanistan, is passing through the House without any division representing the protest

51. "Affairs," *F.R.* 137 (May 1878), 799–800.
52. *Hansard* 240 (May 31, 1878), 1038; (June 3, 1878), 1150–52.
53. "Irish Catholicism and British Liberalism," *F.R.* 139 (July 1878), 30.
54. Thornley, *Butt*, 360–63. The support some Home Rule M.P.'s gave to Disraeli's Eastern policy led Chamberlain to call them a "scurvy lot." Letter to J. T. Bunce, February 16, 1877, Chamberlain Papers, JC 5/8/25.

of the Irish nation; without any demands by the Irish party for the restoration of the Irish parliament or even the redress of grievances. The man who has brought this disgrace upon our country is Isaac Butt."[55]

Chamberlain and Dilke attempted to take advantage of the growing harmony of views by coming to terms with the Irish parliamentary party. On the occasion of the debate on the Zulu War, they met with Parnell and Major J. P. Nolan, the Home Rule party whip. Accounts of the Radical-Irish conversations differ, but probably the four M.P.'s met formally once—at dinner on February 15, 1879—and individually a few other times. Chamberlain indicated in a memorandum of the formal meeting that Nolan "was kindly to the idea of a more cordial understanding between English Radicals and the Irish National Party" but that Parnell "was less opportunist and more irreconcilable than Nolan." Nolan raised two issues on which the Radicals and Irishmen would have to reach agreement: an Irish Catholic university and Irish land problems. Parnell was not much inclined to find agreement with Radicals, and insisted that no arrangement be made that might restrict the Home Rule movement. Chamberlain inferred from his comments that Parnell feared the popularity of land reform, which might divert attention from Home Rule. He concluded that, though Parnell would not exert himself to bring about an alliance between Radical and Irish M.P.'s, the Irish leader believed the Liberals would earn "the support of the Irish people and party for some years at least" if they introduced a good land reform bill.[56]

The conversations did not result in any significant firm agreements between Radicals and Parnellites, though the two factions cooperated in subsequent days on a couple of non-Irish issues.[57] The problem for Chamberlain and Dilke, and for their associate Morley, was to persuade Radicals to support the Irish nationalists on some important questions, while convincing the Irish by word and ex-

55. O'Connor Power to *The Freeman's Journal*, quoted in *The Times*, December 7, 1878.

56. The fullest and most reliable account of the conversations is a memoir by Chamberlain, quoted in Garvin, *Chamberlain*, I, 273–74.

57. The issues were the Radicals' opposition to the government's county boards bill and to the Zulu War. Dilke Memoirs, 43,934, ff. 5, 8.

ample that the Radicals genuinely meant to help them. Chamberlain and Morley recognized that, with a general election in the offing, Radicals had to be shown the possibility and advantage of cooperation with the Parnellites. They also realized that of the two issues raised at the February meeting with Nolan and Parnell, the land question would be a far more satisfactory ground for common action than university education. As Morley wrote in the *Fortnightly*, it was a "foregone conclusion" that Liberals could not satisfy the Irish on education as long as the Irish priesthood felt as they did; but "cordially united action" on Irish land reform would be possible. Land reform would provide the "material guarantee of a genuine and durable alliance between English and Irish Liberalism."[58]

Concentration on the Irish land problem was a shrewd choice, as land reform was a staple item in Radical circles. The Englishman most responsible for the spread of concern about the Irish land problem was G. J. Shaw Lefevre (later Baron Eversley), a Radical who had been investigating Irish land tenure for years. Shaw Lefevre was an industrious and able, though resolutely dull, expert on land questions of all kinds. He had a passion for hard facts and hard work. In 1877 he persuaded the House of Commons by sheer accumulation of detailed evidence to appoint a select committee to investigate the operation of the Bright Clauses (land purchase) of the land act of 1870. The House named Bright and Butt, among others, to the committee, but Shaw Lefevre did most of the work. He tirelessly gathered evidence and promoted his conclusions among leading Liberals. Though the committee rejected his draft for its final report, it proceeded to write in most of his points as amendments to the majority report.[59]

Shaw Lefevre concluded from his investigation that the Bright Clauses had failed: fewer than 600 tenants out of 600,000 in Ireland had purchased their holdings. On the other hand, the purchase

---

58. "Affairs," *F.R.* 147 (March 1879), 488–90; 148 (April 1879), 637.

59. J. L. Hammond, *Gladstone and the Irish Nation* (London, 1938), 160; Lord Eversley, *Gladstone and Ireland: The Irish Policy of Parliament from 1850–1894* (London, 1912), 80; *Report of the Select Committee on the Irish Land Act (1870)*, Sessional Papers, 1878, no. 249, vol. 15, pp. 1–424; Shaw Lefevre to Gladstone, October 11, 1877, Gladstone Papers, 44,153; Shaw Lefevre to Chamberlain, November 8, 1877, Chamberlain Papers, JC 5/52/5.

clauses of the Irish church act had worked. The differences were that the church act had made a higher proportion of the purchase price available as a loan to the tenant, and that the administrators of the church act had provided a simpler and cheaper operation than the administrators of the Bright Clauses. Shaw Lefevre recommended, therefore, an act to establish a commission to relieve the tenants of legal and brokerage costs, and to advance as a loan a larger portion of the sale price. He argued persuasively that for the sake of productivity and stability in Ireland it was necessary to increase the numbers of small owners. As long as there were 600,000 tenants but only 12,000 owners in Ireland, the country would enjoy no political or social security.[60]

Radicals generally agreed with Shaw Lefevre's proposals. The testimony of such a responsible and careful expert lent an aura of respectability to Irish land reform that had seemed lacking before. Radicals could no longer doubt that the Irish had legitimate grievances regarding the land. Bright himself supported Shaw Lefevre's proposals.[61] In the *Fortnightly* Morley added his approval, and expressed the common Radical hope that the spirit of land reform would spread from Ireland to England.[62] Throughout the Radical movement the opinion took hold that proprietorship would transform the Irish tenants from dangerous malcontents into peaceful and loyal citizens.[63]

The Irish M.P.'s, however, were determined to press their case for a Catholic university. This issue laid bare a sensitive root of Radicalism and reduced the middle-class part of the movement to squabbling factions. In February 1879 the O'Connor Don moved the second reading of his Irish university education bill. Almost immediately four divisions of the parliamentary Radicals appeared, some with powerful extraparliamentary support, all with impressive arsenals of principles. First in the field, and backed by the largest forces outside parliament, were Nonconformist Radicals who attacked the bill in the name of nonsectarian education. Henry Rich-

60. *Hansard* 245 (May 2, 1879), 1596–1616; Shaw Lefevre, *English and Irish Land Questions*, 157.
61. *Hansard* 245 (May 2, 1879), 1647–56.
62. "Affairs," *F.R.* 147 (March 1879), 489–90; 150 (June 1879), 964.
63. *Daily News*, May 3, 1879; *The Echo*, May 3, 1879.

ard, parliamentary spokesman for the Peace Society and the Dissenting Deputies, declared that the bill would endow the Roman Catholic priesthood. He could not accept it "without practically repudiating principles which I have professed and proclaimed all my life...."[64] The second group, much smaller than the first and without extensive extraparliamentary support, was composed of Nonconformist Radicals who used the theme of religious equality to support the bill. Osborne Morgan, himself an Anglican but the leader of Nonconformist efforts to break Anglican privileges in the cemeteries, argued that the Irish university problem should be settled, and that any settlement must "recommend itself to the majority of the Irish people."[65] E. A. Leatham, a Quaker, contended that it was precisely because of religious equality that the bill should pass: the Irish Episcopalians and Presbyterians had their universities, but the Catholics, the vast majority of the Irish nation, did not.[66]

Freethinking Radicals split into the other two groups on the university question. Morley, a militant unbeliever, supported the bill on anti-clerical grounds: "There is neither more of bigotry nor rapacity in the present demand of the Irish Catholics, than in the contention of the Irish and English Protestants. Bigotry is not the exclusive note of any one church, but the common quality of all."[67] On the other hand, Radicals like Courtney and Fawcett, as true sons of the Enlightenment, detested the Catholic Church and any measure that tended to establish it in the Irish educational system. Fawcett denied that he would treat Catholics any differently from other sects: he would "sweep away every vestige of denominationalism" in Irish education. He would defend this principle in any country; therefore, he thought that "governing Ireland by Irish ideas" was one of the most unfortunate phrases ever invented.[68]

By the early summer of 1879 the issue of Irish university education was tearing middle-class Radicalism apart. Almost every Radical journal had ferociously attacked the proposal, and some of the most influential Radical newspapers were beginning to criticize the

64. *Hansard* 247 (June 25, 1879), 641–48.
65. *Hansard* 246 (May 21, 1879), 974–77.
66. *Hansard* 247 (June 25, 1879), 630–36.
67. "Affairs," *F.R.* 150 (June 1879), 966–68.
68. *Hansard* 248 (July 24, 1879), 1232–38.

very idea of cooperating with the Irish in parliament.[69] Chamberlain and Morley could only try to shift attention to less divisive issues and to show the Parnellites in other ways that Radicals could be useful allies. In the *Fortnightly* Morley urged Liberals to drop the subject of Irish university education and take up land reform—"the only measure in reference to Ireland which offers Liberalism a prospect of united action: it is the only one also which proposes to strike at the root of Irish discontent."[70] For his part, Chamberlain vigorously joined the Irish in obstructing the flogging provisions of the annual army bill. Though opposing the Liberal party leader, Lord Hartington, Chamberlain and the Irish attracted a good deal of working-class support.[71] Chamberlain also went out of his way to compliment Parnell, first in the House, then in a letter to the *Birmingham Daily Post*. He wrote: "It is impossible to exaggerate the industry of this gentleman—not to admire his unflinching determination, in what he believes to be right—his courage, his coolness."[72] Morley bestowed similarly extravagant praises on the Irish obstructives, and he stated in the *Fortnightly* that Liberals had every reason to find common ground between themselves and the Home Rule party. Again he recommended seeing Ireland through Irish eyes: ". . . a willingness to see Irish affairs from the point of view of the people most immediately concerned, is not necessarily the proof of a spirit of dishonest intrigue."[73]

IV. RADICALS, PARNELL, AND THE ELECTION OF 1880

Parnell remained steadfastly aloof from an alliance with the Radicals. He cooperated with them in the House when their interests happened to coincide with his own, but outside parliament he continued to bring organized electoral pressure on English and Scottish candidates, Radicals included. Early in 1879 he toured the largest

69. *The Nonconformist*, May 21, 1879; *The Liberator*, June 2, July 1, 1879; *The Echo*, May 22, 1879; *The Baptist*, August 1, 1879; *The Congregationalist*, July 1879; *Daily News*, June 25, 1879.

70. "Affairs," *F.R.* 151 (July 1879), 163–64.

71. O'Donnell, *Irish Parliamentary Party*, I, 331–36.

72. O'Brien, *Parnell*, I, 188; Garvin, *Chamberlain*, I, 274.

73. "The House of Commons," *F.R.* 152 (August 1879), 187–92.

British constituencies and attacked the M.P.'s (all Radicals) who had failed to honor Home Rule pledges. In June 1879 the Home Rule Confederation issued a circular to its affiliated associations specifying the terms of the pledge to be submitted to all candidates in the next election.[74] At the annual conference of the Confederation, held in August at the Crystal Palace, Parnell called for a hard line against the British parties. He declared confidently—and correctly—that English and Scottish M.P.'s were concerned about the Irish vote, and forecast that the Irish would control some forty British constituencies. The conference agreed unanimously to a resolution of independence from both parties.[75]

Parnell refused to ally with the Radicals for several reasons. He was by nature a suspicious and cautious man. He also was very wary of political bargains that might compromise his position as nationalist leader. It was far from clear that Chamberlain, Dilke, and Morley spoke for the entire Radical movement, which had so recently proved its fractiousness, and Chamberlain's National Liberal Federation had yet to show its electoral power. Moreover, in 1879 he was involved in an extremely important and delicate development within the Irish nationalist movement, and he did not want to add complications. This development rose from two interrelated causes: a severe agricultural crisis in Ireland, and a tendency among some Fenians toward accepting a constitutional agitation for land reform. A combination of competition from imported foodstuffs and a series of bad harvests had by the winter of 1878–79 brought disaster to Irish farming. As tenant farmers lost the ability to pay rents, evictions increased: from 463 in 1877 to 1,238 in 1879.[76] Popular agitation for relief and reform became intense in the Irish countryside. Impressed by the need for immediate remedy and by Parnell's defiance of the British parliament, many Fenians now thought that Parnell might be able to forge an effective constitutional nationalist movement. In the summer of 1879 Parnell, Michael Davitt (the leading Fenian land reformer), and John Devoy (an American Fenian)

74. *The Times*, June 12, 1879.
75. *The Times*, August 11, 1879.
76. Hammond, *Gladstone and the Irish Nation*, 155; Beckett, *Making of Modern Ireland*, 385.

established the "new departure," which amalgamated the constitutional and revolutionary nationalist movements in a program of land reform. The Land League, founded in October 1879, was the organization for the new departure.[77]

The Land Leaguers did not agree on a single plan for land reform. Davitt wanted to have the land nationalized by an independent national state. Parnell preferred land purchase and redistribution, carried out compulsorily by an Irish state, but with fair compensation to landlords. In either plan the social consequences for Ireland would have been enormous. In 1879, however, the Land League for tactical reasons settled for a less extreme program: security for the tenantry and an improved land purchase system.[78] In this shape the Irish demand for land reforms met a kindred enthusiasm among British Radicals. Working-class Radicals advocated land reforms in Ireland ranging from tenant right to nationalization. Middle-class Radicals sought an *entente* with the Irish nationalists on the basis of increased security for the tenants and land purchase.[79] The spirit of brotherhood in combat against landlordism, growing strong in both the Irish nationalist and Radical movements, operated against Parnell's strategy of strict independence from both British parties.

Examples of cooperation between Irish nationalists and Radicals occurred frequently in the first months of 1880. Some professional English land reformers, notably William E. Bear and James Howard, joined F. H. O'Donnell (who supported land reform but not the Land League) in establishing the Farmers' Alliance in order to coordinate the efforts of land reformers throughout the United Kingdom.[80] In February 1880 representatives of almost every element in both the Irish nationalist and English Radical movements staged a meeting in London to demonstrate their cooperation. Besides in-

77. T. W. Moody, "The New Departure in Irish Politics, 1878-9," in *Essays in British and Irish History in Honour of James Eadie Todd*, ed. H. H. Cronne *et al.* (London, 1949).

78. Eversley, *Gladstone and Ireland*, 101.

79. Bright to J. G. MacCarthy, quoted in *The Times*, December 6, 1879; Bright's speech at Manchester, reported in *The Times*, January 26, 1880; Chamberlain's speech in the House, *Hansard* 250 (February 10, 1880), 388-95; Morley, "Affairs," *F.R.* 156 (December 1879), 917-22; 159 (March 1880), 462-65.

80. O'Donnell, *Irish Parliamentary Party*, I, 347, 354-56; O'Donnell, Bear, and Howard to *The Times*, April 10, 12, 15, 1880, respectively.

dividual Radical delegates, there were representatives of the Land League, the Land Reform Association (an English organization), the London Trades Council, the Agricultural Labourer's Union, and several other trades unions. The end result was to combine the programs of the various nationalist and Radical groups in a broad attack on "landlordism." As chairman, the great atheist Radical Charles Bradlaugh carried resolutions for abolition of entail and the game laws, limitations of family settlements, tenant right, a graduated land tax, and "one and the same land law for Great Britain and Ireland." Joseph Arch, the organizer of English farm laborers, successfully moved a resolution for franchise extension and the redistribution of seats, arguing that these would contribute to the chances of land reform. The meeting ended with an expression of sympathy for the Land League "and its efforts to destroy feudalism and plant the Irish people on the soil of their native land," and with a resolution to establish a Land Law Reform League "for the purpose of agitating for a radical reform in the land laws."[81] Irish land reform, it seemed, had become part of the Radical program.

Disraeli made *rapprochement* between Radicals and Irish nationalists easier by three serious mistakes in late 1879 and early 1880. The first had to do with the agricultural crisis in Ireland. By the winter of 1879 famine threatened Ireland more seriously than at any time since 1848. Disraeli's relief measures were inadequate, and numerous Radicals seized the opportunity to champion justice for Ireland. A. J. Mundella, a businessman and M.P. from Sheffield, even argued that Ireland could no longer be governed "in full accord with those economical theories which worked satisfactorily in England."[82] The second of Disraeli's errors was to sanction the arrest of three Land Leaguers—Davitt, Killen, and Daly. By the time of the arrests (November 1879) the British were watching Irish events with avid attention. Furthermore, the mass of people in the Radical movement believed that the Irish landlords, not the Land League, bore the blame for Irish problems. Popular reaction against the arrests was vigorous. On November 30 more than 100,000 people (according

81. *The Times*, February 11, 1880.
82. *Hansard* 250 (February 10, 1880), 422–27.

to *The Times*) gathered in Hyde Park to protest the arrests and to express approval of the Land League.[83] In the *Fortnightly* Morley voiced the suspicions of most Radicals by contending that the arrests only represented the Tory government's attempt to stir up anti-Irish feeling in England and Scotland for the general election.[84]

Though the arrests may not have been part of his electoral policy, Disraeli did want to exploit anti-Irish emotion in the constituencies. The Home Rule Confederation through all the camaraderie between Radicals and Irishmen had maintained its policy of independence from both British parties. In two by-elections held early in 1880, the Home Rulers' policy roused considerable Liberal and Radical anger. In Liverpool the Liberal candidate, Lord Ramsay, was forced by the Home Rule party to submit to a modified Home Rule pledge. Numerous Liberals resented Ramsay's compact with the Irish and withheld their votes; Ramsay lost the election, amid mutual recriminations between Radicals and Home Rulers.[85] In Southwark an official Liberal candidate named Dunn lost his by-election when a working-class candidate entered the contest, promised to vote for an inquiry into Home Rule, and took the Irish vote. The chairman of Dunn's committee complained that the intervention of the Parnellites against Dunn had cost him his seat.[86] Disraeli, meanwhile, was delighted to see Liberals, Radicals, and Irish so disunited; consequently, he decided on immediate dissolution.[87]

So far Disraeli has played the electoral game shrewdly. The dissolution constituted a serious threat to Radicals in the forty or fifty largest constituencies in England and Scotland, for it found them in a crossfire of Irish pressure from one side and angry Liberal reaction from the other. At this point, however, Disraeli made the third of his mistakes. He failed to notice the genuine desire for amelioration in Ireland widespread among Liberals, and especially among Rad-

---

83. *The Times*, December 1, 1879. Other examples of Radical opposition to the arrests: *The Nonconformist*, November 26, 1879; *The Baptist*, November 28, 1879.

84. "Affairs," *F.R.* 156 (December 1879), 917–18.

85. *The Times*, January 26, 30, 31, February 7, 1880; Edward D. J. Wilson, "Irish Politics and English Parties," *Nineteenth Century* 6 (December 1879), 1068–81.

86. *The Times*, February 13, 14, 17, 19, 1880.

87. Robert Blake, *Disraeli* (New York, 1967), 703–4.

icals. He misplayed his strong hand and forced the Home Rule Confederation to abandon its hard-line policy. Disraeli's misplay took the form of his election manifesto, an open letter to the Duke of Marlborough (the Irish Viceroy) that was supposed to take advantage of Liberal anger toward Irish electoral tactics. Disraeli claimed that Liberals were tampering with the sanctity of the union merely to win the Irish vote. Home Rule, not famine, was the disaster that menaced Ireland, he declared.[88] Only two days after publication of the manifesto, the Home Rule Confederation issued its own election circular, a tirade against the Prime Minister. It said that Disraeli's manifesto amounted to a "declaration of war" on the Irish people. Even if no Englishman had spoken for Ireland, Irishmen had the duty to defeat Disraeli: "Vote against Benjamin Disraeli as you should vote against the mortal enemy of your country and your race."[89]

Radicals were only too happy to see the end, even if temporary, of the Confederation's policy of giving Irish votes to the highest bidder. They refused to play Disraeli's game by denouncing Home Rule. In the election, therefore, Liberal and Radical candidates throughout Britain received Irish votes without being required to promise to vote for an inquiry into Home Rule. Nearly every Radical included Irish land reform in his platform, but only about fifteen Radicals (and one Liberal) who won seats in 1880 definitely pledged to support the Home Rule inquiry.[90] If the Liverpool and Southwark by-elections mean anything, it is that many more Radicals would have been forced into making the pledge, and perhaps into losing the election, had Disraeli's manifesto not caused the Irish in Britain to cease confrontation politics. In the event, a strong Radical contingent, some one-third of the Liberal majority, won seats in the

88. *Ibid.*, 707.
89. Quoted in *The Times*, March 12, 1880.
90. Radicals who won seats in 1880 and who are known to have pledged definitely for an inquiry into Home Rule: Arnold, Barran, Jacob Bright, Broadhurst, Burt, Cowen, Lawson, Macdonald, Samuel Morley, Rogers, Rylands, and Woodall. Bradlaugh also pledged for Home Rule but was not allowed to take his place in the House except from July 1880 to March 1881. The Confederation claimed that Anderson, Cameron, and Middleton (all from Glasgow) had pledged, but they denied it.

new House of Commons. Though they were not by any means Home Rulers, they were prepared to demand extensive reforms in the Irish land system.

Radical attitudes toward Ireland had come a long way since 1874. Indifferent and frequently hostile toward the early Home Rule movement, most Radicals by 1880 had been forced by the rise of Parnellism and the strategy of confrontation, coupled with the major agricultural crisis in Ireland, if not to accept Home Rule, at least to attend to Irish problems. What is interesting is the force that was necessary to get the middle-class Radicals to look beyond their own immediate interests. Butt's powers of persuasion, though formidable and though framed very often in Radical political principles, had not led the Radicals to act favorably on Irish matters. Pressure from the Parnellites was more successful, for while Irish militancy had only alienated Conservatives, Whigs, and most orthodox Liberals, it had begun to work positively on the Radicals. This was true despite the fact that the Parnellite strategy threatened Radical notions about the function of parliament and about their electoral interests.

This first confrontation with militant Home Rulers had revealed other interesting things about late-Victorian Radicalism. The Nonconformity and anti-clericalism which gave rise to principles of religious liberty in Radicalism also tended to produce an ugly anti-Catholic bigotry. The principles of democracy and national self-determination central to the program of Radicalism clashed with ideas about Catholicism, and sometimes about the nature of the Irish "race," rooted in the social soil of the movement. Finally, the main features of the structure of the Radical movement were made to stand out in relief. Even though Radical workingmen seem to have been supportive of Irish claims, they had little direct effect on the votes and attitudes of the Radical M.P.'s, who did not take instructions from below. Moreover, because there was no central organization even at the top level to impose unity on Radical behavior, the leaders of Radicalism like Chamberlain, Dilke, and Morley found it impossible to keep middle-class Radicals from interpreting Irish issues according to mutually conflicting preconceptions. Thus it was difficult for them to bargain effectively with Parnell. When Irish pressure simultaneously demanded answers and divided the Radical movement, the leadership had to find issues pertaining to Ireland on which Radicals *could* agree; by this process the Radical movement began to be turned toward the Irish point of view. The Parnellite strategy of confrontation played directly on Radical weaknesses, and the problem would grow worse, not better.

CHAPTER THREE

Radicals, Coercion, and Conciliation
1880-82

The history of the Radical response to the Irish Question entered a new phase in 1880. Though determined after the general election of 1880 to work important reforms in Ireland, mainly regarding the land laws, Radicals soon were embroiled in Irish affairs much more deeply and fully than they had desired or intended. They expected to grant some kind of security to the Irish tenantry, witness the dissipation of Irish discontent and nationalism, and, while basking in the applause of a grateful Irish people, turn their reforming hands to English problems. Instead, for two extremely turbulent years, Radicals, like all Englishmen, could do little but deal with recalcitrant Irish problems and ungrateful Irish politicians.

Moreover, the Irish Question in these two years came on the British in a form never seen before. Irish agrarian unrest, agitation, and violence created an extraordinary mood of anxiety and alarm among Britons. At the same time, the Parnellites quickly reverted to confrontation politics after the brief detente of 1880. At Westminster, the Irish M.P.'s presented their demands with a force and tenacity new to parliament. The Parnellites displayed organization, discipline, and energy far surpassing the efforts of earlier Irish parties. As the leader of a constitutional party backed implicitly by a violent movement in Ireland, Parnell achieved unusual power in the House of Commons. This double-barreled pressure by the Irish brought about a situation of extreme gravity. Naturally, the British response, both repressive and reformist, went far beyond any made since the act of union.

The unique Irish pressure caught the Radicals in, for them, a unique position. Irish militancy and agitation were now directed against a Liberal government; social disorder in Ireland was now a problem for Liberals, not Conservatives. As a large part of the government party, and as men deeply committed to Gladstone, Radicals felt a new responsibility for governing Ireland. For Chamberlain and Bright, who accepted cabinet office, and for six other Radicals who held subordinate government posts, the problems were especially severe. But all Radicals, both in and out of parliament, had to share the moral responsibility for Liberal party policies. They could no longer treat the struggle of the British government and the Irish nationalists as a war between foreign powers.

The uniqueness of their position would have been serious enough for the Radicals, but in addition the particular shape in which the Irish Question manifested itself caused especially grievous troubles within the Radical movement. By its violence and unruliness, Ireland from 1880 to 1882 tested the social and intellectual bases of Radicalism. It forced Radicals to consider their ultimate values and the extent of their identification with the prevailing social order. Their collective agonizing over these issues went to the heart of the Radical movement.

I. COERCION OR CONCILIATION, 1880

While Gladstone was forming his government in the spring of 1880, the situation in Ireland remained serious. Because of three bad harvests in succession, the winter of 1879–80 had been very bad for Irish tenants, and many were unable to pay their rents. Evictions went on apace. Resistance to evictions naturally followed, accompanied by sporadic agrarian crimes—landlords murdered and shot at, cattle and horses mutilated. The Land League did not encourage terrorism, but it did through massive agitation urge the tenants to cooperate in trying to reduce rents, stave off evictions, and keep new renters away from tenancies from which old occupants had been evicted. In short, much of Ireland seemed to be sinking into general social dissolution.[1]

In Great Britain the upper classes became increasingly concerned about the apparent lack of law and order in Ireland. Conservatives,

1. F. S. L. Lyons, *John Dillon: A Biography* (Chicago, 1968), 29–34.

Whigs, and a great many Liberals as well demanded the imposition of severe legal measures to restore order. Orthodox opinion held that it was worse than useless to conciliate the Irish while disorder flourished; order must precede reform. Radicals, however, believed that problems of land tenure caused the disturbances in Ireland. They expected the new Gladstone government to introduce, not a coercion bill, but a land bill designed to assist the tenants.[2] The problem was that the new Liberal Chief Secretary for Ireland, W. E. Forster, once a Radical himself, fell under the influence of the permanent officials of Dublin Castle almost immediately after his arrival in Ireland. They convinced him to seek a renewal of the coercion act, due to expire in 1880. When Radicals, who already detested Forster for his education act of 1870, got wind of the coercion idea, they unanimously opposed it. They simply did not believe that sufficient reason for coercion had yet been shown, and they thought that rule by the normal law should at least be tried first.[3] Chamberlain and Dilke warned Forster not to ask for coercion; and in order to stop him, Dilke deliberately leaked cabinet information to Frank Hill, editor of the *Daily News*.[4] The most important organ of the Liberal party, the *Daily News* carried strong anti-coercion leaders on May 14 and 15.[5] Whether these efforts were decisive is problematical. At any rate, the cabinet decided to proceed with remedial legislation rather than coercion.

Shaw Lefevre had already advised both Forster and Gladstone what most Radicals regarded as true—that a major revision of the Irish land laws was necessary. However, a major reform would necessarily be an extremely complicated measure, and the cabinet did not have time to undertake such a project in the 1880 session. They decided instead to introduce a temporary bill, which would extend the 1870 land act by providing compensation for disturbance even in cases of eviction for non-payment of rent. This was a very

2. *The Baptist*, January 30, 1880; *The Echo*, January 8, 1880; *Daily News*, April 17, 1880.

3. *Pall Mall Gazette*, May 14, 1880; *Reynolds's Newspaper*, May 23, 1880; *The Echo*, May 17, 1880.

4. Dilke Memoirs, 43,934, f. 182; Dilke Diary, May 13 and 14, 1880, 43,924.

5. The *Daily News* was owned by Samuel Morley, Henry Labouchere, and Dilke.

mild measure compared to what had long been proposed by Irish land reformers. The Parnellites, in fact, regarded it as too limited in application even for a temporary scheme. Yet the bill roused strong opposition from Tories and Whigs, who thought it would allow undue interference with the rights of property.[6] Radicals solidly supported the bill. They did not think that the laws of contract should strictly apply to Ireland. As John Morley wrote in the *Fortnightly*, the Irish landlords would have to realize that their rights "are limited by broad considerations of public utility and of responsibility to the multitude of their countrymen."[7] Within the government, Radicals made their feelings count. Chamberlain and Dilke threatened to resign if the cabinet dropped the bill, as suggested by Lord Hartington.[8] They won this early round, and the cabinet retained the bill. It gained a second reading in the House of Commons with eighty-five of the Radicals voting for it.[9]

The House of Lords promptly rejected the bill. Radicals throughout the country protested the Lords' blatant defiance of the will of the electorate, warning them that such behavior raised the question of maintaining an aristocracy that did not work for its wealth.[10] But the Radicals' protests were to no avail. Events in Ireland were moving rapidly, and the cabinet found by the summer of 1880 that the Land League's agitation and the number of agrarian outrages were increasing. In addition, boycotting by the tenantry had spread widely throughout Ireland. All of the cabinet agreed that a dissolution of parliament and a general election to reassert the authority of the Commons over the Lords was out of the question, as was reintroduction of the compensation for disturbance bill with clear warnings to the Lords.[11] Time for these alternatives had escaped.

6. Eversley, *Gladstone and Ireland*, 115; *Hansard* 253 (June 25, 1880), 862.

7. "Affairs," *F.R.* 163 (July 1880), 133. For similar expressions, see T. Wemyss Reid to Herbert Gladstone, July 18, 1880, Viscount Gladstone Papers, 46,041; and *Hansard* 253 (July 5, 1880), 1692–95; 254 (July 14, 26, 1880), 441–43, 1402–9.

8. Dilke Diary, July 2, 1880, 43,924.

9. *Hansard* 253 (July 5, 1880), 1725–28.

10. *Reynolds's Newspaper*, August 1, 1880; Maccoby, *Radicalism, 1852–86* (London, 1938), 259; O'Donnell, *History of the Irish Parliamentary Party*, I, 484; *The Times*, August 20, 1880.

11. Chamberlain later wrote that he wanted an autumn session so the compensation for disturbance bill could be reintroduced, but there is no evidence that

The only realistic choice for the government lay between continuing the normal law while framing a more comprehensive land bill, or calling a special autumn session of parliament in order to pass coercive measures.

Forster and Lord Cowper, the Lord Lieutenant, believed that the agitation in Ireland was out of control; they opted for a special session to enact coercion. The ensuing debate within Liberal circles revealed the beginnings of serious disagreement among Radicals about the vital issue of Irish disorder. Middle-class Radicals were becoming increasingly troubled by the unruliness of Irish parliamentary tactics and by the violence of the agitation in Ireland. For example, both R. W. Dale, a leading Congregationalist minister and exponent of the Birmingham "civic gospel," and James Kitson, president of the Leeds Liberal Association and vice-president of the National Liberal Federation, expressed disgust with Irish obstruction and belligerence.[12] *The Nonconformist and Independent* declared that the leaders of the agitation in Ireland were "wild demagogues" and that the Home Rule party was alienating Englishmen who might have advocated reforms for Ireland.[13] Even John Morley warned the Irish that if they continued their tendency toward sedition and crime, the government would have to ask for coercive powers.[14]

Inside the cabinet, Chamberlain was put in an increasingly difficult position. He shared the growing concern of middle-class Radicals about disorder in Ireland, but he was not ready to support a coercive proposal. Thus he resisted the pressure for a special session and reaffirmed in public that the government was "pledged up to the eyes to do justice to Ireland."[15] Privately, however, Chamberlain indicated that he had no objections to the *principle* of coercion and

---

he sought to promote the idea. He wrote a memorandum for the cabinet in August 1880, but it called only for a public works relief program. *Political Memoir*, 7.

12. Dale to Chamberlain, June 21, 1880, Chamberlain Papers, JC 5/20/2. Kitson to Herbert Gladstone, July 22, 1880, Viscount Gladstone Papers, 46,027. Even Bradlaugh was becoming angry with the Home Rulers: Walter L. Arnstein, *The Bradlaugh Case: A Study in Late Victorian Opinion and Politics* (Oxford, 1965), 86.

13. August 19, 1880.

14. "Affairs," *F.R.* 165 (September 1880), 401–3.

15. Clipping from *Birmingham Daily Post*, included with a note from Chamberlain to Gladstone, October 1880 (misdated by the B.M. as July 1880), Gladstone Papers, 44,125.

that he too considered the Irish agitation unjustified and illegal. In this mood he agreed to a cabinet decision to prosecute Parnell and other leading Land Leaguers under normal law.[16] He professed to find this step toward repression extremely repugnant, but necessary. He wrote to Dilke:

> I don't half like the Irish prosecutions, but I fear there is no alternative—except indeed the suspension of Habeas Corpus which I should like still less.
>
> Parnell is doing his best to make Irish legislation unpopular with English radicals. The workmen do not like to see law set at defiance, & a dissolution on the 'justice to Ireland' cry would under present circumstances be a hazardous operation.[17]

Undoubtedly Chamberlain and most middle-class Radicals considered the prosecutions by normal law moderate under the circumstances. But many working-class Radicals regarded them as a serious betrayal of Radicalism. To them it was clear that landlordism was the real cause of disorder in Ireland; thus, as *Reynolds's Newspaper* declared, to prosecute the Land Leaguers was to confuse "the cause and the occasion of the disease which troubles the body politic."[18] In the same spirit, delegates from most of the Radical clubs in London gathered on October 30, 1880, to protest coercion. The meeting opposed agrarian crimes, but resolved that "the responsibility for such outrages mainly rests on the landlord party which brought about the rejection of the Disturbance Bill, and it is vain to hope for peace and prosperity in Ireland until the Irish land has been restored to the Irish people."[19]

This working-class Radical opposition to repression in Ireland was a substantial phenomenon. In November 1880 some of the Radicals who had helped organize the London meeting joined the Irish Radical, T. P. O'Connor, in founding the Anti-Coercion Association. They received support from Parnell and some middle-class Radicals, most notably the positivists Henry Crompton and Frederic

16. Joseph Chamberlain, *A Political Memoir, 1880–92* (London, 1953), 5; Dilke Memoirs, 43,934, f. 288.
17. October 27, 1880, Dilke Papers, 43,885.
18. October 31, 1880.
19. *The Times*, November 1, 1880.

Harrison. The Association staged a number of demonstrations and in December began publication of a weekly newspaper, *The Radical*. Edited by two working-class Radicals, Samuel Bennett and F. W. Soutter, *The Radical* urged all Radicals to unite in opposing coercion, criticized Radical M.P.'s for acquiescing in repression, and advocated an alliance of English democrats and Irish Land Leaguers to work a "radical remedy" of the land problem in England and Ireland.[20]

The hostility to repression among working-class Radicals appears to have stiffened the parliamentary Radicals against coercion, at least temporarily. When in November 1880 Forster and Cowper again requested a special session to obtain coercive powers, Chamberlain and Dilke decided that they could not agree unless a strong land bill were to be introduced along with coercion.[21] This proviso, in fact, would rule out any special session at all. Chamberlain wrote Gladstone that he would resign if the cabinet agreed to Forster's proposal without specifying that a land bill would accompany coercion. He argued that coercion without land reform was both "wrong in principle" and "bad in policy"—wrong in principle because Irish disaffection arose from "the causes of just complaint"; bad in policy because a large number of Liberals in and out of parliament opposed coercion and would make its passage extremely difficult.[22]

In public the cabinet Radicals spoke even more uncompromisingly against repression. In Birmingham on November 17 Chamberlain and Bright unconditionally denounced coercion. Some Liberals, Chamberlain said, would "destroy liberty to preserve law," but he felt this was wrong. And Bright declared that the cause of Irish problems was the concentration of land in the hands of a few owners. In words that were to haunt him many times in later years, Bright asked if there was a remedy for this situation: "Force is not

20. *The Radical*, December 4, 1880; F. W. Soutter, *Recollections of a Labour Pioneer* (London, 1923), 100–101.

21. Dilke Diary, November 15, 1880, 43,924.

22. November 16, 1880, Gladstone Papers, 44,125. Chamberlain also wrote a memorandum to the cabinet arguing that it would be impossible to pass a coercion act in a special session, and that even if such an act were passed it would be ineffective—"like firing a rifle at a swarm of gnats." November 18, 1880, Gladstone Papers, 44,125.

a remedy." Reform, not repression, was the only long-term solution.[23] This strong stand by Chamberlain and Bright was successful. Gladstone agreed with them, and their arguments gradually isolated Forster, who once more gave in. The cabinet decided to put off the Irish issues until January 1881, when they would attack the problem as a whole.[24]

II. THE COERCION BILL, 1881

In deciding to attack the Irish Question as a whole, the cabinet implicitly agreed to introduce both a land bill and a coercion bill early in 1881. The only question would be that of priority. Forster and the Whigs thought that first priority had to go to maintenance of law and order, for if a land reform preceded coercion, it would seem to show a weakness in the moral fiber of the cabinet. This would, they believed, destroy the authority of the government and demoralize the Irish people. In this authoritarian attitude, Forster and the Whigs were supported by the great majority of the Conservatives, except that the Tories would have preferred no land reform at all. Chamberlain and Bright contended that land reform should precede coercion, because it might make coercion unnecessary, and in any case would make coercion easier to pass and execute.[25] But this time the Radicals in the government did not threaten to resign over coercion, and this time the authoritarian members of the cabinet won their point. In the Speech from the Throne, the government announced that it would immediately request extra powers for the Irish executive; land reform would follow.[26]

This announcement set off such a ferocious struggle within the British political community that the disputes of the previous year seem like minor scuffling in the ranks by comparison. The Irish nationalist M.P.'s staged spectacular displays of obstruction so that the government had to resort to all-night sittings and suspension of

23. *The Times*, November 17, 1880.
24. Hamilton Diaries, November 26, 1880, 48,630; Dilke Diary, November 20, 24, 1880, 43,924; Reid, *Forster*, II, 271.
25. Bright to Gladstone, December 22, 1880, Gladstone Papers, 44,113; Chamberlain to Gladstone, December 22, 1880, Gladstone Papers, 44,125.
26. *Hansard* 257 (January 6, 1881), 5–7.

Home Rule members in order to get on with their business. The argument within Radicalism was only slightly less explosive than that between the government and the Parnellites. It could easily have split the movement even more seriously than Home Rule later would. From the gravity of this intra-Radical debate, it is clear that the issue of Irish violence, and more generally Irish confrontation politics, raised fundamental problems for Radicals in a way almost no other issue could. It threatened, in fact, the existence of Radicalism itself.

It was the particular nature of the Irish nationalist movement and its strategy that made the issue of coercion so much more divisive to Radicalism than to Conservatives, Whigs, or orthodox Liberals. The function of disorder, criminal acts, disruption, and confrontation, which go together as political violence, is to force the ruling parties to weigh the risks to the social and political order against the costs of repression. As Professor H. L. Nieburg says, political violence "is the ultimate test of viability of values and customary behavior."[27] Most British politicians, indeed most members of the ruling elite, equated the interests of the Anglo-Irish minority with those of the prevailing social order in Britain as a whole. The destruction of property rights and social discipline in Ireland would threaten established society throughout the nation. To them, therefore, it was clear that the agrarian-nationalist threat in Ireland had to be put down at practically any cost. To Radicals the correct response was not so evident. To be sure, some Radicals, despite their desire for reform of various kinds, identified the basic arrangement of British society with the security of the Irish landlords. Thus many middle-class Radicals, deeply disturbed by Irish disorder and intransigence, supported coercion in spite of its stark incompatibility with the Radical tradition. At the same time, however, the very factors that made Radicals of men prevented many of them from supporting repression in Ireland. In other words, people became Radicals in late-Victorian Britain primarily because some particular grievance or other kept them from identifying completely with what they perceived to be the social order itself. Though they de-

27. H. L. Nieburg, *Political Violence: The Behavioral Process* (New York, 1969), 9.

spised and feared Irish political violence, these Radicals refused to pay the heavy moral and intellectual price demanded by coercion. Hardly a single Radical would have opposed repression if the Irish nationalist movement had embarked upon open revolutionary warfare against British authority; in that case, the issue would have seemed different—the existence of Britain itself. But the fact that the Irish agrarian disturbance seemed to have a just cause and was represented by a constitutional, if uncooperative, party made many Radicals reluctant to encourage coercion.

The great majority of the coercionists among Radicals were Nonconformists of the middle class. But it was not, as one might have expected, economic considerations that concerned them. Instead, three factors unrelated to economics contributed to their coercive inclinations: faith in the wisdom of the government, deep distress about disorder, and a misunderstanding of the role of the Parnellites. Coercive Radicals could not believe that a government including Gladstone, Bright, and Chamberlain would resort to coercion unless it was in fact absolutely necessary. As the Scottish Radical, George Anderson, argued, to resist the government's proposal might only bring in the Tories, which would mean even more coercion and less reform.[28] At the same time, these pious and orderly men were extremely concerned about the state of Irish society. *The Congregationalist*, for instance, declared that while Dissenters are by nature reluctant to advocate repression, "they are strenuous supporters of order and law. They would exhaust every expedient before suspending any of the constitutional guarantees of liberty which the heroic endurance and effort of our fathers has secured for us, but they would not be guilty of the insanity of sacrificing freedom itself out of a superstitious regard for its traditions, precedents, and forms."[29] This kind of anxiety led many Radical coercives to distorted conclusions about the sources of agrarian discontent. They increasingly saw the Parnellites and Land Leaguers as causes rather than symptoms of unrest. They incorrectly concluded that Parnell and the Leaguers were using the land agitation

28. *Hansard* 257 (January 13, 1881), 668–70.
29. February 1881.

to destroy the union, and that Parnell had organized a vast conspiracy against the law. As L. L. Dillwyn, a leader of Welsh Nonconformity, said, they believed coercion would be less dangerous to liberty than the Land League's "reign of terrorism."[30]

In reality, the Radical faith in the anti-coercionist bias of Bright and Chamberlain was misplaced. Since the autumn of 1880 Bright, now a man well past his prime, had become virulently hostile toward the Irish nationalists. In December he wrote to Gladstone: "It is evident that Parnell & Co only want men to provoke a revolt, & that their purpose is more revolution than a mere reform, however sound, of their land system."[31] He later told Dilke that he had not only acquiesced in coercion, but positively favored it.[32] He thought that the Land League's advice to the tenantry to resist eviction and to organize boycotts was "illegal and evil . . . to the last degree." By teaching tenants not to pay their rent the League ruined the "honest feeling and sense of honour of the tenants."[33] In earlier years, Bright had been a knowledgeable and sympathetic friend to many demands by Irish nationalists, but after 1880 he became one of their most implacable foes.

Despite his public reputation as an anti-coercionist, Chamberlain in 1881 was one of the government's strongest advocates of repression. He explained in his *Political Memoir* that he had never opposed coercion on principle: "I opposed coercion [in 1880], not because I assumed that coercion might never be necessary, but because I thought it should only come when other means had failed, and that the admitted grievances of the Irish people should be removed before, or at least concurrently with, any proposal for strengthening the criminal law."[34] He wrote to J. T. Bunce (editor of the *Birmingham Daily Post*) at the end of 1880 that, though he still hoped a land bill might settle Ireland, coercion might now be required: "What was not necessary 2 months ago seems to have become so

30. *Hansard* 257 (January 13, 1881), 731–33.
31. December 7, 1880, Gladstone Papers, 44,113.
32. Dilke Memoirs, 43,935, ff. 13–14.
33. *Hansard* 257 (January 27, 1881), 1555–65.
34. Chamberlain, *Political Memoir*, 5.

recently. The agitation is getting out of the hands of the Land League and is more or less used to serve personal ends and purposes of general disaffection."[35]

In defending the government's repressive policy, Chamberlain played on the common coercive themes: Irish disorder and the conspiracy of nationalism. He told his constituents in Birmingham (June 1881) that he and his colleagues hated everything about coercion. "But then," he declared, *"we hate disorder more."*[36] As for the Parnellites and the League, Chamberlain asserted in an open letter to Frank Schnadhorst, secretary of the National Liberal Federation, that they should have tried to discourage crime, but they had not.[37] The reason, he said later, was that they wanted to use the agitation in their campaign to separate Ireland from England. The Parnellites would never be satisfied by reforms because they wanted no settlement.[38] The most authoritarian of the Conservatives could not have put it better. Though Chamberlain did not at all identify with the landowners of Ireland, the unruliness of the Irish agitation disturbed him. Psychologically he needed to feel that he had things under control, that everything around him fit neatly into a preconceived pattern. But the Irish were getting out of control; hence Chamberlain felt that they must be put down.

Opposition to the coercion bill from the anti-repressive Radicals was varied in composition but uniformly passionate in tone. In the House of Commons, perhaps one-third of the Radicals withheld their support from the government, even in the face of demands by the party whips. For example, on a motion by Parnell condemning coercion, while about seventy Radicals voted with the government, seven went into the opposition lobby and perhaps forty abstained—a significant defection in view of the pressure of party discipline.[39]

35. December 30, 1880, Chamberlain Papers, JC 5/8/52.
36. *The Times*, June 8, 1881. Italics mine.
37. Quoted in *The Times*, February 17, 1881.
38. Speech at Birmingham, reported in *The Times*, June 8, 1881.
39. *Hansard* 257 (January 14, 1881), 803–6. On a motion to give precedence to the coercion bill, only two Radicals voted against the party whips, but fifty-two abstained; sixty-five Radicals supported the motion. *Hansard* 257 (January 26, 1881), 1485–87.

This group of anti-coercionist Radicals included a sprinkling of M.P.'s from all sectors of Radicalism, but was most notable for its inclusion of most of the "maverick" Radicals in the House—Joseph Cowen, Charles Bradlaugh, Henry Labouchere, Sir Wilfrid Lawson, and Alexander Macdonald. Dilke also opposed coercion and would have resigned from the government if he had been able to persuade either Bright or Chamberlain to go out with him.[40] As it was, Cowen assumed the leadership of the opposition in parliament, although his role was more moral and spiritual than directive. An extreme individualist, old friend of Mazzini, and fiery orator, Cowen was a loner in British politics. His Radicalism sprang from impassioned sympathy with the underdog—hence his hatred of Chamberlain's efforts to discipline Radicalism in the National Liberal Federation, as well as his defense of Irish nationalism. He argued in his thick North-country accent that the Radical faith demanded reform and not repression in Ireland, and that the British should realize the Irish were "more supremely wretched" than any other people in the world. It could not be right to place this "classic land of misery" in the hands of a prejudiced and bewildered executive.[41]

Outside parliament, opposition to coercion was even more extensive among Radicals. One of the leading forces was John Morley, now editor of the *Pall Mall Gazette* as well as the *Fortnightly*. Unlike Cowen, Morley opposed coercion more on grounds of expediency than of emotion or principle. He did not deny that Britain had the right to suppress Irish agitation. But rights were not at issue, he wrote; remedial legislation would work, while repression would not. The reason for this fact was that the Irish peasant had genuine grievances. By the same token, the Land League had really protected the tenants better than any other Irish agency had ever been able to. To Morley, the facts of history indicated that England would never listen to Ireland until the Irish had made themselves "more than a little troublesome." Those who advocated coercion in actuality only wanted to break up the League; thus they were as re-

40. Dilke Memoirs, 43,935, ff. 9–10.
41. *Hansard* 258 (February 8, 1881), 356–71. See also Evan Rowland Jones, *The Life and Speeches of Joseph Cowen, M.P.* (London, 1885), 193.

actionary as those who had opposed the extension of the franchise in 1867 or the abolition of slavery in America in 1861.[42]

It was in working-class Radicalism that opposition to coercion was most intense. Working-class Radicals, feeling none of the responsibilities of power and no coincidence of interest whatsoever with Irish landlords, pitched into Dilke, Chamberlain, and Bright more freely than did Cowen or Morley. *Reynolds's* called the coercion bill "deformed and wicked," and urged Bright, Chamberlain, and Dilke to oppose it.[43] *The Radical* explicitly attacked Chamberlain and Bright. The coercion bill, wrote the editors, represented a victory of Whiggery over Radicalism, for Whigs concern themselves with order while Radicals must advocate reform. *The Radical* even argued that, for the Irish, violence was a legitimate method of redressing grievances, and that maintaining order in Ireland really meant giving license to landlords to evict helpless tenants.[44] The Radical clubs of London, which had founded the Anti-Coercion Association, now established a second Radical organization devoted to opposing coercion. The leader of this new effort was H. M. Hyndman, a Marxist who had close personal ties with members of several metropolitan Radical clubs. Hyndman found that, despite his general belief in imperial unity, he shared with many Radical clubs a hostility to coercion and to the National Liberal Federation, which had loyally followed Chamberlain's Irish policy. Together they established in March 1881 a new democratic party, the Democratic Federation. Cowen and some English positivists joined the movement. By midsummer of 1881 the Democratic Federation was an organization of considerable importance in working-class Radicalism.[45]

Concern for Ireland provided the adhesive to keep the Democratic

42. For Morley's opinions, see the following articles in the *Fortnightly*: "Affairs," 169 (January 1881), 119–26; 170 (February 1881), 261–65; 171 (March 1881), 397–402; "England and Ireland," 172 (April 1881), 407–25; and "Conciliation with Ireland," 175 (July 1881), 1–25. In addition, see his leaders in the *Pall Mall Gazette*, January 1881.

43. February 6, 1881.

44. January 8, 15, 22, 29; February 5, 19, 1881.

45. Chushichi Tsuzuki, *H. M. Hyndman and British Socialism* (London, 1961), 36–47; Pelling, *Origins of the Labour Party*, 18–23; Cole, *British Working Class Politics*, 82–87.

Federation together. At a general meeting in July the Federation promulgated a program that included planks for nationalizing the land throughout Britain and legislative independence for Ireland. It organized mass anti-coercion meetings and established relations with the Land League. It sent an inquiry team to Ireland, the forerunner of many Radical tours, and published the team's report. This document attacked coercion, criticized John Bright, and advocated land nationalization and Home Rule for Ireland.[46] But the range of ideologies in the Democratic Federation proved to be too diverse once problems besides Ireland were raised. In the autumn of 1881 Hyndman denounced the "hollowness and hypocrisy of capitalist Radicalism" while campaigning for a Land League candidate in Tyrone.[47] This was too much for most Radicals, and all but one of the Radical clubs withdrew from the Federation. Yet, however short-lived, working-class Radical participation in the Democratic Federation signified extensive hostility to coercion; it represented an important step in working-class consciousness as well.

III. THE LAND BILL, 1881

The dispute over coercion within Radicalism was so intense during the first half of 1881 that only a general expectation of a strong land bill held the movement together. Whatever their attitudes toward repression, all Radicals looked to an extensive reform of the land system for at least a partial solution to the Irish Question. Their main concern here was to make as extreme as possible the government's bill. On the other hand, most Whigs, including some very influential members of the cabinet, wanted to limit the bill as much as they could. Hartington, for example, thought that the Irish landlords already had surrendered as much of their rights of property as they could. Gladstone himself, though he has the reputation of the innovator in Irish matters, had to be led by the Radicals on this issue. He wanted to restrict the new land bill to an extension of the 1870 act; that is, to provide that a tenant could not be evicted for non-

---

46. Jesse Craigen, *Report on a Visit to Ireland in the Summer of 1881* (Dublin, 1882).

47. Tsuzuki, *Hyndman*, 47; Pelling, *Origins of the Labour Party*, 18–23.

payment of rent if the default arose from causes beyond his control. Radicals did not think that such a measure would be adequate; consequently, they sought to convince Gladstone to introduce a bill along the lines of Butt's proposal of 1876.

For most Radicals in and out of parliament the best plan would consist of the "three F's"—fixity of tenure, fair rents, and free sale by the tenant of his share in the holding. Apparently Chamberlain and Bright in December 1880 suggested to the cabinet a plan for a large-scale land purchase and redistribution to the tenants, desiring not merely to provide for easier transactions, but to carry out a mass conversion of large estates into small properties.[48] Gladstone rejected this plan outright, and both Chamberlain and Bright resorted to the three F's. In response to a request from Gladstone, Shaw Lefevre composed a long memorandum on the land question that eventually formed the nucleus of the government's bill. In it Shaw Lefevre advocated a three F's measure. He explained that he still favored extension of the land purchase clause, but now thought that only the three F's could be of such extensive application as to be of use to all the tenants. He considered the most novel and contentious feature of this three F scheme to be a proposal for fixing fair rents by a court of arbitration. He believed, however, that such a system in practice already existed in Ulster and could easily be extended to the rest of Ireland. As to purchase, Shaw Lefevre rejected the idea of having the government lend all of the money for the purchase of a holding, but he recommended that four-fifths instead of two-thirds be advanced.[49]

Gladstone initially regarded Shaw Lefevre's plan as too extreme. He thought that it would destroy the balance between landlord and tenant by abolishing the ultimate weapon of the landlord—eviction.[50] Even after the Richmond and Bessborough royal commissions produced reports generally supporting arguments for the three F's, Gladstone resisted. His original draft bill only resembled the com-

48. Hamilton Diaries, December 17, 19, 1880, 48,630; Chamberlain to Gladstone, December 22, 1880, Gladstone Papers, 44,125; Bright to Gladstone, December 24, 1880, Gladstone Papers, 44,113.

49. Shaw Lefevre to Gladstone, December 25, 1880, Gladstone Papers, 44,153.

50. Gladstone to Shaw Lefevre, December 27, 1880, Gladstone Papers, 44,153; Eversley, *Gladstone and Ireland*, 146.

pensation for disturbance bill of 1880, and it caused much dissension among the Radicals who knew about it.[51] Finally, in late January 1881 he gave way and turned to the three F's. The Duke of Argyll, the leading Whig expert on the rights of property, resigned from the cabinet.

Having won their point, Radicals of all kinds gave a friendly reception to Gladstone's land bill of 1881. *Reynolds's* said that the bill had "at last lifted the gloomy pall which hung over the country . . . it is a real invasion of feudalism."[52] *The Radical* agreed that the bill was "far more Radical than either the friends or the opponents of the present Government anticipated," and urged that all true friends of progress accept it.[53] *The Nonconformist and Independent* labeled it "a great and statesmanlike measure."[54] Shaw Lefevre thought that the bill exactly fulfilled the need. As he wrote to Frederic Harrison, in his opinion the three F bill would have settled the Irish land problem a year before if Gladstone had taken his advice then.[55] After more than a year of effort, Radicals had an Irish bill that pleased them.

In fact, the enthusiasm of middle-class Radicals for the land bill was such that they regarded it not only as a step in the right direction but also as the final solution to the most important aspect of the Irish Question. While most working-class Radicals thought the bill would be a blessing, they did not think that it would end the land problem.[56] But the majority of middle-class Radicals believed that the bill would remove the just cause of Irish discontent, return prosperity to Ireland, and destroy the power of the Land League.[57] Only this fact can account for the widespread Radical disgust and anger with Parnell's attitude toward the bill. Parnell wanted to make it possible for the Irish people to own their farms; consequently, he

51. Dilke Diary, January 8, 1881, 43,924.
52. April 17, 1881.
53. April 9, 1881.
54. April 14, 1881.
55. April 13, 1881, Harrison Papers, Additional Papers, Box 6.
56. Henry George, very popular in working-class Radical circles, called the three F's the "three frauds": *The Irish Land Question* (New York, 1881), 38–39.
57. See the speeches by Shaw Lefevre and Thorold Rogers, *Hansard* 260 (May 2, 1881), 1586–1602, 1606–10; and by John Bright, *Hansard* 261 (May 9, 1881), 94–113.

did not regard the bill as satisfactory. He feared that in practice it would not benefit the tenantry. Moreover, Parnell stood in an exceedingly difficult political position. If he showed enthusiasm for the bill, extremists within the nationalist movement might well abandon him; if he neglected the bill altogether, the tenants might ignore his leadership in their desire to take advantage of the measure. Parnell thus had to walk a narrow line. He did not oppose the bill, but he and some other Home Rulers abstained from the vote on the second reading and generally failed to show any gratitude for the bill.[58] To most Radicals this was an unexpected display of insolence. More seriously, many Radicals incorrectly interpreted Parnell's response as a deliberate attempt to sabotage a peaceful solution to the main problem in Anglo-Irish relations. As the editor of *The Echo* put it, Parnell denounced the land act because he wanted social and political chaos in Ireland.[59] Chamberlain felt the same way. He told his constituents that the land bill was a "message of peace" that the Irish ought to accept, but the Land League wanted no settlement. He also warned that, as the government had staked its existence on the land bill, it would use every instrument in its power—including coercion—to assure that the bill got a fair chance to work.[60]

IV. The Arrests, 1881

Considering the economic condition of Ireland, the land act worked fairly well, but it neither ended the Irish Question nor reestablished the conditions for good relations between Radicals and Irish nationalists. The Irish remained extremely embittered toward the Radicals because of support so many of them gave to coercion and to rules of closure aimed at breaking obstruction.[61] Furthermore,

---

58. Lyons, *Dillon*, 49; Conor Cruise O'Brien, *Parnell and His Party, 1880–90* (Oxford, 1957), 62–63.

59. *The Echo*, October 1, 1881.

60. *The Times*, June 8, 1881.

61. One Irishman living in England complained to T. P. O'Connor: "I went without my dinner to vote for Mr. Bryce, and now Mr. Bryce is voting for coercion." O'Connor himself recalled that one of the "most painful and even disgusting experiences" of the coercion matter was the desertion of Ireland by English Radicals. T. P. O'Connor, *The Parnell Movement* (London, 1886), 313, 429.

Parnell still dared not welcome the land act. He had to adopt a middle course of "testing" the act by sending select cases to the new land court. But Gladstone, like the middle-class Radicals, believed that everything depended on the successful operation of his act. Advised by several of the leading authorities on Ireland, including Spencer, Forster, and Cowper, that Parnell and the Land Leaguers meant to subvert the new law, Gladstone in October 1881 denounced Parnell. He warned the Irish agitators that the "resources of civilization" had not yet been exhausted. Parnell replied with a blunt and insolent challenge. The cabinet had him arrested, and so began Parnell's famous stay in Kilmainham prison.

The imprisonment of Parnell and some other Land Leaguers revived the corrosive dispute about coercion within the Radical movement. If anything, this round of the Radicals' intramural struggle was more bitter than ever. The alignment of factions remained the same. *The Radical* denounced the arrests as "one of the most cowardly and thoroughly unjustifiable actions which have disgraced even the present Government's tenure of power."[62] *Reynolds's* considered it a bitter satire that a Liberal ministry should rule Ireland by "buckshot, bayonet, and bludgeon."[63] Large popular demonstrations were held in Hyde Park and Trafalgar Square.[64] On the other side, many Radicals, again mostly from the middle class, showed deep hostility to the Land League because of their treatment of the land act. *The Nonconformist and Independent*, for instance, regretted that the arrests had to be made, but thought they were necessary because the Irish nationalist leaders were trying to deny the benefits of the land act to the Irish people.[65] John Bright wrote to Gladstone:

> I have felt a strong inclination to say what I have thought of Mr Parnell. . . . He is open to a tremendous assault on the ground of his lying statements, & of the unsound sentiments he is spreading among the Irish people. . . .

62. October 15, 1881.
63. October 23, 1881.
64. *Daily News*, October 24, 1881.
65. October 20, 1881. Similar attitudes were shown by the *Daily News* (October 10, 1881) and A. J. Mundella (letter to Robert Leader, September 2, 1881, Mundella-Leader Letters).

His main belief is a break-up of the United Kingdom, for he hates us & England even more than he loves Ireland. . . .[66]

The two most important Radicals to engage in the dispute over coercion were Chamberlain and Morley. Their disagreement, as in 1877, threatened to separate the chief Radical politician from the leading Radical intellectual. By October 1881 Chamberlain had begun to wish that he and Dilke had resigned over coercion earlier in the year. But he also thought that Parnell now had gotten beyond control; the Irish leader wanted only "No Rent & Separation," which Chamberlain did not consider just cause for agitation.[67] After Parnell's challenge to Gladstone, Chamberlain readily accepted the policy of arresting the Irish leaders.[68] As he told a conference of the National Liberal Federation, sometimes Radicals must support coercion: "We, Liberals or Radicals, are alike prepared, if necessity arises to put down rebellion."[69] To him, as to most other Englishmen of the ruling classes, the authority of the law was the issue.

Morley could not agree. As he wrote Gladstone, he had criticized the passage of the coercion act and now found it difficult, even under the influence of deep sympathy for the Liberal government, to support a particular application of the act.[70] Though he tried to soften the blow to his friends by placing the arrests in broad historical context, Morley condemned coercion in both the *Fortnightly* and the *Pall Mall Gazette*.[71] When this criticism brought a plea from Chamberlain not to "wobble," Morley replied in an impassioned letter. It showed that he believed the issue to be, not the authority of the law, but the justice of the Irish grievances:

Of course if I were like the Daily News, I would turn round straight in a night. Hill doesn't mind being told that he is a spaniel who will run to pick up any dirty stick that Gladstone throws. I do mind

66. October 4, 1881, Gladstone Papers, 44,113.
67. Chamberlain to Dilke, October 4, 1881, Dilke Papers, 43,885.
68. Chamberlain to Dilke, October 12, 1881, Dilke Papers, 43,885. Edward Hamilton also recorded in his Diary that the cabinet was united in its severe attitude toward the Irish: October 16, 1881, 48,631.
69. *The Times*, October 26, 1881.
70. October 17, 1881, Gladstone Papers, 44,255.
71. "Affairs," *F.R.* 179 (November 1881), 660–64.

rather—and I mind it the more because in my heart I feel that the League has done downright good work in raising up the tenants against their truly detestable tyrants; and with this leaning at the back of my mind, I have not been able all at once to call the League bad names.[72]

Morley was well aware that the Land League's agitation probably inspired some criminal acts. As he wrote Chamberlain, this was a fact he could accept: "Of course *I* shd. say—'Well, if we can't have agitation without disorder, we'll have the disorder, and be hanged to you.' "[73] In other words, Morley refused to pay the heavy price demanded of Radicals to maintain what he regarded as an unjust economic and social system in Ireland. Chamberlain would pay that price, for to him disorder in Ireland seemed a grave threat. He wrote to Morley: "You can't fight with gloves on & I am prepared to use every means likely to succeed in putting down the present agitation which I believe to be based on no real grievance but to be largely an agitation directed from America & supported by American money for revolutionary objects with which the mass of the Irish people have no sympathy whatever."[74]

By December 1881 Chamberlain's vigorous defense of the government's repressive policy had attracted much personal criticism from Radicals. For example, *Reynolds's* compared some of his speeches to the efforts of Strafford and George III.[75] A very serious criticism came from John Page Hopps, a Nonconformist minister from Leicester. In a closely reasoned public letter to Chamberlain, Page Hopps argued that the Land League was a legitimate voice for Irish grievances, and that it had not commanded the tenantry to refrain from using the land act. He thought it very dangerous to make the leaders of a political agitation responsible for crimes committed during the general conditions of disturbance. Like Morley, Page Hopps believed that reforms rarely are granted without political pressure; therefore, "a clear distinction ought to have been resolutely drawn

72. October 19, 1881, Chamberlain Papers, JC 5/54/384.
73. December 5, 1881, Chamberlain Papers, JC 5/54/415.
74. December 30, 1881, Chamberlain Papers, JC 5/54/432.
75. October 30, 1881; see also the issues for November 20, 1881, and January 1, 1882; and *The Radical*, December 17, 24, 1881.

between the agitation that was demanded and the crime no one could prevent."[76]

This letter, printed or excerpted in many newspapers of importance in England, caused Chamberlain much concern. He consulted Morley in preparing his reply and had it published in several newspapers, including *The Times*. Essentially Chamberlain repeated the argument that the Land League did not want the land act to work because they feared it would reconcile the Irish people to English rule.[77] Whatever the merits of his views, Chamberlain was plainly disturbed by the extent of the criticism from Radicals about coercion, particularly by the evidence of significant opposition to coercion within Nonconformity, the section of Radicalism peculiarly crucial to Chamberlain.[78] Even before the exchange with Page Hopps, Chamberlain privately expressed the opinion that Liberal discontent would force the government to resist new demands for repression. He wrote to Gladstone: "On purely party grounds, therefore, I feel sure that we should do serious harm by yielding to the cry which the 'Standard' and the 'Telegraph' & to some extent, the 'Times' are trying to palm off as a genuine outburst of public opinion."[79]

Radical opposition to coercion, though far from the unanimous opinion of Radicals, had made itself felt. The unquestioning faith in the Gladstone government prevalent in the left wing of the Liberal party had been shaken. At least as far as the British side was concerned, this fact contributed much to the origins of the conciliatory policy symbolized by the Kilmainham Treaty.

V. The Kilmainham Treaty, 1882

From December 1881 Chamberlain increasingly became the cabinet's leading advocate of a policy of conciliating the Irish and the

76. Page Hopps to Chamberlain, December 16, 1881, Chamberlain Papers, JC 8/4/2/8.

77. Chamberlain to Page Hopps, quoted in *The Times*, December 26, 1881; also the *Daily News*, December 26, 1881.

78. The growing hostility to coercion among middle-class Nonconformist Radicals can be seen in: *The Echo* (October 14, December 23, 1881), *Daily News* (April 6, 17, 1882), and *The Nonconformist and Independent* (April 6, 1882).

79. December 14, 1881, Gladstone Papers, 44,125.

focal point of Radical desire to return Anglo-Irish relations to normal. Concern for the internal health of the Liberal party was not the only reason Chamberlain began to lean toward conciliation. Another was his perception that the cabinet's policy was defeating Irish extremism. In part, this perception was accurate, for the land act of 1881 was working, in the sense that many tenants were using its provisions. Moreover, John Givan, an Irish M.P., told Chamberlain that the situation in Ireland was improving because the power of the Land League had been broken. Yet to some degree Chamberlain's view of the Irish situation must have resulted from his capacity —exhibited fairly often in his later career—to see whatever his political considerations *required* him to see. The coercion act had in reality increased the rate of agrarian crime.[80] Nevertheless, Chamberlain at the end of 1881 chose to believe Givan's assessment that with firmness and patience by the government, "all would be well," for any attempt by the Parnellites to break English authority in Ireland "will assuredly fail as all our people, Radicals included, will resist them to the death."[81]

In this frame of mind Chamberlain was ready to welcome a sign of conciliation from the Irish nationalists. It came initially from E. D. Gray, owner and editor of the *Freeman's Journal* and Home Rule M.P. In a friendly letter Gray told Chamberlain that he regretted necessity of opposing the government, and he proposed what Chamberlain had so long desired—namely, cooperation between Home Rulers and Radicals: "There are so many things which a government like yours could do for Ireland and so many ways in which the Irish Members might help the advanced Liberal Party in England that I for one regret seeing them playing the game of the Kilkenny cats."[82] Gray went on to suggest that the government make some provision for the arrears of rent that so many tenants now owed. Chamberlain passed Gray's letter to Gladstone with a recommendation that his proposals regarding land problems be followed.[83]

---

80. Lyons, *Dillon*, 64.
81. Chamberlain to Morley, December 18, 1881, Chamberlain Papers, JC 5/54/421.
82. January 5, 1882 [misdated 1881], Gladstone Papers, 44,125.
83. January 9, 1882, Gladstone Papers, 44,125.

Gray's letter and Chamberlain's response can be seen as the first steps in the negotiations involving Chamberlain that ultimately produced the Kilmainham Treaty. In the first months of 1882 Chamberlain in private worked to stave off a renewal of coercion and to promote a policy of conciliation. Morley vigorously supported him, stating plainly in the *Fortnightly* that an attempt by the ministry to renew coercion might break up the cabinet, and that a "strong contingent of English Radicals" would join the Irish in resisting the policy.[84] On April 3, 1882, Morley caused a minor sensation with a leader in the *Pall Mall Gazette* calling for Forster's resignation from the Chief Secretaryship and for the development of an entirely new and conciliatory program for Ireland.[85] Morley's words spoke for nearly all Radicals. By April even the former coercionists among the Radicals had given up on repression and were demanding concessions to Ireland.[86] Radical opinion clearly pitted Chamberlain and conciliation against Forster and coercion. The near unanimity of this view among English democrats was a powerful turn of events. Parnell did not doubt that the "new departure" in English attitudes would prevail. He wrote Mrs. O'Shea: "I think it very likely that something will be done by the Government shortly on the arrears question. If this be so, things will undoubtedly quiet down a great deal, and it will give us an opportunity of coming to some arrangement."[87]

For his part, Parnell now had strong reason to reach a settlement with the government. He was anxious to leave Kilmainham prison, because he wanted to be with Mrs. O'Shea, who was about to give birth to their child, and because he wanted to resume active leadership of the nationalist movement, which had fallen into extremist hands during his imprisonment. These converging forces produced

84. "Affairs," *F.R.* 284 (April 1882), 541–42.

85. It is commonly believed that in this leader Morley urged the government to replace Forster as Chief Secretary with Chamberlain. He did not do so explicitly, though well-informed political observers would have known that Morley and Chamberlain were usually close allies.

86. *Daily News*, April 10, 13, 1882; *The Nonconformist and Independent*, April 6, 13, 1882; *The Baptist*, April 7, 1882.

87. Quoted in Katherine O'Shea, *Charles Stewart Parnell: His Love Story and Political Life*, 2 vols. (London, 1914), I, 242.

delicate and complicated communications between Chamberlain and Parnell, conducted mainly through the unfortunately chosen medium, Captain William O'Shea, husband of Parnell's mistress and inveterate meddler in affairs beyond his ability. O'Shea initially had attempted without success to interest Gladstone in an agreement with Parnell, and had turned to Chamberlain because he regarded the Birmingham Radical as "a Minister without political pedantry. . . ." The bargain that he offered Chamberlain went beyond the exchange of Parnell's release for Parnellite influence for peace in Ireland. He asked Chamberlain: "Leaving aside other matters which are not to my present purpose, such as the effects of an extended franchise, I ask you how the Liberal party is to get on in the next election, and at the one after, and so on, against the Irish vote? And if by any chance it did get in, how on earth is it to get on?"[88]

O'Shea's offer, it seems clear, was of the same variety as Gray's: it promised not only to end the current difficulties between the government and the nationalists, and so let the Radical coercionists off the hook, but also to ally the Parnellites with the Liberal party, or more precisely, the advanced wing of the party. These were exactly the kind of terms to interest Chamberlain, who had tried to strike a similar bargain in 1879. An alliance would tame the Irish nationalists, and it would also link them to efforts by advanced Liberals to force land and franchise reforms on the Whigs and Conservatives. From the beginning of his negotiations with the nationalists, therefore, Chamberlain had an objective over and above that of Gladstone and most of the cabinet. While Gladstone wanted simply to break the impasse in Ireland, Chamberlain wanted also to arrange an alliance with the nationalists, of which the beneficiaries would be his section of the party.[89]

The result of these communications was a justly famous letter from Parnell to Chamberlain in which the terms of the agreement were established: the government would concede certain points regarding the arrears of rent accrued by Irish tenants and the admission of leaseholders to the provisions of the 1881 land act; Parnell would try to prevent crime in Ireland; and the Parnellites would

88. Quoted in Chamberlain, *Political Memoir*, 29–30.
89. *Ibid.*, 34–35.

cooperate with reform efforts of the Liberal party: "The accomplishment of the programme I have sketched out to you would in my judgment be regarded by the country as a practical settlement of the Land Question and would enable us to co-operate cordially for the future with the Liberal Party in forwarding Liberal principles and measures of general reform."[90]

To Forster, who was the symbol and substance of the resistance within the party to conciliation of the Parnellites, this letter made it certain that his colleagues had been bargaining with confessed criminals and, even worse, now wished to release them from prison in return for a promise of political support. Gladstone did not see it in that light, and, while rejecting the alliance *"hors d'oeuvre,"* he was pleased that the Parnellites wanted to help restore peace to Ireland.[91] On May 1, the cabinet decided to release the prisoners from Kilmainham without meeting a demand by Forster that they first obtain passage of a new coercion law or require a public promise of lawful behavior from Parnell. The next day, Forster sent his resignation to Gladstone. Conciliation had won.

The release of the Land Leaguers from Kilmainham and the resignation of Forster symbolized a "new departure" for the government; it was greeted with great satisfaction by the Radicals. They believed, not so much that Irish agitation had been justified, as that Forster and coercion had failed and that a new policy had to be tried. Many Radicals hoped and expected that Chamberlain would be appointed Chief Secretary, for he appeared to be the main force behind the conciliatory move.[92] Chamberlain himself expected to be appointed, and although he did not want the position, he would have accepted it.[93] Gladstone, however, seems to have been unaware of the sentiment for appointing Chamberlain; moreover, he and his Whig advisors, Grosvenor and Hartington, rightly thought that Chamberlain's Radicalism would have terrified the Irish landlords.[94] In the

90. Quoted in full *ibid.*, 49–50. See also O'Brien, *Parnell*, I, 341–42; O'Shea, *Parnell*, I, 255.

91. Reid, *Forster*, II, 436–40.

92. *Daily News*, May 3, 1882; *The Echo*, May 3, 4, 1882.

93. Chamberlain, *Political Memoir*, 60; Dilke Memoirs, 43,936, f. 97.

94. Hamilton Diaries, May 4, 1882, 48,632; Grosvenor to Gladstone, May 3, 1882, Gladstone Papers, 44,315.

event, Lord Frederick Cavendish, younger brother of Hartington and nephew of Gladstone, received the post. Radicals expressed some disappointment but did not despair of the policy of conciliation.

Cavendish crossed over to Ireland on May 5. On May 6 he and the undersecretary were assassinated in Phoenix Park. These brutal murders threw the British political world into a turmoil and threatened to abort the conciliatory policy. The great bulk of orthodox opinion in Ireland and England raged with anger and called for renewed and stronger coercive laws. It was perfectly clear to most of the ruling orders that appeasing the nationalists had led to the disaster, because the Irish could not be trusted to behave as responsible people without the firm hand of authority to restrain them.[95] But Radical opinion sharply differed. The greatest concern of the Radicals in this new crisis was to preserve the "spirit of Kilmainham," although the assassinations had changed the situation too much to retain the details of the agreement. Nearly all Radicals, both middle and working class, urged Chamberlain and the cabinet to keep the conciliatory policy intact. For example, A. J. Mundella, who had once been a strong coercionist, wrote a friend: "I hope the Government will persevere in their good work. I think my friend Forster is in the wrong, and *so do all* his colleagues."[96] Radicals, therefore, were very pleased when Gladstone chose Trevelyan, a well-known Radical, to succeed Cavendish.[97]

The appointment of Trevelyan, however, did not mean that the government—or Trevelyan, for that matter—was willing to forego a new coercive law. Public opinion plainly demanded that strong medicine be administered to the Irish. A few of the more rebellious Radicals, like Labouchere and Cowen, opposed the passage of the new coercion bill, but most agreed with Chamberlain that the public demand for strengthening the law in Ireland was irresistible. The

---

95. *The Times*, the *Standard*, and the *Daily Telegraph*, all for May 8, 1882.

96. To Robert Leader, May 8, 1882, Mundella-Leader Letters. Other expressions of Radical desire to maintain the treaty: *The Echo*, May 8, 1882; *The Nonconformist and Independent*, May 12, 1882; *Reynolds's Newspaper*, May 14, 1882; *The Radical*, May 13, 1882; Collings to Chamberlain, May 7, 1882, Chamberlain Papers, JC 5/16/17; Morley to Chamberlain, May 8, 1882, Chamberlain Papers, JC 5/54/455.

97. *Daily News*, May 10, 1882; *The Echo*, May 10, 1882.

main hope of the Radical movement was that the government's policy of conciliation would make extensive use of the law unnecessary. They wanted to minimize the powers of the coercion bill during its passage, then to proceed as quickly as possible to the arrears bill. Thus the acceptance by many Radicals, including most of those in parliament, of a new measure of coercion did not spring on their part from any renewed anger with the nationalists or anxiety over the disorder in Ireland. Rather, it came from the feeling that coercion was the inevitable, regrettable, and tiresome result of an extraordinary situation. Chamberlain worked in vain to get the cabinet to make concessions to Parnell on the crimes bill, just as he tried without much effect to persuade Parnell to restrain the Home Rulers' opposition to it. Yet in general the spirit of Kilmainham survived, for the cabinet followed coercion with the arrears bill, and the Home Rulers settled down to a period of relative calm.[98]

By the summer of 1882 the Radicals had taken another important step in the evolution of their attitude toward Ireland. After two years of the most intense debate and concern over the Irish Question, they had decided that coercion was an ineffective and inappropriate long-range policy for Ireland. Even the flexible Mr. Chamberlain, who had never opposed the principle of coercion, found that the pressure of opinion and the threat of division within the Radical movement for the time being made the policy implicit in older coercive acts inexpedient. It is remarkable how the issue of disorder in Ireland had divided the Radicals. Many Radicals, especially those of the middle class, had advocated strong repressive measures, declaring that a devotion to law and order took precedence over protection of civil liberties. Further, their behavior made it clear that Radical principles were not made for export, even for such a short distance as to Ireland, and that reforms, if any, were to be granted to, not demanded by, the Irish. An authoritarian tendency limited Radicals in the same way (though not to the same degree)

98. Chamberlain, Memorandum to the Cabinet, May 20, 1882, Chamberlain Papers, JC 8/5/1/4; Chamberlain to Spencer, May 20, 1882, Chamberlain Papers, JC 8/9/3/7; Dilke Diary, June 7, 1882, 43,924; Chamberlain to Gladstone, June 7, 9, 1882, Gladstone Papers, 44,125; O'Shea to Parnell, June 23, 28, 1882, copies in Chamberlain Papers, JC 8/8/2G/1-2; Hammond, *Gladstone and the Irish Nation,* 300; O'Brien, *Parnell and His Party,* 80.

as it limited most Victorians. This was not the case among working-class Radicals, perhaps because they found it easy to equate the predicament of the Irish tenantry with their own. Whatever the reason, the opposition to coercion which appeared within working-class Radicalism contributed strongly to that increase in working-class consciousness so evident in the late-nineteenth century and eventually so damaging to the Radical movement itself.

Even for the Radicals most inclined to support authoritarian policies, coercion came at a high price, so high in fact that few were willing to pay it for very long. The Irish strategy of confrontation, including political violence, forced the Radical elite to decide how much they would pay, in terms of damage to political principles, to revered traditions, and to the unity of their movement, in order to maintain social discipline in Ireland. By mid-1882, most of them found the cost too high; thus they turned against coercion as an acceptable means of keeping order in Ireland. Again, as in 1874–80, the level of effort required to force many of them to act upon basic Radical principles was high, when the people concerned did not belong to their movement. Moreover, the Radicals had not as a whole responded to stress with the graceful imperturbability characteristic of the British ruling orders. But at least they had altered their position, and few Radicals would ever seriously consider a coercive policy again. Ireland had revealed some of the boundaries of Radicalism, and had drawn an important new one as well.

CHAPTER FOUR

Coming of the Storm
1883-85

From 1874 to 1883 two sets of factors had largely determined the response of Radicals to Ireland. The first was the very nature of Radicalism, which equipped individual Radicals with a cumbersome burden of English-made principles, prejudices, values, and habits of thought. The second was Parnell's strategy of confrontation, which forcibly turned most Radicals toward the Irish point of view. Not that the Radicals became spokesmen for Irish nationalism, but at least they had developed a concern for Irish problems, had arrived at an analysis of those problems that emphasized the detrimental role of the landlord class rather than the characteristics of the Irish race, and had moved away from the idea of maintaining political and social order in Ireland by coercion.

From 1883 to 1885 these determinants continued to operate, but considerations arising from the immediate political situation in Britain also came to exert heavy influence. By 1883 the Radicals, like all Englishmen, were weary of battling Irish nationalists. As men with a reformist goal, they were especially eager to free parliament from the Irish imbroglio in order to enact domestic legislation. In addition they felt more and more the need to prepare for the great moment in their political scenario, the climax of their striving for power both within and without the Liberal party. Thus the Radicals wanted to streamline the House of Commons, reform the national franchise, and formulate their program for the day when they would sweep the electorate, rid the Liberal party of Whigs, and do battle with the Tories for the land and the Church. Everything pointed to the next general election as the critical moment in nineteenth-century politics. To most Radicals, it seemed essential that Ireland not interfere.

For a time the Parnellites cooperated with the English desire for a calmer period. Parnell did not take nearly so active a role in the House in 1883–84 as in previous years. He dissolved the Land League and replaced it with the less militant National League. The Irish parliamentary party refrained from introducing Home Rule motions and from serious obstruction. Yet the nationalists did not by any means cease all activities. They incessantly criticized the administration of the crimes act of 1882. They spread the Home Rule gospel throughout Ireland, and they reorganized the old Home Rule Confederation of England and Scotland as the Irish National League of Great Britain. After cooperating for a time with the Liberals, Parnell revived his efforts to bring about a stalemate between the English parties. He gradually forced the Gladstone government to consider long-range Irish programs, so that by the summer of 1885 the Irish Question again had risen to the top rank. How the Radicals responded to Ireland in this new situation proved to be crucial in their history.

I. Two Radical Chief Secretaries

The period of relative calm in 1883–84 failed to give any respite to G. O. Trevelyan, successor to Lord Frederick Cavendish. For two years the Irish tangle tore at him, finally transforming him from a rising Radical politician to a rather querulous defender of the Irish status quo. He never completely recovered from the experience. The Irish task would have broken many men. John Morley, who knew from experience, aptly described the office of the Chief Secretary as "that grim apartment in Dublin Castle, where successive secretaries spend unshining hours in saying No to impossible demands, and hunting for plausible answers to insoluble riddles."[1] Such a post would have been difficult for most Radicals, who were perhaps better suited for criticism and legislation than for administra-

---

1. John Morley, *The Life of William Ewart Gladstone*, 3 vols. (New York, 1903), III, 67.

tion, but it was especially hard for a limited and unimaginative man like Trevelyan.

The causes of Trevelyan's inaptitude for the position were two-fold: one might be called personal mental and temperamental qualities, the other his Radical characteristics. Like his father, Sir Charles Trevelyan, who had been largely responsible for Irish affairs during the Famine, G. O. Trevelyan proved to be an energetic administrator, but one without intuitive sympathy or warm feeling for the Irish people. Curiously, although Trevelyan was a well-known historian, and in his major works an ardent advocate of the American point of view in the revolutionary period, he showed no historical sense about the Irish nation or culture. To make matters worse, he was too proud and sensitive. Constant hounding by the Irish nationalists was standard treatment for Chief Secretaries, but Trevelyan took it personally. He struck back with injudicious words and only aggravated the situation. Here a strong measure of aristocratic disdain would have served him better.

The turn of mind arising from his Radicalism was perhaps an even more serious impediment. The problem was that Trevelyan was too much the typical parliamentary Radical, inclined to apply certain Radical nostrums without much regard for the real situation in Ireland. Yet he did not act according to the Radical spirit, perhaps mythical, of getting to the root of things. He had experience as an administrator in both India and Whitehall, but he had learned mainly to regard economy in government finance as the highest virtue. By a cruel repetition of history, he tried to employ Manchester School economics as rigidly as had his father. There was in Radicalism enough liking for root-and-branch reform and enough hostility for the landed orders for Trevelyan to have cleaned house in Dublin Castle and made the Irish executive more responsive to the Irish people; but in this he failed, for he could not see beyond the information fed to him by the Castle bureaucracy. Like most parliamentary Radicals, he could not translate his Radicalism into a different context.

Trevelyan's main duty as Chief Secretary was to administer the crimes act. He intended to do so reasonably. He went to Dublin in 1882 with the entirely Radical intention of ending the landlord bias in the Castle, writing Gladstone that the Irish executive should

never use coercion unless there had been a "pointed and practical
... incitement to a definite crime. ..." Furthermore, he would teach
his subordinates in the Irish government that he and Lord Spencer,
the Viceroy, were masters in Ireland: "It will never do to glide into
a system in which Ireland is permanently ruled by prefects: and
that is what things were fast coming to."[2] But the subordinates soon
mastered him, and converted him to their view of the Irish agitation.
As early as January 1883 he wrote Chamberlain that the tenants
really disliked the nationalist turmoil, and that the movement was
kept alive only by professional agitators.[3] In February 1883 he complained in a speech that the Irish were divided into two parties:
those for law and those opposed. The National League, he said,
only wanted to terrorize the tenantry and separate Ireland from
England.[4]

During 1883 Trevelyan and Spencer—with Spencer the dominant
figure—began to stop nationalist meetings and to prosecute some of
the most vituperative nationalist leaders, including Davitt, Healy,
and Biggar. They tried to silence the strongest nationalist paper,
United Ireland, by prosecuting its editor, William O'Brien. None
of these attempts was successful, and nationalist criticism only increased. Forced on the defensive, Trevelyan was soon defending
the very administrative system he and other Radicals had formerly
criticized. Once committed to administering rather than reforming
the system, an inflexible man like Trevelyan had no choice but to
protect it. For instance, he declared in a speech in Scotland that the
officials in the Irish government were as high-minded and honorable
as any in Great Britain. He even argued that Irishmen should not
complain about their lack of self-rule, for many officials in Ireland
were Irish, and Irishmen also got plenty of opportunity to exercise
their capacity for ruling in various posts throughout the Empire.[5]
To the appropriate complaint that Irish Catholics, the great majority
of the population, supplied only a small number of the Irish magistrates, Trevelyan lamely replied that gentleman magistrates were

2. September 11, 1882, Gladstone Papers, 44,335.
3. January 7, 1883, Chamberlain Papers, JC 5/70/4.
4. Quoted in *The Times*, February 10, 1883.
5. *The Times*, December 7, 1883.

necessary, and that the landlord class alone had the requisite "leisure and education."[6] That was hardly talk for a Radical.

Yet even the landlords and the Castle machinery provided trouble for Trevelyan. Both the Royal Irish Constabulary and the local police were discontented with their onerous duties and mistrustful of their superiors; sometimes they showed entirely too much vigor in breaking up meetings and carrying out evictions. Beginning in 1883, the landlords of Ulster responded to nationalist advances in the northern province by reviving Orange lodges, staging counter-demonstrations, and arming themselves. Trevelyan and Spencer soon had to stop Orangist as well as nationalist meetings. On one occasion they had to remove an Ulster magistrate from the Commission of the Peace for his flagrant attempt to provoke a fight between his Orange following and nationalist demonstrators.[7] Thus Trevelyan, like Spencer, received fierce criticism from both sides. He complained to his constituents that while Orangemen accused the Irish executive of allying with the Parnellites, Parnellites called him and Spencer the meanest and most malicious men ever to rule Ireland.[8] Spencer, a staunch, red-bearded Whig, could take the punishment; Trevelyan could not. His Radicalism paralyzed by overwhelming administrative duties, Trevelyan proposed only a small legislative program for Ireland. He pressed for bills to improve the Constabulary's pay and pension, to ease voter registration, to close pubs on Sunday, and to raise teachers' salaries.[9] He also supported the extension of Irish tramways and the inclusion of Ireland in the 1884 franchise reform bill. The nationalists, with some justice, regarded Trevelyan's plans as most significant for what they failed to do. In particular, the Parnellites criticized his determination not to undertake public works or poor law extension for relief of

6. *Hansard* 286 (April 4, 1884), 1658, 1700–1708.

7. The magistrate was Lord Rossmore. Trevelyan to Chamberlain, December 27, 1883, and January 2, 1884, Chamberlain Papers, JC 5/70/6 and 7; *Hansard* 284 (February 8, 1884), 374–92.

8. Quoted in *The Times*, December 7, 1883.

9. Spencer to Gladstone, May 3, 1883, and January 29, 1884, Gladstone Papers, 44,310, 44,311; Trevelyan to Spencer, February 6, 1884, Gladstone Papers, 44,311; Trevelyan to Edward Hamilton, April 7, 1884, Gladstone Papers, 44,335; *Hansard* 282 (August 4, 1883), 1541–52.

poverty. Trevelyan believed that the English work house test should be copied in Ireland, for outdoor relief would "demoralize" the Irish people. He much preferred emigration, long the bane of Irish nationalists, as a relief measure.[10] The nationalists, however, considering that Ireland faced a crisis of hunger in the winter of 1882–83, called Trevelyan's a "pinch-of-hunger" and a "deportation" policy.[11]

From early 1883 nationalist criticism of Trevelyan intensified. In February 1883 Parnell strongly attacked both Spencer and Trevelyan in the House of Commons, stating baldly that they were "unfitted" for their posts. Several days later he moved an amendment to the Address, declaring that their administration of the coercion act was tyrannical.[12] In February 1884 he accused Spencer and Trevelyan of "wanton prohibition of legal and constitutional public meetings throughout Ireland...."[13] In *United Ireland* O'Brien and Healy unmercifully assaulted the Viceroy and the Chief Secretary for a wide variety of sins, including judicial tyranny and harboring criminals among the Dublin Castle bureaucracy.[14] The heaviest attacks pertained to the Maamtrasna murders, the Parnellites claiming that Spencer and Trevelyan had judicially murdered Myles Joyce, one of the men executed for the crime. By the same token, the Parnellites accused the executive of deliberately allowing the guilty man to go free.[15]

Although Spencer received even more intense criticism than his Chief Secretary, it was Trevelyan who broke down. Trevelyan found his parliamentary function especially nerve-wracking. Day after day he had to face as many as twenty bad-tempered questions from the Irish M.P.'s on topics ranging from specific cases of eviction to the statistics of poor relief. In August 1883 Trevelyan wrote

10. *Hansard* 276 (February 27, 1882), 1063–73; *The Times*, April 24, 1883; Trevelyan to Gladstone, April 3, 1883, Gladstone Papers, 44,335.

11. Resolutions of a nationalist meeting at Limerick, quoted in *The Times*, May 14, 1883.

12. *Hansard* 276 (February 23, 26, 1883), 723–24, 854–75.

13. *Hansard* 284 (February 8, 1884), 321–37.

14. Eversley, *Gladstone and Ireland*, 237; William O'Brien, *Evening Memories* (London, 1920), 12–32.

15. See Timothy Harrington's speech, *Hansard* 293 (October 23, 1884), 127–48.

to Gladstone of "this terrible office." No one, he wrote, could understand "what it is to be the representative of the central government in the face of the false and unscrupulous men who are forever seeking to discredit English rule in Ireland by the personal ruin of the Minister who represents it in the House."[16]

To strengthen his position, Trevelyan asked for a seat in the cabinet, but Gladstone refused on grounds that the Viceroy already was a cabinet member.[17] By May 1884 Gladstone's secretary, Edward Hamilton, had heard that Trevelyan was "breaking down under his work." He told Gladstone correctly that Trevelyan was "too highly strung to stand the bully-ragging of the Parnellites. . . ."[18] On July 10, 1884, the Parnellites during question-time gave Trevelyan an especially fearsome treatment, and two weeks later Trevelyan asked to be relieved of his post. He wrote Gladstone: "The life I lead is, indeed, not a human life at all." The functions of the office could be carried out only by "the sacrifice of one man's nerves, health, happiness, and self respect. . . . I feel as if at any time I might break down."[19] On August 6 the government announced that due to "fatigue and indisposition combined" Trevelyan would take no further part in the parliamentary session.[20] In October 1884 Gladstone shifted Trevelyan to the Chancellorship of the Duchy of Lancaster. By then Trevelyan's fine black hair and beard had turned white. *United Ireland* exulted that Trevelyan had "fled like a rat to his hole."[21]

The cabinet chose to replace him with Henry Campbell-Bannerman, an easy-going Scottish Radical who at the time was secretary to the admiralty.[22] Although Campbell-Bannerman professed absolute ignorance of Irish affairs as well as disbelief in the Dublin

16. August 20, 1883, Gladstone Papers, 44,335.

17. Gladstone to Trevelyan, August 23, 1883, Gladstone Papers, 44,335.

18. Hamilton Diaries, May 7, 1884, 48,636.

19. July 26, 1884, Gladstone Papers, 44,335.

20. *The Times*, August 6, 1884; Spencer to Gladstone, September 20, 1884, Gladstone Papers, 44,311.

21. Quoted in *The Times*, August 6, 1884.

22. The offer went initially to Shaw Lefevre, who refused because he opposed coercion. Eversley, *Gladstone and Ireland*, 256; Shaw Lefevre to Gladstone, October 10, 11, 1884, Gladstone Papers, 44,153.

Castle system, Spencer and Gladstone finally prevailed upon him to accept the office.[23] Once in the position he became an exemplary Chief Secretary—largely because he willingly put Radicalism aside. He was a good administrator and got on well with all kinds of people. In public he maintained absolute loyalty to Spencer, the government, and Dublin Castle. Above all he remained remarkably calm and good-tempered, even in the face of Irish attacks in the House. It was frequently said that Campbell-Bannerman ruled Ireland with Scottish jokes. If that remark was unfair, certainly he sought to make his speeches as short and dull as possible in order to expose the minimum target for assault.[24] As he held office only nine months before the government fell, Campbell-Bannerman offered no significant legislation for Ireland. Yet the Irish never criticized him as they had Spencer or Trevelyan. He left Dublin with the respect of the Parnellites and the appreciation of the Liberal party. He also kept his own perspective of Ireland and in 1885 significantly influenced the debate in Liberal and Radical circles about Irish policy. His record, as contrasted with Trevelyan's, suggests that if Radicals were to take part in the governing of Ireland by Britain, they were well advised to forget their Radicalism entirely.

II. Radicals and Irish Problems, 1883–84

Radicals were too concerned with English reforms and with preparing for the future to trouble themselves about the lessons inherent in Trevelyan's downfall. As Schnadhorst wrote Chamberlain, the English constituencies had no more enthusiasm for Irish reforms: "... we cannot win the General Election of '85 as we did that of '68 on the issue of 'Justice to Ireland' *by itself*."[25] Yet the Irish Question succeeded in forcing itself on the attention of the Radicals

23. Spencer to Gladstone, October 13, 1884, Gladstone Papers, 44,311; Campbell-Bannerman to Spencer, October 13, 1884, Campbell-Bannerman Papers, 41,228.

24. J. A. Spender, *The Life of the Rt. Hon. Sir Henry Campbell-Bannerman, G.C.B.*, 2 vols. (London, 1923), I, 66–69.

25. January 29, 1883, Chamberlain Papers, JC 5/63/5; also, E. A. Freeman to James Bryce, April 17, 1883, Bryce Papers, MS 7; G. W. E. Russell, "The Coming Session," *F.R.* 193 (January, 1883), 1–18.

in the years 1883–84 precisely because of the importance of the political struggle in England and Scotland. That is, the Irish Question kept inserting itself into what Radicals regarded as the central political issue of the day—the battle between Radicals and Whigs for power in the Liberal party.

This battle seemed more urgent after 1882 because of the impending retirement of Gladstone. Since the 1870's Radicals and Whigs alike had recognized that only Gladstone could hold the left and right wings of the party together. But from the summer of 1882 on, the Grand Old Man seemed to be on the verge of retirement.[26] Anticipation of a Radical triumph under a newly widened franchise, to which the government was committed, intensified the air of crisis. Radicals thought it necessary to stake out their position in order to assure themselves of the fruits of victory. Chamberlain wrote Morley: "The time is coming when our Party (of three or four) must have a Programme & know exactly what it is aiming at."[27] Shortly afterward, in August 1883, the Radical Programme began to appear in the *Fortnightly*. Thus, for the Liberal party at least, the political context consisted of intense preparation by Radicals and corresponding apprehension by Whigs. And, instead of staying out of the way, Ireland provided a number of the sorest points of contention between Radicals and Whigs.[28]

Curiously enough, the Irish land problem, the most hotly contested issue between Radicals and Whigs before 1882, now played a relatively insignificant role. This was mainly due to Radical reluctance to raise the issue again. The Irish nationalists were not satisfied with the 1881 land act. Even those who rejected Davitt's idea of land nationalization saw serious flaws in the working of the 1881 law. Parnell asked Gladstone in October of 1882 to amend the land act by allowing leaseholders into the fair rent clauses, and by extending the purchase provisions so as to lend all of the purchase

26. Gladstone brought up the question of retirement in July and October 1882 and again in February 1883: Dilke Memoirs, 43,936, ff. 150–51; Hamilton Diaries, October 18, 1882, 48,633; Bernard Holland, *The Life of Spencer Compton Eighth Duke of Devonshire*, 2 vols. (London, 1911), I, 377–79; Dilke Memoirs, 43,937, ff. 47–48.

27. May 19, 1883, Chamberlain Papers, JC 5/54/505.

28. Hartington recognized this: Holland, *Life of Devonshire*, I, 378.

money to the tenant.[29] In 1883 and 1884 he introduced bills drawn along these lines into the House of Commons, but in each case without favorable action.

Even though W. H. Smith, a leading Tory, committed himself to a scheme of land purchase early in 1882, Gladstone and most of the Liberal leaders were extremely reluctant to reopen the land question. The Whigs thought that property already had been too much tampered with. Moderate Liberals agreed that if they entertained any amendments to the land act, the Parnellites might seize the opportunity to demand extreme changes. They also believed that the business of the House demanded attention to other problems.[30]

Most Radicals agreed with this reasoning. In part their sentiments were expressed by T. H. S. Escott, successor to Morley as editor of the *Fortnightly*: "... it is intolerable that the Irish peasant should always be allowed priority in the deliberations of the Government over the labouring classes of England."[31] Radical M.P.'s gave Parnell little assistance when he presented his land bills in the House.[32] Of course all Radicals still wanted to free the Irish tenant from the arbitrary control of the landlords, and they spoke highly of the potential benefits of a peasant proprietary.[33] But they objected to spending the huge sums of money necessary under any purchase plan. Here their basic anti-landlord attitudes reemerged. Both Alfred Russell Wallace and Henry George, the most influential Radical land theoreticians, thought that purchase would only lead to further concentration of ownership in a few hands.[34] Further, working-class militants objected to purchase because it would force

29. K. O'Shea to Gladstone, October 6, 1882, Gladstone Papers, 44,269. The term "land purchase" hereafter will be used to mean purchase by loans to the tenant amounting to the full purchase price.

30. Gladstone to Spencer, March 12, 1883, Gladstone Papers, 44,310.

31. "Affairs," *F.R.* 196 (April 1883), 609; also *The Echo*, March 14, 1883.

32. In March 1883, 18 Radicals voted for the Parnellites' land reform bill, and 42 against; in March 1884, 23 voted for the Parnellites and 34 against. *Hansard* 277 (March 14, 1883), 450–509; 285 (March 5, 1884), 551–607.

33. "Irish Land Reforms," *British Quarterly Review* 143 (July 1880), 135–37; attitudes of the Trades Union Congress, reported in *The Times*, September 20, 1882.

34. A. R. Wallace, "How to Nationalize the Land: A Radical Solution of the Irish Land Problem," *Contemporary Review* 38 (November 1880), 716–34; George, *Irish Land Question*, 20–21.

English workmen to help compensate Irish landlords.[35] Middle-class Radicals opposed purchase because of the adverse moral effects they thought it would have. As the *Daily News* argued, land purchase schemes could provide no "test of the fitness of a tenant to become an owner"; therefore, they would allow "a lazy thriftless, ne'er-do-weel" as well as a provident tenant to buy land.[36]

The security of Treasury funds involved in purchase was another concern of Radicals. In this they agreed with their Liberal and Whig colleagues. For example, in response to a motion for land purchase by Lord George Hamilton, Trevelyan contended that the scheme would set purchase payments below the levels of the tenant's rent, so the tenant would have no incentive to drive a good bargain for which he was using government money. Furthermore, in bad times, the tenantry would agitate to force the government to remit all purchase payments.[37] This line of thinking hamstrung the Liberal party. In the spring of 1884 pressure from Tories, Parnellites, and Irish Liberals forced the government to produce a proposal for extension of the purchase clauses. In the cabinet discussions Chamberlain advocated a plan for advancing 100 percent of the money, and Trevelyan finally agreed. But the bill that Trevelyan actually introduced into the House (May 1884) was so restricted by safeguards for Treasury funds that the Parnellites received it very skeptically.[38] The government abandoned the bill, and not a Radical expressed regret.

The idea of reforming Irish local government provided a much more contentious point between Radicals and Whigs. The reason is that while purchase proposals seemed likely only to embroil parliament more than ever in Irish affairs, local government reform promised to relieve parliament of precisely those duties. Thus by 1883, while few Radicals advocated Home Rule, all favored some kind of reform to give Irishmen a degree of control over their own affairs. Radicals were not entirely alone in this sentiment. Gladstone wanted to go at least as far as most Radicals toward Irish self-rule;

35. *Reynolds's Newspaper*, April 30, May 7, 1882.
36. *Daily News*, April 8, 1882.
37. *Hansard* 280 (June 12, 1883), 427–35.
38. John E. Pomfret, *The Struggle for Land in Ireland* (Princeton, 1930), 226–27; *Hansard* 288 (May 27, 1884), 1510–28; Hamilton Diaries, May 13, 1884, 48,636.

consequently, he made common cause in 1883–84 with Radicals against the Whigs and Conservatives, who regarded the prospect of local Irish self-rule as the elephant views the mouse.

Although most Radicals would have in principle agreed with John Morley that "... you cannot have liberalism in England without liberalism in Ireland," by 1883 they were increasingly motivated for Irish governmental reform by the simple desire to be rid of Irish business. With them, the general concern about the overburdening of parliament was an especially serious problem, as they wanted parliament to be an active, reforming agency. They concluded that some form of local self-rule for the various parts of the kingdom would be necessary to break the parliamentary deadlock, to which Ireland had long been the heaviest contributor.[39] Radicals also believed that Irishmen would not settle down and spare parliament their demands until they felt that Irish opinion carried weight in Irish legislation. By the same token, most Radicals agreed with Gladstone that a "bulwark" of local government in Ireland was needed to protect the English government from Irish agitation.[40] Put another way, a system of local government in Ireland would act as a ground for the lightning of Irish storms. Trevelyan wrote: "Our general view is that to engage the people in the management of their own affairs is the best means for withdrawing them from the barren quarrel with the Central Government which constitutes so large a part of politics in Ireland."[41]

In accordance with these ideas, Radicals expressed support for a number of plans to give the Irish limited control over their own affairs. One such scheme proposed the establishment of a "Grand Committee" in the House of Commons, to be composed mainly of Irish M.P.'s, for handling the details of purely Irish legislation.[42]

39. Frederic Harrison, "The Deadlock in the House of Commons," *Nineteenth Century* 55 (September 1881), 317–40; John Morley, "Affairs," *F.R.* 184 (April 1882), 537–40; Thomas Shaw, "The Union with England of Scotland and Ireland," *British Quarterly Review*, 150 (April 1882), 396–419.

40. Hamilton Diaries, December 7, 1882, 48,633; John Morley, "Irish Revolution and English Liberalism," *Nineteenth Century* 69 (November 1882), 647–66; Escott, "Affairs," *F.R.* 193 (January 1883), 147–50.

41. To Gladstone, December 23, 1882, Gladstone Papers, 44,335.

42. Hammond, *Gladstone and the Irish Nation*, 198–204; Chamberlain, *Political Memoir*, 9; *Hansard* 275 (November 29, 1882), 315–18; John Boyd Kinnear, *Ireland*

Impeded by opposition within the cabinet and by technical complexities, however, the Grand Committee idea was soon replaced by other plans. The one most favored by Radicals would have set up elective county councils in Ireland. The Liberal government had pledged to establish county councils throughout Britain as early as 1881, but could not proceed with its plans because of Irish and Egyptian problems until the winter of 1882–83. By then the Whigs, especially Hartington and Spencer, strongly believed that Ireland should be omitted from any county council measure. As Hartington put it, the Whigs felt it would be "madness" to give Ireland any self-government without assurance that the Irish would not use it as a base for agitation.[43] A bitter cabinet quarrel followed, with Gladstone, Chamberlain, and Dilke opposing Hartington and Spencer. The two Radicals argued that Irish agitators would feed on the obvious grievance if England and Scotland got county councils and Ireland did not. They were determined for purposes of pacification to give Ireland at least, as Dilke said, "fair words for the future."[44]

Despite vigorous efforts by Chamberlain to rally public opinion for giving Ireland institutions of local government, the Whigs won the struggle.[45] The Queen's speech in 1883 did not mention the subject. The loss to the Whigs seems only to have hardened Radical attitudes, and they campaigned vigorously for Irish local government reform throughout 1883.[46] By 1884 Radical opinion had evolved considerably and was beginning to go beyond county councils. It was finally obvious that even a Radical Chief Secretary (Trevelyan) could not make the Dublin Castle administration work to the satisfaction of Irishmen. During the course of 1884 the great

---

(London, 1880); John Morley, "England and Ireland," *F.R.* 172 (April 1881), 423–24.

43. Holland, *Life of Devonshire*, I, 384.

44. Dilke to Chamberlain, February 3, 1883; also Chamberlain to Dilke, February 4, 1883, both in Dilke Papers, 43,886.

45. See the speech by Chamberlain, quoted in Stephen Gwynn and Gertrude M. Tuckwell, *The Life of the Rt. Hon. Sir Charles Dilke*, 2 vols. (London, 1918), I, 516.

46. Speeches by: Chamberlain at Birmingham, *The Times*, March 31, 1883; Morley at Liverpool, *The Times*, May 19, 1883; Dilke at Glasgow, *The Times*, October 31, 1883.

bulk of the Radical movement inclined toward giving Ireland, as Thomas Burt stated, "all the self-government consistent with the Union."[47] This catch-all phrase, convenient for Radicals in distinguishing themselves from Whigs, covered a multitude of positions. A few Radicals like Cowen, Labouchere, and the followers of Henry George supported Home Rule outright.[48] Most of the rest preferred some type of elective national board. Because of his activities in 1885, Chamberlain got credit for this idea, but the evidence is clear that he did not originate it. As early as 1882 Morley had suggested that an elective tribunal in Dublin could deal with Irish private bills, and that men responsible to the Irish people should exercise the functions of the Irish Board of Works and the Local Government Board.[49] Various schemes along these lines were elaborated by Radicals in 1883 and 1884. The objective of all of them was to do away with Irish problems by deflecting Irish energy away from Westminster and away from British politics.[50]

The most significant example of this shift in Radical opinion was the assistance given by a number of Radical M.P.'s in forming a standing agency to promote, among other Irish policies, an extensive measure of self-government. Led by James Bryce and Alfred Illingworth, who were no eccentrics but respectively a professor of civil law and a wealthy manufacturer, these men joined Irish Liberals in February 1884 in establishing a Committee on Irish Affairs.[51] According to a booklet by Bryce which set out the views of the Committee, the near future weighed heavy with them.[52] The Committee thought at the next general election the Parnellites would win three-fourths of the Irish seats. It was important to formulate a program to answer this powerful demand for "separation." They

47. From a speech at Blyth, quoted in *The Times*, February 3, 1883.

48. Labouchere, "Radicals and Whigs," *F.R.* 206 (February 1884), 222–24; Henry George, "England and Ireland: An American View," *F.R.* 186 (June 1882), 780–94; *The Radical*, October 29, 1881.

49. "Irish Revolution and English Liberalism," 658–60.

50. Escott, "Affairs," *F.R.* 193 (January 1883), 149–50; Samuel Laing, "Rational Radicalism," *F.R.* 205 (January 1884), 86–87.

51. Bryce's introductory letter, February 15, 1884, Bryce Papers, Ireland Box, p. 20. There were twenty-seven other Radicals on the Committee.

52. James Bryce, *England and Ireland: An Introductory Statement* (London, 1884).

made the crucial admission that Irish disaffection rose, neither from the character of the Irish people nor from the agitation of a few, but from the fact that English administration in Ireland was a "foreign government." Furthermore, the English party system inevitably resulted in vacillating Irish policies. Ireland therefore had to be governed by Irish ideas, hence by Irishmen. The Committee also recognized what most Englishmen were unable to see: that the Parnellite party was a mixed bag, in which some ingredients were fundamentally more moderate than Repealers or Fenians had been. They argued that Parnell had to present a hostile facade to the British or be branded with timidity at home. They urged, therefore, that the nationalists be treated with patience and understanding. Finally, the Committee tried to associate Irish self-rule with the advent of British democracy by declaring that the English "popular party" must predominate before Ireland could win justice.

The Committee's conclusions marked an important turn of Radical opinion toward the Irish point of view. Their analysis of the Irish problem no longer simply blamed landlordism, but now looked to the very political relations between the two countries. It is impossible to know how many Radicals shared precisely these attitudes, but as the Committee consisted mainly of moderate Radicals, their opinions probably represented a substantial part of the movement. In the meantime, Ireland embroiled Radicals and Whigs in a dispute in which Radical opinion was nearly unanimous: extending the franchise.

The Liberal party came to office in 1880 intending to broaden the county franchise. But in the autumn of 1883, when the cabinet finally got around to consideration of a scheme, Hartington urged that Ireland be excluded from the reform. He wrote Gladstone that franchise extension in Ireland "would have the effect of strengthening the party of rebellion, and of discouraging, if not crushing, the remaining supporters of order in Ireland."[53] Hartington proposed that if the franchise reform included Ireland, then it be accompanied by a redistribution of seats, by which he planned to salvage at least part of the Protestant minority's power.[54] Preserva-

53. Quoted in Holland, *Life of Devonshire*, I, 400.
54. Hamilton Diaries, December 14, 1883, 48,635.

tion of public order and the position of the Anglo-Irish elite was to him the issue. The Radicals, however, wished to include Ireland and have no redistribution. To them, English political affairs constituted the problem. They thought that redistribution by its very nature would be very difficult to pass, and to add it to the franchise bill would endanger the whole package. Moreover, they wanted to wait until the reformed parliament met to draw up a seats bill, for the new parliament would more likely favor Radicals. The Radicals also considered it tactically impossible to omit Ireland from the reform.[55] The Whigs would sacrifice reform if necessary to keep the Irish in order, but the Radicals could not wait. Trevelyan made the most significant contribution of his term as Chief Secretary in arguing the Radicals' position on this point.[56] In the cabinet Chamberlain and Dilke stood firm against Hartington's threats of resignation. In public Chamberlain spoke strongly for the inclusion of Ireland, in order to build such a wave of opinion that Hartington could only submit or resign.[57] His tactics of speaking before the cabinet had made its decision upset Gladstone, but the Radicals succeeded in this phase of their struggle with the Whigs. The franchise bill that the House of Commons passed (April 1884) included Ireland and abolished no Irish seats.

III. CHAMBERLAIN AND THE NATIONAL COUNCIL PLAN, 1884–85

Radicals had to carry on their efforts against the Whigs for Irish local government and franchise reform without substantial support from the Parnellites. The Irish leader fulfilled his part of the Kilmainham bargain in 1882 and 1883, supporting, for instance, Chamberlain's bankruptcy and merchant shipping bills. Chamberlain publicly acknowledged Parnell's loyal fulfillment of his engagements, and Parnell deliberately excluded Chamberlain from his

55. Except for Leonard Courtney, who hated the Parnellites and denied that they represented the true feeling of the Irish people. See his memorandum to Gladstone, November 8, 1884, Courtney Collection, IV.

56. Trevelyan to Gladstone, October 26, 1883, Gladstone Papers, 44,335.

57. Speeches at Wolverhampton and Bristol, quoted in *The Times*, December 5, November 23, 1883. According to Dilke, Chamberlain was "very anxious to 'make Hartington go out on Franchise.'" Dilke Memoirs, January 28, 1884, 43,938.

criticism of British rule.[58] But in 1884 the nationalists began to turn against their allies. Twice in the first half of 1884 the Parnellites joined the Tories in votes of censure against the government's Sudan policy.[59] In the summer of 1884 Radicals sought nationalist assistance in agitating against the Lords for the reform bill, only to hear the Parnellites declare that extension of the franchise in Ireland was not essential and bitterly denounce the Radical requests for support.[60] Irish nationalists in Britain reaffirmed their old policy of bringing about a stalemate between parties. *United Ireland* declared that the "wishy-washy Radicals who at present supply the British workman with his political spoon-feeding" were useless.[61]

The reasons for the reversal of Irish opinion were complex. A few of the militant Home Rulers believed that Radicals had betrayed pledges to Ireland. Moreover, as Conor Cruise O'Brien suggests, the Irish Catholic clergy began to sway the nationalists against the Radicals.[62] But the main reason probably was that the nationalists' anger at the Liberal government's coercive policy spilled over to the Radicals. While Radicals were concerning themselves with English and Scottish plans in 1883 and 1884, the Irish nationalists were fighting what they regarded as the really crucial battle at home. Increasingly they tended to feel that Radicals who did not speak out or resign were actually supporting coercion. Thus, though bitter against nearly all Englishmen, the nationalists in 1884 seemed to direct their most intense hostility toward Radicals.

The Irish disaffection was a very serious matter for the Radicals. For one thing, the franchise bill had been rejected by the House of Lords and hung in the balance, and with it a Radical redistribution of seats. Radicals knew a general election would follow hard upon

58. Chamberlain to O'Shea, August 2, 5, 15, 1883; O'Shea to Chamberlain, April 16, 1884, JC 8/8/1/16, 17, 18, 24; Parnell to Chamberlain, April 10, 1884, JC 8/6/3L; *Hansard* 276 (February 26, 1883), 873.

59. *Hansard* 284 (February 19, 1884), 1458–62; 288 (May 13, 1884), 302–6.

60. See the article on the attitude of the Irish National League of Great Britain in *The Times*, July 28, 1884; the letter by Matthew Harris to Cowen, quoted in *The Times*, August 25, 1884; and Healy's article, "The Irish and the Government," *F.R.* 215 (November 1884), 649–56.

61. November 22, 1884.

62. O'Brien, *Parnell and His Party*, 89–90.

the reform bills, and the final retirement of Gladstone as well. The new Irish crisis threatened their plans by turning the Parnellite vote in the House and in the British cities against the Liberal party. No one saw this more clearly than Chamberlain. Busy constructing a program with which to swamp the Whigs, he realized that the Irish behavior threatened to associate Radicalism with an oppressive policy in Ireland, which he thought the British masses at the moment would not tolerate. Chamberlain concluded that the Radicals needed an Irish policy which would be distinct from that of the Whigs; one which could be presented to the British electorate as a generous —but safe—concession to Ireland; which could unify Radicals on a potentially divisive issue; which also could win enough support in Ireland to prevent the nationalist leaders from rejecting it outright; and which might remove the Irish Question once and for all from British politics. The national council plan was his solution.

Chamberlain's decision to take up the national council idea was crucial to the history of both his own career and British politics in general. It propelled him to center stage in the Anglo-Irish drama, where he remained for several years, and it promoted to legitimacy what was to be until the twentieth century the most serious rival to Home Rule. Chamberlain put his national council proposal in a famous letter to W. H. Duignan in December 1884. Chamberlain declared that he would never consent to the nationalist program if it meant independence for Ireland "as a separate people with the inherent rights of an absolutely independent community."[63] But he said that he believed the Irish had a right to extensive self-government, which he hoped the first session of the reformed parliament would meet. Chamberlain stated that he would grant even more than elective county government; for there should be a national board to deal with exclusively Irish matters—education, land, railways and other communications, and with taxation "in Ireland for these strictly Irish purposes." The Irish people "would have entire independence as regards all local work and local expenditure." He added that he was not sure British public opinion would support "so great a change; but if I were entirely free I should be greatly

63. December 17, 1884, Chamberlain Papers, JC 8/3/1/24.

inclined to make a speech or two in Ireland submitting these proposals." Two days later Chamberlain authorized Duignan to show the letter to the Irish leaders.[64]

Several aspects of this letter should be noted. First, Chamberlain's adoption of the national council idea arose entirely from his perception of the state of party politics in Britain, and not from altruism or conscious extension of Radicalism to Ireland. Second, his plan crystallized ideas already generally held by most Radicals. Third, the scheme shows that Chamberlain did not accept Home Rule in the sense that the Irish had given the term since the days of Isaac Butt; indeed, Chamberlain made it clear that he believed an Irish legislature would be tantamount to separation. He distinctly held that Ireland was as much a part of the British community as Scotland or Wales, or even Sussex or London. Fourth, although the national board would have mainly administrative functions, it would also have important *legislative* powers in dealing with land and education and the associated taxation. This would establish a kind of dyarchy in Ireland. Finally, Chamberlain hoped—no more or less than hoped—that the plan would diminish the demand for Home Rule. Like all Radicals, he wanted to divert the attention of Irishmen from the English government. Although his scheme has sometimes been regarded as a trap for the Parnellites, it was a trap only insofar as any appeasement is a trap; it was a gamble that something less than Home Rule would satisfy Irish nationalism.[65]

Duignan showed Chamberlain's letter to most of the leading nationalists, including Parnell. The letter worried the Uncrowned King. He wanted to improve Irish local government, but he did not want anything to distract attention from Home Rule during the coming general election or afterward. He responded, therefore, by offering a plan of his own for a national board that would constitute an important administrative reform yet provide no competition for Home Rule. Strict limitation of the legislative power was the key to his solution. His formula called for an elective central board that would control the administrative functions of a number of pub-

64. December 19, 1884, Chamberlain Papers, JC/8/3/1/25.
65. Peter Fraser, in his *Joseph Chamberlain: Radicalism and Empire, 1868–1914*, 60–61, says that Chamberlain tried to trap Parnell into an anti-separationist scheme.

lic agencies like the Irish Board of Works and National Education Board. However, the central board would exercise no legislative functions; it would serve primarily as an agency for administering laws made at Westminster.[66]

A complicated series of indirect communications between Chamberlain and Parnell ensued. If they had come to an agreement on some formulation of the national or central board idea, the history of the next year, if not many years, would have been very different. But the two men were extremely cautious and suspicious, a situation sharply aggravated by their choice of a go-between: again the incompetent but dangerous Captain O'Shea. Chamberlain's proposal was to get Parnell's commitment to his national board scheme, but not to tie Parnell to a complete political alliance. O'Shea, however, in his simple way, interpreted the Parnell-Chamberlain communications as negotiations leading to an alliance, the reward for his part in the affair to be the Chief Secretaryship of Ireland.[67] Muddled by his clumsy diplomacy, the communications never had much chance of success. Eventually Chamberlain had to rebuke O'Shea and back away from the initiative he had taken.[68]

The replies Chamberlain received from his letter to Duignan confirmed Chamberlain in his retreat. E. D. Gray, editor of the *Freeman's Journal*, liked the plan, but William O'Brien, editor of the more extreme *United Ireland*, opposed it.[69] Other Irish leaders insisted that, however important the national board would be, only an Irish parliament would suffice. T. M. Healy, one of the most virulent of Irish nationalists, responded very angrily to the proposal. He refused comments on the details of the plan, because he thought Irish trust would simply be betrayed when the English found it useful to do so. Individual Englishmen might wish to act nobly, he admitted, but they were restricted by "the hogs who mostly composed the

66. Parnell's plan is in a memorandum written by O'Shea and given to Chamberlain: January 14, 1885, Chamberlain Papers, JC 8/8/1/36.

67. O'Shea, *Parnell*, II, 206.

68. January 21, 1885, Chamberlain Papers, JC 8/8/1/37; Chamberlain, *Political Memoir*, 138–39; Chamberlain, letter to *The Times*, August 11, 1888, copy in the Chamberlain Papers, JC 8/7/3/10; O'Shea to Parnell, January 19, 1885, copy in the Chamberlain Papers, JC 8/8/2G/7.

69. Chamberlain, *Political Memoir*, 138; O'Brien, *Parnell and His Party*, 91.

House of Commons." Englishmen would never give anything unless forced to; thus the Irish should hold out for a parliament.[70] These responses caused Chamberlain temporarily to give up his proposal. He wrote Duignan: "We know generally how such a proposal would be regarded & it is evident from Healy's letter that the simplest action may be misconstrued." He added that reconciliation with the nationalists at the moment seemed impossible.[71]

IV. RADICALS AND THE GOVERNMENT'S IRISH POLICY, 1885

During the first half of 1885, the last months of the second Gladstone administration, Radical attitudes toward Ireland were relatively unified. In regard to the land problem, most Radicals still held the landlords guilty of much of the troubles of Ireland, but they had no specific reforms in mind. They liked the idea of a peasant proprietary but continued to be unwilling to risk the credit of the Treasury for a policy of purchase that would benefit the landlords. The Committee on Irish Affairs, probably because of the influence of Irish Liberals, constituted a notable exception to this rule.[72] Nearly all Radicals agreed on the way Ireland should be governed. In the first place, they thought that coercion should be abandoned. It was not that they felt any less concerned about Irish disorder; rather, they saw that coercion had failed to pacify the country. As W. S. Caine, a Yorkshire coal mine owner, said, "we could not go on forever renewing coercion bills."[73] In the second place, even the few Radicals, like Trevelyan and Bright, who had strong reservations about dropping coercion, agreed that Ireland needed representative county government and some type of national board. Yet this sentiment did not go as far as Home Rule for many: indeed, most Radicals, especially in the middle class, still equated Home Rule with separation.[74]

70. Healy to Duignan, January 11, 1885, Chamberlain Papers, JC 8/3/2/2.
71. February 7, 1885, Chamberlain Papers, JC 8/3/1/28.
72. *The Times* and the *Daily News*, June 9, 1885.
73. Quoted in *The Times*, January 2, 1885. Other expressions of opposition to coercion: *Reynolds's Newspaper*, May 31, 1885; John Morley's speech at Islington, reported in *The Times*, June 6, 1885; Escott, "Affairs," *F.R.* 222 (June 1885), 879.
74. For example, Osborne Morgan spoke favorably of the nationalism of the

It remained for the Radicals in the ministry to try to attach these policies to the government's program. Although none expected the points to be enacted before the end of the session, all considered it essential to commit the Liberal party to a progressive program, even pertaining to Ireland, before the next general election and Gladstone's retirement.[75] In reaction to a set of proposals by Spencer, Chamberlain wrote a long memorandum expressing the Radical position. Noting that renewal of coercion, proposed by Spencer, would arouse strong opposition among both Liberal and nationalist M.P.'s and would hurt the Liberal party in the general election, he suggested limiting any coercion bill to a duration of one year. As to land purchase, Chamberlain dismissed it on grounds that the Irish were satisfied with the 1881 act. What he thought important was reform of Irish local government—"in my opinion the only hope of ultimately securing better relations between the two countries." Thus he urged adoption of his plan of county councils plus a national board. He suggested that a national board scheme might induce the Irish to restrain their objection to a coercion bill. He also linked his own acceptance of coercion to the national board: without cabinet support for his scheme, he would not accept even a limited measure of coercion.[76]

Chamberlain and Dilke, however, faced a stalemate in Spencer's determined opposition to a national council. Spencer, as always concerned primarily with orderliness, feared that a national board would assume the right to speak for the Irish nation and would, as a rival administrative body, conflict with the Irish executive. An opportunity to break the stalemate came from Cardinal Manning, who in April 1885 offered Chamberlain and Dilke the prospect of clerical approval of the national council idea. A lengthy set of communications followed, in which Manning tried through episcopal influence to obtain Parnell's support of the national council plan, and Cham-

---

four main parts of Great Britain, but distinctly rejected "separation." *The Times*, March 2, 1885.

75. C. H. D. Howard has a full account of the development of the cabinet's policy: "Joseph Chamberlain, Parnell and the Irish 'Central Board' Scheme, 1884–85," *Irish Historical Studies* 8 (September 1953), 324–61.

76. Memorandum on Spencer's Irish Program, April 11, 1885, Chamberlain Papers, JC 8/5/1/11.

berlain attempted to win cabinet approval of it as well as strict limitation of coercion.[77] For a time Chamberlain and Dilke thought they had secured agreement between all parties.[78] On May 9, however, the cabinet rejected the national council plan, with all of the peers except Granville voting against it, and all of the commoners except Hartington voting for it. Chamberlain and Dilke would have liked to resign, but they had not won Parnell's support for such a move, and without his approval their resignation would have been an empty gesture. Further maneuvering inside the cabinet succeeded only in confusing the issues of coercion and land purchase. Finally, on May 20, Dilke and Chamberlain resigned out of exasperation with their colleagues, and Shaw Lefevre reluctantly went with them.[79]

In any case time was running out on the government, as many Radicals had decided to act in order to prevent the cabinet from renewing coercion even in limited form. In this important regard they had gone beyond Chamberlain, though Chamberlain seems not to have realized it. On June 4, 1885, John Morley, the leader of anti-coercionist opinion among parliamentary Radicals, gave notice of a resolution against any renewal of repression. By then the Parnellites believed that the Conservatives would be more inclined to abandon coercion than the Liberals. On June 9 Parnellites and Tories combined to defeat the government on a detail of the budget. Twelve Radicals deliberately abstained from the division as a protest against coercion.[80] Dilke, Chamberlain, and Shaw Lefevre were relieved

77. Howard, "Chamberlain, Parnell and the Central Board Scheme," 341–61; Shane Leslie, *Henry Edward Manning: His Life and Labours* (London, 1921), 387–411; O'Brien, *Parnell and His Party*, 93; Dilke Memoirs, 43,939, f. 123; Gwynn and Tuckwell, *Dilke*, II, 130; Memorandum by Chamberlain, April 24, 1885, Chamberlain Papers, JC 8/7/2/12. Chamberlain to Manning, April 25, 1885; and "Local Government in Ireland" (a memorandum), both in Dilke Papers, 43,887.

78. Chamberlain, *Political Memoir*, 148; notes by O'Shea, April 28, 29, 30, 1885, Chamberlain Papers, JC 8/8/1/41; Dilke Memoirs, 43,939, f. 130; Manning to Chamberlain, May 4, 1885, copy in Dilke Papers, 43,887.

79. Chamberlain to Gladstone, May 12, 1885, Gladstone Papers, 44,126; Spencer to Gladstone, "Notes to Mr. Chamberlain's ideas as stated by Mr. Gladstone," May 6, 1885, Gladstone Papers, 44,312; *Hansard* 298 (May 20, 1885), 971–72; Hamilton Diaries, May 15, 18, 20, 21, 1885, 48,640; Dilke to Gladstone, May 20, 21, 1885, Gladstone Papers, 44,149; Chamberlain to Gladstone, May 20, 1885, Gladstone Papers, 44,126; Shaw Lefevre to Gladstone, May 21, 1885, Gladstone Papers, 44,153.

80. *The Times*, June 10, 1885, lists all the Liberals who were paired in the di-

to have the faltering, stifling government gone. They had failed to commit the ministry to Irish governmental reform, but at least they had thwarted pressures for more coercion. The general election could be faced without fear.

V. THE GENERAL ELECTION OF 1885

The next six months, culminating in the general election, did not at all work out the way Radicals wanted or expected, and largely because of the Irish Question. Perhaps most severely treated by events was Joseph Chamberlain, who was very confident of his position in June 1885. He wrote Bunce that, if the government had not fallen, Radicals would have been hobbled by commitment to some degree of coercion; but now that the Tories had to cope with Ireland, he was free to campaign for his national council scheme.[81] This he did, notably at Islington, where he described Dublin Castle as an "absurd and irritating anachronism."[82] He also arranged for publication of a version of the national council idea in the July issue of the *Fortnightly* and as the last chapter of the *Radical Programme*. In his view, all that remained to put his political plans in order was to reconfirm the support of the Irish Catholic bishops and Parnell for his policy.

This last decision led to disastrous results, for while Chamberlain was campaigning for his national council, the bishops and the Parnellites were turning against it. Anxious to promote Catholic education in Ireland, the bishops had recognized that they had more to gain from the Tories than from the Radicals.[83] In addition, the militant Parnellites were furious with what they regarded as the tacit support given to coercion by Chamberlain and Dilke.[84] The na-

---

vision, plus those who abstained. There is no evidence that Chamberlain "arranged" the defeat of the government, but there is much evidence of Radical opposition to coercion; *Daily News*, May 21, 1885; *Birmingham Daily Post*, May 22, 23, 1885.

81. June 11, 1885, Chamberlain Papers, JC 5/8.

82. *The Times*, June 15, 18, 1885.

83. C. H. D. Howard, "The Parnell Manifesto of 21 November, 1885, and the Schools Question," *English Historical Review* 62 (January 1947), 42–51.

84. *United Ireland*, May 30, 1885; speech by Healy, quoted in *The Times*, May 20, 1885; interview by Justin McCarthy, *Birmingham Daily Post*, June 27, 1885.

tionalists had won much from the Tories, who had decided to drop coercion and institute an enquiry into the Maamtrasna case. Also, the Conservative Lord Chancellor of Ireland, Lord Ashbourne, in July introduced a land purchase bill into the House of Lords. Indeed, the Parnellites believed that the Tories would be at least as likely as the Liberals to carry Home Rule, for Lord Randolph Churchill, the bright light of the party, seemed favorable to Ireland, and the Tories alone had a real chance of putting Home Rule through the House of Lords.[85] By mid-June 1885 the Parnellites saw no reason to meddle with so partial a reform as a national council.

Unaware of this change in Irish attitudes, Chamberlain took steps to cement an alliance with the nationalists and the bishops. He sent O'Shea to tell Parnell that, contingent upon Parnell's support, he and Dilke would refuse to join any cabinet that did not put a national council in its program.[86] He and Dilke also asked Cardinal Manning for letters of introduction to the Irish bishops. They intended to go to Ireland to speak to the bishops about a national council. Much to their dismay, Manning refused. "I am afraid of your Midlothian in Ireland," he wrote Dilke; "How can I be godfather to Hengist and Horsa?"[87] No promises of public silence from Dilke could change his mind. And at the same time, the Parnellites fell upon the idea with stunning gusto. Reminding them of their complicity in coercion, *United Ireland* warned Chamberlain and Dilke to stay out of Ireland: "We tell Mr. Chamberlain that our people fully understand that he would be unwilling to grant us one single concession which he felt himself able to withhold, and that if he imagines he can dupe the National party with his bastard out-of-date sympathy, he has a much higher opinion of his powers than is entertained on this side of the Channel."[88]

Chamberlain resented the attacks and naturally blamed Parnell, but he did not yet give up his plans. He wrote Dilke that he was losing confidence in Parnell's honesty, but that "neither he nor anyone else will succeed in Boycotting us." Perseverance would win

85. O'Brien, *Parnell*, II, 44–46; Healy to Labouchere, October 15, 1885, Viscount Gladstone Papers, 46,015.
86. Chamberlain, *Political Memoir*, 150.
87. Quoted by Gwynn and Tuckwell, *Dilke*, II, 149.
88. June 27, 1885.

out: "A little patience & we shall secure all we have fought for."[89]
A favorable letter from Davitt kept his hopes up.[90] But in a subsequent exchange of communications with Parnell, Chamberlain discovered that the Irish leader now doubted it would be "worth while to encumber the Irish question at present with a larger extension of local government to Ireland than to England."[91]

Parnell's response ended Chamberlain's efforts to win Irish support, and it set his anger toward the Irish to smoldering. Confident that the Irish would not hold the balance of parties after the election and that the Tories would not grant Home Rule, Chamberlain claimed that the Parnellites would learn a "healthy" lesson from their experience.[92] He grew increasingly bitter and hostile toward the Irish in the next few months. Ruthless and imperious, and never a man to be thwarted, Chamberlain was particularly disturbed by what he regarded as a personal rebuff. Clearly he had developed a heavy ego investment in the national council plan. To reject it not only unsettled his plans for a crucial election, but also hurt him personally. He wrote O'Shea: "As regards the Irish, they are gone, and I am not certain that I regret it. I am inclined to give them a bit of my mind in public some day but perhaps discretion will be the better part of valour."[93] Edward Hamilton recorded in November 1885 that he had heard "Chamberlain's latest object of animosity is Parnell with whom he declares after what has happened he will never make peace on any terms; and Chamberlain's animosities once formed are implacable."[94] Indeed, Chamberlain began to go beyond simple anger. He seems to have concluded that the Parnellites could not be trusted; consequently, they must be firmly and authoritatively dealt with. Ironically, his efforts to deal with the Irish nationalist party had only stirred within himself strongly authoritarian attitudes.

During the campaign Chamberlain concerned himself mainly

89. June 30, 1885, Dilke Papers, 43,887.

90. Garvin, *Chamberlain*, II, 18.

91. O'Shea to Chamberlain, July 13, 1885, quoted in Chamberlain, *Political Memoir*, 154–56.

92. To Henry Labouchere, July 18, 1885, Chamberlain Papers, JC 5/50/20a.

93. August 3, 1885, Chamberlain Papers, JC 8/8/1/51.

94. Hamilton Diaries, November 1, 1885, 48,641.

with elaborating a distinctly Radical program for the Liberal party. His first aim still was to construct a situation in which Whigs would have to submit to Radicalism or leave the party. In regard to Ireland, he held not only to the letter of the national council scheme but also to the spirit of his hostility to Irish nationalism. Crucial to this stance was his supreme confidence that if *he* had not been able to reach an understanding with the Irish, then no one else could. Eventually the Parnellites would have to come to him on his own terms. This attitude made Chamberlain one of the most outspoken anti–Home Rulers in the Liberal party. It also threw him into direct confrontation with Parnell, who in August 1885 declared that the *only* plank in the nationalist platform would be Home Rule. Furthermore, Parnell explicitly included the right to establish protective tariffs among the necessary functions of an Irish parliament. Chamberlain responded with an uncompromisingly severe statement at Warrington on September 8. He flatly rejected Home Rule on a number of grounds. It would establish a hostile power within thirty miles of English shores. It would give independence to people who had no more right to self-determination "without regard to the rest of the community than . . . the five millions of persons who inhabit the metropolis." And it would empower a man who intended the "first object" of the Irish legislature to be tariffs "against all English manufactures."[95] This was the tone Chamberlain maintained throughout the campaign. When Parnell in November instructed the Irishmen in Britain to vote Tory, Chamberlain expressed no surprise. He wrote Labouchere that Parnell "will force us all, Radicals & Liberals, to reject all arrangements with him. If we had a good Speaker with dictatorial powers he could stop Irish obstruction & P.'s power in Ireland would be shaken as soon as the people saw he was impotent in Parliament."[96]

In assuming that his hard line against the Irish had no rivals within Liberal opinion, Chamberlain neglected to take into consideration the wondrous, some might say malignant, durability and flexibility of Gladstone. Instead of retiring, as Chamberlain expected and

95. Quoted in *The Times*, September 9, 1885.
96. November 22, 1885, Chamberlain Papers, JC 5/50/26a.

hoped, the Grand Old Man decided to remain in politics through the general election. Two beliefs moved him to this decision: first, that only the Liberal party would be likely to settle the Irish Question; and second, that only he could hold the left and right of the party together. Gladstone correctly realized that the return of eighty to eighty-five Parnellites in the election, which everyone expected, would be so serious as to "shift the centre of gravity in the relations between the two countries."[97] Thus during the summer and autumn of 1885 Gladstone began to think that he had a special mission to solve the Irish problem. Therein lay the roots of a grave division between Gladstone and Chamberlain.

An important movement away from Chamberlain's stance was also beginning to grow within Radicalism itself. A number of Radicals, like Labouchere, Cowen, and some extreme working-class Radicals, supported Home Rule outright, as they had done for some time.[98] More seriously, a number of influential Radical M.P.'s increasingly tended to accept the concept of Home Rule. Dilke, who in public supported the national council policy, in private had never abandoned an old commitment to an Irish parliament. James Bryce now considered Home Rule inevitable and believed that the more the Irish controlled their own affairs the better.[99] Shaw Lefevre, thinking it necessary to satisfy Irish national sentiment, advocated the simple expedient of calling the national council a parliament.[100] Perhaps most important of all, John Morley had concluded, like Gladstone, that Ireland would be the crucial question for the next parliament, no matter what programs the Radicals put forward. Obviously hinting at Home Rule, he argued that no solution should be met with a closed mind. He refused to be shocked by Parnell's

97. Gladstone to Spencer, June 30, 1885, Gladstone Papers, 44,312; Philip Magnus, *Gladstone: A Biography* (New York, 1964), 330–37.

98. *The Democrat*, a land nationalizer, Henry Georgeite paper, applauded Home Rule on December 12, 1885, for instance. Other Radical Home Rulers: Samuel Storey, Jacob Bright, Samuel Montagu (Whitechapel), Alderman Scarr (Halifax), Dr. Pankhurst (Rotherhithe), and Miss Helen Taylor (Camberwell).

99. H. A. L. Fisher, *James Bryce (Viscount Bryce of Dechmont, O.M.)*, 2 vols. (London, 1927), I, 200; Bryce to H. Gladstone, November 8, 1885, and December 11, 1885, Viscount Gladstone Papers, 46,019.

100. Eversley, *Gladstone and Ireland*, 280; *The Times*, June 26, 1885.

talk about an Irish tariff, for he recognized that all the colonies with responsible government had such a power. In each of these aspects he was evolving a position diametrically opposed to that of his old friend and ally, Chamberlain.[101]

In connection with Irish issues, the rest of the Radical movement fell into two groups: those who agreed with the spirit, and those who agreed with only the letter, of Chamberlain's attitude. The former, much the smaller of the two groups, equaled Chamberlain in the intensity of their personal hostility to the nationalists. These were men like Trevelyan, whose memories of his treatment by the Irish still rankled; Bright, who as deeply as ever regarded the Parnellites as "rebels"; and Leonard Courtney, who distrusted the Parnellites so much that he convinced himself proportional representation would prove the nationalists did not represent the overwhelming majority of the Irish people.[102] The second group, comprising the bulk of Radicalism, agreed with all the surface level of Chamberlain's policies regarding the Irish, but did not share either his psychological involvement with the national council plan or his increasingly authoritarian spirit. For the most part their attitudes revolved around the problems raised by Parnell's confrontation strategy. They opposed both Home Rule and Parnell's political maneuvering. They were angry with Parnell's cooperation with the Conservative government and with his determination to bring about a political stalemate. Most of them approved of the hard-line tactics in Chamberlain's Warrington speech. As for specific policies, they opposed renewal of coercion and supported the idea of granting Ireland "all the self-rule consistent with the Union," by which they meant elective county and national councils. In each aspect their attitudes appeared to coincide with Chamberlain's, but under the surface there was a difference. They were angry with the Parnellites and afraid of their power, while Chamberlain was coldly

101. Morley to Chamberlain, September 19, 1885, Chamberlain Papers, JC 5/54/627; speeches quoted in *The Times*, September 17, October 16, November 12, 1885.

102. G. P. Gooch, *Life of Lord Courtney* (London, 1920), 231–35; speeches by Trevelyan, quoted in *The Times*, June 4, July 2, 16, 23, October 19, 1885; Bright's speech in *Hansard* 300 (July 28, 1885), 259–66; Bright to Blennerhassett, quoted in *The Times*, November 4, 1885.

vindictive. Their attitude was normal in political struggle; his went beyond that. For this reason they would be better prepared than Chamberlain to respond to new political realities.[103]

Parnell and his colleagues cared less about earning Radical approval than about checkmating the two English parties. In their election manifesto, instructing all Irishmen in Britain to vote Tory, they exempted among the Radicals only Labouchere, Storey, and Cowen. Irishmen even cast their ballots against Morley, Dilke, and Shaw Lefevre. The Irish vote was effective, providing, according to estimates, from twenty-five to forty seats to the Conservatives.[104] As the Irish vote was centered in the large cities, many of these seats were won from Radicals. An examination of the constituencies where Irish voters were numerous and where the margin of loss for the Radical candidates was small indicates that between fifteen and twenty Radicals lost because of the Irish vote.[105]

103. Escott, "Affairs," *F.R.* 277 (December 1885), 879; "Lord Spencer's Irish Administration and the Conservative Government," *British Quarterly Review* 164 (October 1885), 325–38; *Daily News*, September 9, 1885; *The Nonconformist and Independent*, August 27, September 10, 1885; *The Echo*, August 26, September 9, 1885; *The Congregationalist*, August 1885; *Methodist Times*, August 27, September 3, 10, 1885; *The Baptist*, November 27, 1885.

104. Robert Ensor, *England, 1870–1914* (Oxford, 1936), 95. The Irish National League of Great Britain issued a circular listing 117 M.P.'s who had voted frequently against Irish interests; Chamberlain, Dilke, Bright, Courtney, Mundella, Rylands, Bryce, and Illingworth all ranked among the top thirteen Liberals in "opposing Irish interests." *The Times*, weekly edition, December 11, 1885.

105. Radical candidates who probably would have won if the Irish vote had not gone to the Tories:

Candidate	Constituency	Margin of loss
G. Shaw Lefevre	Reading	129
C. H. Hopwood	Stockport	12
Dr. H. Watney	Greenwich	356
Hugh Mason	Ashton-under-Lyne	46
W. E. Briggs	Blackburn	686
Samuel Smith	Liverpool	807
Jacob Bright	Manchester	567
E. L. Stanley	Oldham	145
Arthur Arnold	Salford	176
William Summers	Salford	219
W. S. Caine	Tottenham	735
G. W. E. Russell	Fulham	52
John Holmes	Hackney	193

With or without the Irish vote, the Radicals would have been severely disappointed with the results of the election. They ran well in the counties but not nearly as well as they had hoped in the cities. Even after all the expectations and preparations since 1882, Radical M.P.'s still would not have a majority in the parliamentary Liberal party. During the campaign Chamberlain had written: "The Tories will be smashed & the Whigs will be extinguished."[106] But the defenders of the old order had proved to be remarkably resilient. Furthermore, Radicals had tried to keep the tentacles of the Irish problem away from the great struggle between themselves and the landed classes, but they had failed. They had wanted during the election of 1885 to see the Liberal party win a majority over Tories and Parnellites combined, so that they would be able to deal with Ireland from a position of strength. But Parnell's strategy of confrontation had very nearly paid off, and, as so many times before, it had confounded Radical plans. As a result of the election, the number of Parnellite and Tory M.P.'s equaled the Liberals: 335 Liberals, 249 Conservatives, and 86 Home Rulers. Parnell at last held the balance.

The Radicals' growing expectations of power and their consequent attention to English issues paradoxically had forced them to devise extensive Irish policies. They distinguished themselves from other Liberals from 1883 to 1885 by their hostility to coercion, and by their willingness to support a substantial measure of local self-

---

Candidate	Constituency	Margin of loss
Dr. Pankhurst	Rotherhithe	527
A. Pease	Whitby	340
John Barran	Leeds	314
J. Glover	Scarborough	148

In addition, the following Radicals were defeated in London, but with the complicating factor of a second Liberal candidate who split the Liberal vote:

Candidate	Constituency	Margin of loss	Votes to other Liberal
William Willis	Peckham	433	580
W. Wren	Lambeth	178	692
A. G. Henriques	Walworth	89	246

The Irish National League claimed to have defeated thirty-seven Liberals, of whom more than twenty were Radicals. *The Times*, weekly edition, December 11, 1885.
106. To A. J. Mundella, October 7, 1885, Mundella Papers, Folio II.

rule in Ireland. But several other aspects of Radical behavior toward Ireland in those years are also worth noting. One was the inability of a man like Trevelyan to see the implications of Radicalism for a subject, such as the Irish Question, standing outside the essential, narrowly English, concerns of the movement. Another was the disinclination of Radicals to take up Irish issues, such as land purchase, which required them to risk English treasure and transcend standard Radical principles. Radicals were willing voluntarily to take up Irish causes for the most part only when their own political and financial interests were not endangered. Finally, the parliamentary Radicals, including Chamberlain, turned to a policy of substantial self-rule by the Irish, not out of conviction that the situation in Ireland justified the program of the nationalists or that the principles of Radicalism demanded it, but because it was in the Radical interest to win the support of the Parnellites and get Irish problems out of the British parliament. Their concern for social discipline in Ireland had conflicted with, and had been replaced by, their vital desire for reform in England.

CHAPTER FIVE

Radicals and the Home Rule Parliament
1886

The return of eighty-six Parnellites and the consequent possibility of stalemate in the House of Commons completely altered the context of British politics. The onrush of Radicalism no longer seemed the crucial factor. Even during the electoral campaign moderate Liberals and Radicals had to cooperate in order to save themselves. After the election the struggle between Radicals and Whigs had to take a back seat to Parnell's more immediate—and, in the minds of many, more serious—threat. Ireland would have to be dealt with in one way or another; there could be no more delay. For a great many Englishmen, including all but a few of the Conservatives and most of the Whigs, the way to handle the Irish was clear, though difficult: the English parties must stand together to reject the Parnellite demands, and if necessary put an end to agitation by coercion in Ireland and cloture in the House of Commons. Because the fate of landowners, Protestantism, and law and order were at stake in Ireland, there could be no compromise with Parnell. For those of the Radical persuasion, however, the answer could not be so clear; hence their response is more interesting—and informative. The big question would be how and why they reacted to the most critical challenge in late-Victorian politics. Put another way: what features of Radicalism would stand out under the most severe examination?

I. RADICALS AND RADICALISM, 1886

The first questions to be answered concern the composition of the Radicalism of 1886. How many Radicals were there? Who were they? What were they like? Contemporary observers estimated that between 60 and 150 Radicals won seats during the general election of 1885.[1] The reason for the unusually wide range of the estimates is that the new constitutional arrangements established by the reform acts of 1884 and 1885 produced an abnormally large number of new, relatively obscure M.P.'s. Multiple discriminant analysis of voting during the 1886 parliament sets the number of Radicals as slightly greater even than the higher estimate: it shows that 165 Radicals sat in the House, about 160 at any one time. (Appendix C gives the divisions used for the analysis and lists all of the Radical M.P.'s.) They amounted to a 33 percent increase in the Radical parliamentary faction over 1880–85. Radical M.P.'s now made up about 25 percent of the House and, even more important, about 48 percent of the parliamentary Liberal party. Many Radicals expressed disappointment over their record in the election, for they had expected something like the 50 percent increase in M.P.'s they had won in 1880, and hoped to win an outright majority of the Liberal members. Their disappointment hid from them two significant facts: first, they now represented the largest single faction within the Liberal parliamentary party; and second, if the Whigs were to secede from the party, as most Radicals expected and desired, then Radicals would at least have a clear majority of Liberal M.P.'s. Indeed, the day of victory, so long anticipated, was on the horizon.

The social structure of parliamentary Radicalism remained essentially what it had been in the two previous parliaments. Most of the Radical M.P.'s were either big businessmen or successful lawyers (75 percent; see Appendix C). Only 6 percent had traditionally aristocratic occupations. As before, most of them had already achieved considerable wealth and civic prestige by the time they arrived in parliament. The only important variation from these generalizations was a group of eleven workingmen, who represented almost a 300 percent increase in working-class M.P.'s. If we can assume that Radical M.P.'s in broad social patterns resembled their

1. *The Times*, December 19, 1885, reported that estimates varied from 60 to 150; Randolph Churchill wrote Lord Salisbury: "The party more immediately under the control of Messrs. Chamberlain, Dilke, Morley and Labouchere may be estimated at sixty-five votes." Quoted in Winston Churchill, *Lord Randolph Churchill* (London, 1952), 406. Grosvenor estimated to Gladstone that there would be 232 Liberals and 101 Radicals. December 12, 1885, Gladstone Papers, 44,316.

constituents, then it is clear that Radicalism was still essentially a movement with middle- and working-class wings, with the working-class part becoming rather better organized than before, but still not granted anything approaching an appropriate status in the movement's structure of power.

If anything, the Nonconformist character of Radicalism had become more pronounced. *The Liberator* calculated that 230 men committed to one or another form of disestablishment were returned to parliament; of these, the editors later reckoned that about 170 supported disestablishment of the Church of England itself.[2] Of the Radicals whose religion is known (about 82 percent of them), 76 percent were Nonconformists, and a total of 85 percent stood outside the established Churches. (See Appendix C.) These figures were less than the Dissenters had hoped for, but they were greater than in any earlier parliament.

Despite the passage of the reform acts of 1884 and 1885, the regional pattern of Radicalism had not changed. Radical M.P.'s still tended to represent the Nonconformist areas of Britain. More than three-fourths of them still sat for constituencies north and west of a line from the mouth of the Severn to The Wash. About 75 percent of them, as in the two previous parliaments, represented English constituencies; 10 percent represented Welsh and 15 percent Scottish constituencies. Radicals apparently had continued to make impressive strides in Wales and Scotland: they now represented 50 percent of all Welsh seats, and 33 percent of all Scottish seats.[3] (See Appendix C.)

The Radical prototype from the 1886 parliament would resemble in almost every respect that from either of the two previous parliaments. The main difference was not of social background, but of tone and temper. The Radicals in the 1886 parliament appear to have been more aggressive, more eager than before. For example, they introduced measures to disestablish the Churches in Wales and Scotland for the first time since 1873. They more directly attacked aristocratic privilege by assailing the power and the hereditary

2. January 1, August 2, 1886.
3. There is a massive amount of information on constituencies in Henry Pelling, *Social Geography of British Elections*.

basis of the House of Lords. These were not new directions for Radicalism; rather, they expressed a new confidence among Radical M.P.'s. This fresh confidence in turn was the result of a crystallization of issues that took place in 1885, of the marked increase in the number of Radicals in parliament, and of the appearance of new faces in the Radical rank and file. Not surprisingly, a number of men who had been Radicals before 1885 now found the spirit of Radicalism uncomfortable and dropped out of the movement.[4]

II. From the General Election to the Formation of the Gladstone Government

The growth of Radical power, however, could have little effect until the Home Rule problem was disposed of. Because the victory of eighty-six Parnellites authoritatively represented the opinion of Ireland and gave Parnell the power to make any government impossible, Gladstone believed that the time had come for a final settlement of the Irish Question. He also thought that, as any solution would depend on acceptance by the Irish M.P.'s, Home Rule would be the only one possible. Gladstone considered that both practical and constitutional reasons gave the initiative to the Conservative administration. If they proved unwilling, the Grand Old Man believed it his constitutional duty to try himself. This was a momentous decision, but because he did not wish to appear to bid for Irish support, Gladstone did not consult his fellow party leaders in reaching it. Instead, his approach to Ireland was a night cavalry ride around the flank of his own army; its secrecy would cost him much later.[5]

Meanwhile, many—it is impossible to say precisely how many—Radicals were arriving independently at the same conclusions as Gladstone. There were, for the moment, three interrelated issues to be faced: whether to accept Home Rule or some modification of it, whether to deal with Parnell in arriving at a plan for Ireland, and whether the Conservative government should be left in office

4. W. Agnew, D. Davies, Dr. R. Farquharson, Sir C. Forster, H. H. Fowler, C. H. James, and J. C. Stevenson.

5. Hammond, *Gladstone and the Irish Nation*, 459; Morley, *Gladstone*, III, 256–76.

for the time being. The first problem was the most intensely debated in the movement as a whole. Here the very results of the elections were decisive, for most Radicals, sobered by the Liberal party's inability to get a majority independent of Parnell, quickly admitted that some kind of Home Rule was inevitable. As the *Daily News* put it, the Irish demand for Home Rule had been shown to be a genuinely national demand, and under the circumstances, the only question was what kind of legislature the Irish should have.[6] There was a feeling of resignation rather than eagerness about Home Rule in this attitude of the Radicals, but the force of reality moved them nonetheless quickly. Not only could they as Radicals no longer deny the intent of the Irish voters, but also the parliamentary situation made conciliation of Irish demands necessary. The obstacles that such a large body of nationalist M.P.'s could throw in the path of parliamentary business made it more important than ever to remove the Irish from the House of Commons. A leader in the *Daily News* declared: "Instead of coveting the presence of the Irish members in London, the one thing to be desired is that they should take themselves and their business to Dublin."[7] To reject Home Rule altogether would be to require the House of Commons to pay a huge cost, both in terms of the effort to pass a coercion bill, and in terms of the time lost to reform measures. A great many Englishmen were prepared to pay that cost, but few Radicals were. They had already decided that coercion was politically and ideologically too expensive, and that the existing social and economic order in Ireland was not worth the price of defending it. For them to have decided otherwise would have required that they alter their values so extensively as to set high store by landed society. As Radicals, this they could never do.

Unbending opposition to Home Rule would also have required Radicals to regard the Parnellites as dangerous, if not criminal, men. But most Radicals stood ready to sanction discussions with Parnell about Home Rule. A few even saw him as the genuine leader of the Irish democracy, with whom British Radicals on principle ought to ally. Most would not go that far, but at least their willingness to

6. December 12, 1885.
7. December 14, 1885.

consult Parnell rested on an assumption that he *might* be a reasonable and safe person. The great majority of Radicals would not accept an arrangement that did not keep constitutional supremacy securely in British hands, but the course of events was forcing them to recognize that some forms of Home Rule might be compatible with imperial union, and that Parnell might be willing to accept some such formula. Besides, as many Radicals thought, the natural rivalry of parties in Britain made all other alternative policies impossible—this much the events of 1885 had clearly taught.[8]

On the third issue, whether to leave the Conservative government in office for a time, there was more diversity in Radical opinion. Some, responding quickly to what they regarded as necessity, and no doubt to the lure of office, advocated overturning the Tories as soon as possible. But others, including both pro- and anti-Home Rulers, preferred to leave them in for a while. Some shrank from dealing with such an extraordinarily difficult challenge. Others, like Dilke, who would have supported a Home Rule bill, thought that any Liberal government would be weak, due to its dependence on the Irish M.P.'s, and should not be formed.[9] Those who opposed Home Rule altogether, like Bright and Trevelyan, simply wanted to let the Tories cope with the Irish.[10] Like them, Chamberlain strongly opposed the formation of a Liberal government. He shared all the doubts about the difficulties of the situation and wanted the Tories to teach the Irish a lesson; in addition, he was concerned about the response of the Radicals throughout the country to Home Rule. He wrote Labouchere: "I am convinced, from personal observation, that the workmen will not stand much more in the way of Irish conciliation or concessions to Parnell."[11] But in this view, Chamberlain almost certainly was reading his own attitude into

8. *The Echo*, December 8, 14, 15, 1885; letter to *The Democrat* by J. Morrison Davidson, published December 12, 1885; *The Nonconformist and Independent*, December 17, 1885; *Daily News*, December 18, 1885.

9. Dilke, speech in Chelsea, reported in *The Times*, December 15, 1885; Dilke Memoir, 43,940, ff. 82–83.

10. Bright to Chamberlain, December 15, 1885, Chamberlain Papers, JC 5/7/25; Trevelyan to Chamberlain, December 13, 1885, Chamberlain Papers, JC 5/70/12.

11. December 11, 1885, quoted in Algar Thorold, *Labouchere: The Life of Henry Labouchere* (London, 1913), 250; also Chamberlain to Labouchere, December 4, 1885, Chamberlain Papers, JC 5/50/30a.

those of working-class Radicals. There is no evidence that he was surveying Radical opinion or that anti-Home Rule messages from workers were streaming to him. Working-class Radicals all along had been comparatively willing to accept Home Rule, and there was no sign that they were changing their views. More likely, Chamberlain was assuming that Radical opinion must agree with his own, and was arguing against Home Rule in a narrowly political way, simply because these were the terms that meant most to himself. Chamberlain's self-confidence, ability, and ruthlessness always had the potential of setting him apart from most Radicals, as the events of 1886 would make painfully clear.

Meanwhile, some of Gladstone's immediate circle of advisers concluded that Chamberlain and Dilke were, for reasons of mere personal ambition, trying to keep Gladstone from forming a government. Among these was Gladstone's son Herbert, who decided to circumvent the stalling tactics of the two Radical leaders.[12] The famous "Hawarden Kite" was the result. Herbert told the manager of the National Press Agency on December 16 that his father supported Home Rule. The next day several newspapers carried summaries of Herbert's private opinion as authoritative statements of Gladstone's views. This revelation caused a thrill of fear throughout Britain, for it meant that Parnell now would have no reason to settle for anything less than a Liberal government committed to passing Home Rule. However, in Radical circles, though the Kite was talked about, it did not have decisive influence. It probably convinced some Radicals that Home Rule would inevitably be a question of practical politics, but most of those who said so already had become Home Rulers.[13]

Chamberlain was furious about the Kite. He had no doubt that it accurately represented Gladstone's views. He told Labouchere that it would "ruin the Radicals for years to be allied with such proposals," for the Tories would appeal to the country on the theme of the empire in danger and would "carry everything before

12. Hamilton Diaries, December 15, 1885, 48,642; H. Gladstone to T. W. Reid, December 14, 1885, Viscount Gladstone Papers, 46,041.
13. For example, *The Nonconformist and Independent*, December 24, 1885.

them."[14] But Chamberlain realized that he could not publicly repudiate Gladstone because the Grand Old Man had too much popular support. His position, enunciated in a speech at Birmingham, was that the Irish deserved all the self-government consistent with the empire, but that Parnell must be made to deal first with the Conservatives. When the Irish chief discovered he could get nothing from them, he would approach the Liberals in a more contrite spirit.[15] Privately he confided to Dilke:

> Finally, my view is that Mr. G.'s Irish scheme is death and damnation; that we must try and stop it; that we must not openly commit ourselves against it yet; that we must let the situation shape itself before we finally decide; that the Whigs are our greatest enemies, and that we must not join them if we can help it; that we cannot take office, but must not offer assistance to the Tories publicly; . . . that even if they bring in good measures they will also bring in bad, which we shall be forced to oppose; and that the less we speak in public for the present, the better.[16]

Clearly Chamberlain was feeling the pinch of a new situation—one in which people and events were going beyond the roles assigned to them in his contingency plans. Things were getting out of control.

Most annoying of all to Chamberlain, John Morley was not cooperating; indeed, Morley was rapidly making himself the leading Home Ruler among the Radicals. This was both the cause of the final, most bitter, dispute between the two old friends and a symptom of the division of the Radical leadership. During the campaign of 1885 Morley had argued that Ireland should take precedence over all other political questions, including even the Radical program. By December 1885 he believed that Ireland required immediate attention and that the Tories would not take adequate steps. Consequently, Morley differed from Chamberlain, Dilke, and Trevelyan, his colleagues in the Radical "junta" or "cabal," in wanting to turn out the Tories as soon as possible.[17] Nor did he wish to see Glad-

14. From a conversation reported by Labouchere to H. Gladstone, December 17, 1885, Viscount Gladstone Papers, 46,015.

15. *The Times*, December 18, 1885.

16. December 18, 1885, quoted in Gwynn and Tuckwell, *Dilke*, II, 197.

17. Garvin, *Chamberlain*, II, 131.

stone's Irish intentions thwarted. He wrote Spence Watson, his political agent in Newcastle: "Much dirty intriguing is going on. I won't be party to snubbing the old man."[18] On December 21 at Newcastle Morley delivered a hearty endorsement of Home Rule, arguing that the eighty-six Parnellite M.P.'s must represent to all democrats an irresistible demand for self-rule, and that the failure of government in Ireland and of parliament at Westminster made Home Rule necessary.[19]

Morley's speech elicited a firm reprimand from Chamberlain, who argued that Morley was raising "false hopes by vague generalities." He believed that Morley simply did not understand the inevitable practical consequences of Home Rule: separation of Ireland from England and the destruction of the unity of the empire.[20] To allege that Morley failed to understand practical problems struck at the deepest regions of Morley's psyche. Ever since early adulthood, Morley had been extremely sensitive about being an intellectual. He always had stressed the practical rather than the theoretical side of issues.[21] He responded to Chamberlain with a kind of declaration of independence:

> I submit that you should not be in such a hurry to sever old political connections. As you know, I have no sort of ambition to be an admiral of the fleet. But I'll be hanged if I'll be powder-monkey. I have thought, read, written about Ireland all my life. Here comes a crisis. Am I to be debarred from saying what I think—saying it, mind you, as I did at Newcastle, in particularly careful, sober, well-weighed words? Are the Tories and Whigs to say what they like, and I to stand by in silent acquiescence? Well, I won't. Don't be too exacting. We may part company over Irish affairs before they are done. The journey may be trying. But it's childish for men like you and me to quarrel at the first jolt.[22]

18. Quoted in F. W. Hirst, *Morley*, II, 271–72.

19. *The Times*, December 22, 1885.

20. Chamberlain to Morley, December 24, 1885, partially quoted in Garvin, *Chamberlain*, II, 147–48.

21. See D. A. Hamer, *John Morley: Liberal Intellectual in Politics* (Oxford, 1968), Chs. 1–4.

22. December 28, 1885, quoted in John Morley, *Recollections*, 2 vols. (New York, 1917), I, 206–7.

Despite this closing plea for patience, the two Radicals already had parted company, for they were poles apart on Home Rule as it was coming to be formulated. By the middle of December, Labouchere, who had excellent personal connections with some Home Rulers, and T. M. Healy had brought together the ideas for self-rule most favored in Radical and Parnellite circles.[23] The plan consisted of: 1) an Irish parliament for Irish affairs; 2) reservation of military, foreign, and colonial affairs to the imperial parliament; 3) retention of Irish M.P.'s at Westminster for imperial affairs only; 4) an Irish ministry responsible to the Irish parliament; 5) the power of veto to be exercised by the Viceroy, not by the British parliament; and 6) protection of minorities by explicit guarantees of the sanctity of contracts and of the right of landlords to sell their land to the Irish government. This was a scheme for a full-scale responsible government, and Chamberlain objected to almost every aspect of it. He thought that retention of Irish M.P.'s at Westminster would enable the Irish to continue to overturn governments, even those with majorities on purely English and Scottish issues, and to disrupt the House of Commons.[24] He believed that the Healy-Labouchere formulation, by denying the authority of Westminster over the Dublin parliament, would abolish effective control over Ireland, for the veto by the Viceroy was a "transparent fraud."[25] Moreover, the guarantees of minority rights would be useless, because the Irish parliament would be dominated by Fenians, who intended to make any guarantees "absolutely illusory." To Chamberlain it was perfectly plain that an Irish parliament would agitate for complete separation; that it would establish conscription; and that agitation and conscription would cause war between Britain and Ireland.[26]

In order to expose the weaknesses in Home Rule and to divert public attention from it, Chamberlain suggested a plan of federation

---

23. Thorold, *Labouchere*, 260–62; *The Times*, December 28, 1885; also Labouchere to H. Gladstone, December 19, 1885, Viscount Gladstone Papers, 46,015.

24. Chamberlain to Morley, December 21, 1885, Chamberlain Papers, JC 5/54/668; Chamberlain to Dilke, December 26, 27, 1885, Dilke Papers, 43,887.

25. Chamberlain to Labouchere, December 24, 27, 1885, Chamberlain Papers, JC 5/50/37a, 40a.

26. Chamberlain to Dilke, December 26, 1885, Dilke Papers, 43,887.

modelled after the United States. He would erect legislatures for England, Scotland, Wales, Ulster, and Southern Ireland, all clearly subordinate to an imperial parliament. He contended that, unlike Home Rule, his system would work because the imperial parliament would retain complete supremacy over the provincial assemblies. Yet it is important to note that Chamberlain did not offer his scheme as a genuine alternative to Home Rule. He purposely included in it as many controversial features as he could—for instance, abolition of the British House of Lords, a forecast of the end of the monarchy, and the separate Ulster legislature—in order to support his belief that a workable plan of Irish self-rule necessarily involved revolutionary changes. Rather patronizingly, and hypocritically, he declared that he, as a Radical, did not fear such changes, but that he realized the public was not ready for them.[27]

In stark contrast to Chamberlain, Morley agreed with almost every point of the Labouchere-Healy plan. The one aspect on which he sympathized with Chamberlain (ironically enough!) pertained to retention of the Irish M.P.'s at Westminster. Like the majority of Radicals, Morley wanted to remove the Irish from parliament once and for all. To placate this attitude among Radicals, and particularly Chamberlain's criticisms, Labouchere publicly acceded to complete exclusion of the Irish from Westminster.[28] Morley wrote Chamberlain in the same vein: "I am for no plan of Thorough, unless it involves the disappearance of the Irish members from our House. If that be not possible, I would almost try to muddle and potter on."[29] On January 7, 1886, Morley "shot his bolt for exclusion" in an important speech at Chelmsford. The more we consider Home Rule, he stated, "the more we shall feel the cardinal point on which all hangs is the restitution to the House of Commons of the power of being able to carry out the will and wishes of those who elect its members."[30] But agreement on this point could not hide the grave

27. Chamberlain to Labouchere, December 26, 1885, quoted in Thorold, *Labouchere*, 272; Chamberlain to Labouchere, December 27, 1885, Chamberlain Papers, JC 5/50/40a; Chamberlain to Dilke, December 26, 1885, Dilke Papers, 43,887.
28. Labouchere to *The Times*, December 30, 1885.
29. January 1, 1886, quoted in Hirst, *Morley*, II, 276.
30. Quoted in *The Times*, January 8, 1886.

differences between Chamberlain and Morley: to Morley, exclusion was one of many advantages offered by Home Rule; to Chamberlain, it was the only redeeming feature. Chamberlain wrote to Labouchere: "I believe the anti-Irish feeling is very strong with our best friends—the respectable artisans & the non-Conformists. One thing I am clear about. If we are to give way it must be by getting rid of Ireland altogether. . . . The difficulties of any plan are almost insurmountable, but the worst of all plans would be one which kept the Irishmen at Westminster while they had their own Parliament in Dublin."[31]

Chamberlain's immediate concern was to prevent Gladstone from pursuing what he was sure would be a disastrous policy for the Liberal party. Late in December he suggested to Harcourt that they meet with Hartington and Dilke in a combined operation to stop Gladstone. Although the four complained bitterly to each other about Gladstone's advance toward Home Rule, and especially about the Hawarden Kite, they could not find an effective mode of opposition, for they dared not oppose the Grand Old Man, and all but Hartington reluctantly conceded that some form of Home Rule policy was inevitable.[32] Although Chamberlain still lamented Morley's "literary nonsense" in connection with Home Rule, he grudgingly realized that the Liberal M.P.'s would not support a Tory government.[33] He concluded that a non-Irish issue must provide the occasion of turning the Tories out, for it would not commit the Liberals to a specific Irish policy. Consequently, he and Dilke drew up an amendment to the Address calling for enactment of the Radical scheme of rural allotments—the "three acres and a cow" amendment presented in the House by Jesse Collings.[34]

Chamberlain, however, had not yet abandoned all hope of short-

31. January 3, 1886, Chamberlain Papers, JC 5/50/43a.

32. A. G. Gardiner, *The Life of Sir William Harcourt*, 2 vols. (London, 1923), I, 556–57; Dilke Diary, January 1, 1886, 43,927.

33. Chamberlain to Dilke, January 8, 1886, Dilke Papers, 49,610; Gardiner, *Harcourt*, I, 557; Holland, *Life of Devonshire*, II, 110; Chamberlain to Labouchere, January 3, 1886, Chamberlain Papers, JC 5/50/43a; Chamberlain to Bunce, January 12, 1886, Chamberlain Papers, JC 5/8/81.

34. Chamberlain, *Political Memoir*, 177.

circuiting Gladstone. About January 10 he took interest in a scheme of land purchase recently described in *The Times*.[35] It occurred to him, as in 1879, that he might distract attention from Home Rule by offering a plan for massive land purchase designed to establish a peasant proprietary in Ireland. In mid-January he wrote an article for the February *Fortnightly Review* setting out his argument. Contending that the land problem lay at the root of Irish disaffection, Chamberlain urged the English and Irish democracies, while putting aside the demand for separation, to join in settling Ireland's legitimate grievances—the distribution of land. He explicitly called on Parnell to take up this challenge.[36] On January 22 he followed up his article with a memorandum for Parnell. Arguing that Gladstone could neither pledge himself to nor carry into legislation a Home Rule bill, he offered the land question as the only opportunity for agreement: "The question is, would Mr Parnell co-operate with a Radical or Liberal Government in the endeavour to make a final arrangement by means of some large operation of land purchase, without pressing for an immediate consideration of Home Rule proposals?"[37]

This last-minute effort by Chamberlain was bound to fail. It was a solution of the Irish Question that most Radicals at one time would have welcomed but by 1886 had left behind. Furthermore, Parnell would have none of it, for he now firmly believed that Gladstone would do more for Home Rule than any other Englishman, and he rightly interpreted Chamberlain's offer as an obvious attempt to supplant Gladstone. On January 23 Parnell let Gladstone know that the Irish M.P.'s would help defeat the Tories on Collings's amendment if Gladstone, rather than Hartington or Chamberlain, would form the new government. On January 26 the Conservatives, having rejected all notions of conciliating the Irish demand for self-rule, announced their intent to introduce a coercion measure. Most Liberal leaders and nearly all the Radicals inside the House and out agreed that under no circumstances could they support coercion. Consequently Parnellites and Liberals, including most Radical M.P.'s, combined later the same day to defeat the Tories on Collings's

---

35. Chamberlain to Dilke, January 10, 1886, Dilke Papers, 43,888.
36. "A Radical View of the Irish Crisis," *F.R.* 230 (February 1886), 282–84.
37. Quoted in Chamberlain, *Political Memoir*, 177–78.

amendment. Everyone recognized the vote to be a protest to co-ercion. Eighteen Liberals, primarily Whigs, voted with the Con-servatives, and seventy-six abstained. Whig participation in the Liberal party had ended; the Radicals had reached their goal of many years, and it was Ireland that provided the occasion.[38]

III. THE IRISH BILLS, 1886

Gladstone formed his government with the intent of framing a Home Rule bill satisfactory to both his cabinet and the Parnellites. His selection of John Morley as Chief Secretary revealed his purpose. Morley already was known as one of the most ardent Home Rulers in England; indeed, in his Chelmsford speech, in which he called for exclusion of the Irish M.P.'s, Morley had gone further than Glad-stone himself, who leaned toward retention.[39] This fact made it dif-ficult for Chamberlain and Trevelyan to join the government, and Gladstone made matters worse by slighting Chamberlain somewhat in several ministerial arrangements. But these slights, however an-noying, did not contribute to Chamberlain's attitudes on the Irish Question, despite historical interpretations to the contrary.[40] The Radical leader already had formed his hostility to Irish nationalism and had committed himself very strongly against Home Rule. Be-sides, the issues at stake in the Home Rule crisis were so great that it is extremely unlikely he would have let these minor personal ir-ritations determine his course. With the Whigs gone, Chamberlain stood to win or lose for himself and for Radicalism the leadership of the Liberal party. He was far too intelligent and calculating to let any but the gravest issues stand in his path.

Meanwhile, the decision of the Conservatives to seek coercive power and the successful effort by Gladstone to form a government confirmed and crystallized in the minds of most Radicals the urgent need for Home Rule. Even a number of waverers began to come

38. *Hansard* 302 (January 26, 1886), 525–29. Three Radicals opposed Collings's motion: Courtney, Dixon, and Westlake.

39. Morley, *Recollections*, I, 213–15.

40. In his *Political Memoir*, 188, Chamberlain declares that personal irritation with Gladstone had nothing to do with his opinion regarding Ireland. For a dif-ferent view, see Magnus, *Gladstone*, 347.

over, for, as the days passed and the novelty of the idea of Irish autonomy wore off, it appeared increasingly clear that the only alternative to Home Rule was coercion—a course that was unacceptable. Moreover, the solidification of orthodox opinion against Home Rule had the reverse effect of persuading some Radicals that Home Rule must be a good thing. The evolution of the opinion of the editor of *The Congregationalist* is illustrative. The paper had vigorously appealed for a majority independent of the Parnellites during the general election of 1885, and it had been very slow to adjust to the defeat of this desire. But by February 1886 *The Congregationalist* admitted that Britain must face the problem of eighty-six Parnellites in the House and that Parnell must be reckoned with. By April the paper had gone over fully to Gladstone, for the editor now saw the Irish controversy as "but one of the many phases of the conflict between privileged classes and the people." By dickering with the Irish, the Tories had made coercion impossible and Home Rule inevitable. Though he reserved judgment on the details of Home Rule, the editor was now confident that Gladstone would present reasonable proposals.[41]

Of course there remained a substantial opposition to Home Rule among Radicals, especially among those who believed that the Irish Catholics would persecute or destroy the Protestant minority.[42] But with the bulk of Radicalism moving toward Home Rule, several influential Radicals tried to persuade Chamberlain to abandon or modify his opposition. Dilke, for instance, argued to Chamberlain

41. *The Congregationalist*, January, February, April 1886. For other interesting statements of support for Home Rule, see *The Inquirer*, February 20, 1886; Mundella to Leader, March 14, 1886, Mundella-Leader Letters; and H. J. Wilson to his family, February 12, 1886, Wilson Papers, MD 2564-1. This Wilson correspondence shows a remarkable enthusiasm for Home Rule among some of the leading Puritans in the House: Wilson, J. E. Ellis, Illingworth, Brunner, and Rowntree. See also: James Bryce, "Alternative Policies in Ireland," *Nineteenth Century* 108 (February 1886), 312–28; E. A. Freeman, "Some Aspects of Home Rule," *Contemporary Review* 49 (February 1886), 153–86; Frederic Harrison, "The Radical Program," *Contemporary Review* 49 (February 1886), 278–79; and Shaw Lefevre, "The Two Unions," *Contemporary Review* 49 (April 1886), 560–78.

42. For example, W. S. Caine, a leading temperance advocate, won a by-election in Barrow on the prediction that Home Rule would destroy the Protestant and landlord minorities. John Newton, *W. S. Caine, M.P.: A Biography* (London, 1907), 140–46; *The Times*, March 30, April 5, 7, 1886.

that by opposing Home Rule he would isolate himself from "the great mass" of the Liberal party, who would support Gladstone.[43] Schnadhorst, who kept close contact with Radical organizations, warned Chamberlain that most Liberals and Radicals would favor Home Rule because they had "an eager desire if possible to get Ireland out of the way so that the rest of the Kingdom may secure some attention for its pressing needs."[44] Labouchere begged Chamberlain to seize the opportunity presented by Home Rule to forge a Radical party against "tories, Whigs, & Lords."[45]

Yet Chamberlain remained adamant against Home Rule. He could not see that either principles or expediency made support for Home Rule necessary. He had never opposed the principle of coercion, only its tactical advisability. Now, in 1886, he was convinced that the voters of Britain would support coercion if that was the only alternative to Home Rule.[46] As to the danger of becoming isolated and missing the chance to succeed Gladstone, Chamberlain as yet had little worry. In fact, he believed that firm opposition to Home Rule would bring him ultimate political triumph. He wrote his brother Arthur:

> As regards Ireland I have quite made up my mind—indeed I have never felt the slightest hesitation. If M^r G's scheme goes too far, as I expect it will, I shall leave him.
>
> The immediate result will be considerable unpopularity & temporary estrangement from the Radical party.... I shall be left almost alone for a time. I cannot of course work with the Tories & Hartington is quite as much hostile to my radical views as to M^r G's Irish plans.
>
> But in time the situation will clear. Either Mr G will succeed and get the Irish question out of the way or he will fail.
>
> In either case he will retire from politics and I do not suppose the Liberal Party will accept Childers or even John Morley as its permanent leader.[47]

43. April 7, 1886, Chamberlain Papers, JC 5/24/166.
44. February 13, 1886, Chamberlain Papers, JC 5/63/9.
45. March 31, 1886, Chamberlain Papers, JC 5/50/50.
46. Chamberlain to Labouchere, February 15, 1886, Chamberlain Papers, JC 5/50/49a.
47. March 8, 1886, Chamberlain Papers, JC 5/11/5.

His predictions as to the nature of the government's Irish policy turned out to be accurate. Under pressure from a few colleagues, mainly from Morley and Spencer, Gladstone agreed that Home Rule would have to be accompanied by land purchase, likely to be unpopular with Radicals, to protect Irish landlords; and he accepted the idea of excluding Irishmen from parliament.[48] The prime minister presented the first part of his policy, land purchase, to the cabinet on March 13, 1886. His scheme provided for purchase of land from the landlords by an Irish authority—to be described in another bill—and, after amendment, for resale of the land to the tenantry.[49] Chamberlain, who had recently suggested land purchase himself, and Trevelyan, who had long opposed purchase proposals, both objected to Gladstone's measure for reasons largely extraneous to purchase *per se*. Chamberlain wanted to know whether the Irish authority referred to would be under the control of parliament in London; thus he forced Gladstone to sketch out the general lines of his Home Rule proposal even though the bill was not yet complete. He and Trevelyan found the powers of the proposed Irish parliament too extensive and on March 15 sent letters of resignation to Gladstone. Trevelyan stated simply that Gladstone's plans would "lead the deliberations of the Cabinet in a direction quite opposite to that which I can follow."[50] Chamberlain contended that the land purchase bill would add a huge burden to the national debt only in order to "purchase the repeal of the Union and practical separation of Ireland from England and Scotland."[51]

Gladstone rightly appealed to both Radicals to postpone their resignations at least until the Home Rule measure was formally submitted to the cabinet, and they agreed. On March 26, Gladstone brought Home Rule before his colleagues. He cagily attempted first to obtain their commitment to a general resolution approving the

48. Morley, *Recollections*, I, 221; speech at Newcastle, quoted in *The Times*, February 12, 1886; Hamilton Diaries, February 24, 1886, 48,643; Harcourt to Gladstone, March 7, 1886, Gladstone Papers, 44,200; Morley to Gladstone, April 13, 1886, Gladstone Papers, 44,255.

49. Gladstone, Memorandum on Irish Land, copy in Chamberlain Papers, JC 8/4/3/16.

50. March 15, 1886, Gladstone Papers, 44,335.

51. March 15, 1886, quoted in Chamberlain, *Political Memoir*, 194–96.

establishment of an Irish legislative body for Irish affairs, but Chamberlain immediately protested that the resolution was too vague. He demanded that Gladstone answer four test questions concerning the degree of independence for the Irish legislature: 1) would Irish M.P.'s be excluded from Westminster; 2) would the Irish parliament have the power of taxation, including customs and excises; 3) would the Irish parliament have the power to appoint judges and magistrates; and 4) would the Irish parliament have control over every matter not specifically enumerated by the act. Gladstone in effect answered yes to each question. Chamberlain and Trevelyan immediately resigned.[52]

Why did the two Radicals leave the cabinet? Could adjustments in the bill have been made to keep them in the government? For Trevelyan the issue ultimately was one of law and order. Deeply affected by his experience as Chief Secretary, he doubted that the Irish tenantry would pay annuities to the state as required by the land purchase plan. To insure that collections were made, and that the laws were enforced, the Irish executive, particularly the police, would have to remain in British hands. He would accept local elective boards in Ireland, but he believed that the Irish central government had to be responsible to a British, not Irish, parliament. It is difficult to see how the cabinet could have met his objections without abandoning the principle of responsible government.[53]

Chamberlain's case was more subtle. By the very questions he put to Gladstone he seemed to imply that with certain restrictions he would accept an Irish parliament. However, his evident haste to resign and his private correspondence at the time of resignation reveal that he would not have accepted an Irish parliament in the full sense of the term—a representative assembly with responsible government. On March 17 he had his secretary send a memorandum to Bunce that shows he objected to essentials and not details of Home Rule. He argued that there were only two ways of enacting Home Rule: by exclusion or by retention of the Irish members. He objected to both methods. If Irishmen were excluded, the Dublin parliament would be outside the control of Westminster, and separation

52. *Ibid.*, 198–99.
53. Hamilton Diaries, March 20, 1886, 48,643.

would follow. If the Irish were retained, they would devote all their powers of "obstruction and opposition" toward throwing off English control; again, separation would follow. The memorandum concluded that any scheme "of the kind attributed to Mr. Gladstone will lead in the long run to the absolute national independence of Ireland, and that this cannot be conceded without serious danger and the heaviest sacrifices on the part of Great Britain."[54]

Similarly, Chamberlain outlined for Hartington a plan of local government for Ireland that shows he could not have, at the time of resignation, accepted an Irish parliament. In it he proposed the establishment of two "Provincial Assemblies"—one for Ulster and the other for the rest of Ireland. These assemblies would have been larger than national councils, but almost the same in function. They would control a specifically enumerated list of topics, including public works, education, and (apparently) land purchase. The executive government of Ireland would be represented in the British cabinet by a secretary of state, and in the House of Commons by M.P.'s.[55] Now this plan would have made a significant change in Irish local government, but it would not have established an Irish national legislature or even less a responsible government. Chamberlain could not have been kept in the cabinet except by abandonment of Home Rule. To him, unity of the United Kingdom was right by reason of both principle and expediency. The determination of the Irish nationalists to extract concessions from England by confrontation politics had convinced him that they could not be trusted with a parliament. Nothing would ever alter his attitude toward Irishmen, and only a change in his perception of his political need would alter the policy he derived from it.

IV. RADICALS AND THE IRISH BILLS, 1886

Gladstone introduced the Home Rule bill to a crowded and tense House of Commons on April 8, and the land purchase bill on April 16. The Home Rule bill would create an Irish parliament consisting

54. Copy in the Chamberlain Papers, JC 5/8/83.
55. Memorandum for Hartington, n.d. (probably March 27, 1886), Chamberlain Papers, JC 5/22/110.

of two orders, which would control all Irish affairs not specifically denied them. The Irish executive would be responsible to the Irish parliament. The Irish would collect their own taxes and contribute a fixed annual sum to the imperial treasury. Irish representatives would return to Westminster only when the fixed sum or any part of the Home Rule act itself was to be altered; otherwise, they would be excluded from the British parliament. The British parliament would retain control over Irish customs and excises. The land purchase bill provided that all landowners with lands in tenancy could sell to the government if they chose. Tenants could purchase their holdings by 100 percent loans from the government, repayable at low interest over forty-nine years.

Everyone agreed that Gladstone's speech introducing the Home Rule bill was a magnificent performance, but of course that admission did not diminish the opposition of the Conservative party or most of the Whigs. They felt certain that Home Rule would be disastrous to both Ireland and England; that the Parnellites, who were not much better than criminals, would dominate the Irish parliament; and that neither property nor Protestantism could long survive the establishment of an Irish legislature. All safeguards would be useless. Civil war in Ireland and conflict between England and Ireland would result. In sum, the Irish were not fit to rule themselves, and it would be a tragic denial by Englishmen of their responsibilities to let the empire be so severely damaged at its very base.[56]

It was immediately clear that Conservative, Whig, and Ulster Protestant opposition would come very close to defeating both bills. The decisive factor would be the opinion of moderate Liberals and Radicals, and as Joseph Chamberlain already had made himself one of the most vigorous opponents of Home Rule, attention in the country naturally became fixed on the Radical wing of the party: would the Radicals go with Chamberlain or remain loyal to Gladstone? The reception given by Radicals to the Home Rule bill showed that most of them in the House and in the country alike approved at least of the principle of Home Rule. Their arguments were essentially pragmatic, not doctrinaire. As John Morley put it, the

56. There is a brief discussion of the anti–Home Rule argument in Curtis, *Anglo-Saxons and Celts*, Ch. 8.

crucial issue was how to govern Ireland; coercion had failed and English policy had vacillated to the extreme; therefore, Home Rule was the only solution. Furthermore, Home Rule would free parliament from the Irish entanglement that had choked and hobbled it for years. As to the character of the Irish people, many Radicals recognized a risk in putting Protestants at the mercy of Catholics, but they also contended that Irish nationalists were not criminals and were not likely to persecute their Protestant compatriots. Here the intensely moralistic orientation of the Radicals emerged. The *Methodist Times* called Home Rule the "Christian" policy for Ireland, for it was what Jesus would have done in the circumstances. According to *The Congregationalist*, one thing was clear: no country holding such derogatory views of a subject people as expressed by the anti-Home Rulers was capable of governing them. As to imperial unity, Radical Home Rulers continued to be concerned about the empire, but they agreed that the empire already was becoming disunited; Home Rule might tend to reunify it.[57]

There was nothing peculiarly "Radical" in the reasoning of pro-Home Rule Radicals. Their arguments did not significantly differ from those of more moderate Liberals. Only their recognition that the massive electoral victory of the Parnellites was an imperative to men of democratic views can be regarded as an essentially Radical point—and even this argument every Liberal Home Ruler employed. Indeed, what is striking about the thinking of Home Rule Radicals is its pragmatic content; very little of it derives from Radical principles. This fact suggests that these Radicals had arrived at Home Rule, not through rational application of Radical beliefs, but through adjustments to the immediate political situation. Although they naturally would not admit it, Parnell's confrontation strategy had made Home Rule expedient for them. Once having found it

57. *Methodist Times*, April 15, 1886; *Congregationalist*, May 1886; *Reynolds's Newspaper*, April 11, 1886; *Inquirer*, May 1, 1886; *Daily News*, April 9, 10, 1886; *The Nonconformist and Independent*, April 15, 1886; Arthur Arnold, "The Irish Crisis. I.—Mr. Gladstone's Policy," *F.R.* 233 (May 1886), 697–706. Speeches in the House by Radicals, for Home Rule (all references to *Hansard* 304): W. S. Shirley (April 8, 1886), 1100–1101; John Morley (April 9, 1886), 1263–78; Joseph Arch (April 13, 1886), 1482–83; and Alfred Illingworth (April 16, 1886), 1840–43.

expedient, they characteristically adopted a moralistic tone in their rhetoric.

But why did they find adoption of the Parnellite policy expedient, when Britain's traditional rulers did not? The answer lies in what kind of men the Radicals were. Whereas Conservatives and Whigs (not to mention a great many moderate Liberals) identified with the existing order of society, Radicals, at least in some important ways, did not. To the traditional rulers, it was clear that Parnell and his gang of Catholic agrarian reformers threatened a part of their social order. Many of them either owned land in Ireland or had friends who did; thus their sense of the threat posed by the Irish nationalists was urgent. Under certain circumstances, the Radicals would have sympathized with the view that public order in Ireland was an extension of public order in England, the circumstances consisting of an easily ignored request by respectable and patient Irish M.P.'s for self-government, and of some alternative other than coercion to Home Rule. But Parnell had made it his business to destroy exactly those circumstances. He had forced Englishmen to pay attention to Ireland, to develop an analysis of the Irish problem, and to decide only between coercion and Home Rule. While orthodox English politicians had rapidly arrived at an analysis emphasizing the depravity of the nationalist leaders, Radicals, who could not by their very nature credit the traditional rulers of Irish society with wisdom and righteousness, had since the 1870's gradually evolved an analysis stressing the illegitimacy of the Irish social and economic structure. Coercion, which they thought was the only alternative to Home Rule, demanded great sacrifices to uphold that illegitimate structure. Moreover, they had come to see Parnell less as a criminal or unprincipled demagogue than as the natural result of the Irish environment. A just political arrangement would teach him to be a reasonable man. Thus to the majority of Radicals both inside the House and out, Home Rule was the only possible solution to the Irish Question.[58]

Even among the Radicals generally favorable to Home Rule, how-

58. Curtis emphasizes the "environmentalist" aspect of pro-Home Rule arguments in *Anglo-Saxons and Celts*, Ch. 8.

ever, there were important reservations about Gladstone's specific policy. Very few Radicals liked the land purchase bill. While it is true that some, including the editors of the *Daily News*, agreed with Gladstone and Morley that the landlords would need protection from the Irish nationalists, most believed that the price required from the British taxpayers was too high. Opposition to purchase in working-class Radical circles was downright vicious: *Reynolds's Newspaper* predicted that no Radical would ever "so provide for the handful of miscreants who have ruined Ireland and brought indelible disgrace to the English name."[59] In view of such ardent opposition, the cabinet made no attempt to proceed with the land purchase bill. They faced a stickier problem with the reservations concerning Home Rule. A good many of the Radical friends of Irish self-rule, perhaps as many as one-third, believed that exclusion of the Irish from Westminster would tend toward separation. As long as Irishmen were represented in the House of Commons, then Ireland would be bound by the decisions of parliament. If, however, the Irish were excluded, then they would feel no responsibility for parliamentary actions, and the tie with England would depend on the continued good will of Irishmen and the tenuous power of the Irish Viceroy.[60]

This reservation about the formulation of the Home Rule bill was serious, for it threatened to divide the Radicals who were concerned about imperial unity from those who wanted most of all to get the Irish out of the House of Commons. And it was upon this issue that the diehard Radical opponents of Home Rule focused. Some Radicals—no one knew how many, and estimates ranged from a handful to as much as a third or more—from the beginning of the crisis had

59. *Reynolds's Newspaper*, April 4, 1886. Also: *Daily News*, April 17, 1886 (favorable to land purchase); *Inquirer*, April 24, 1886 (opposed to the land purchase bill). Radical speeches against land purchase: by Dilke, *The Times*, March 27, April 6, 1886; by H. P. Cobb and A. Williams, *The Times*, April 29, 1886.

60. Radical expressions of reservations about exclusion: *Inquirer*, April 17, 1886; *Congregationalist*, May 1886; speeches by Bradlaugh and Burt, *Hansard* 304 (April 12, 1886), 1376–81, 1368–73; a speech by A. Thomas and a letter by W. Summers, reported in *The Times*, April 29, 1886; and reports of a conference of workingmen from labor and Radical societies held at the Walworth Radical Club, and of the St. James Hall Radical meeting, in *The Times*, April 12, 23, 1886.

opposed Home Rule. Angry because Gladstone had failed to consult Liberal or Radical opinion, these men felt that Home Rule had been inadequately considered, and that Gladstone in old age was becoming tyrannical. They had not been able to adjust to the idea of dealing with Parnell, for they believed that the Parnellites were criminals and traitors, that Catholics would seek revenge on loyal Protestants for centuries of mistreatment, and that law and order—cherished by all Englishmen regardless of political party—would be swept away in Ireland as soon as the Irish obtained self-rule. To these Radicals, exclusion compounded the sins of Home Rule. As democrats they had long contended that the only legitimate authority in the constitution derived from the House of Commons; hence they believed that the surest way to separation of Ireland from England, and to all the consequent terrors they foresaw, was to exclude Irish representatives from parliament. The exclusion issue, therefore, was for Radical opponents of Home Rule no minor detail. They might tolerate limited Irish self-government within a tight federal system, but only if the Irish legislature was directly subordinate to the British parliament. Such a plan, they thought, was possible only if the Irish retained representatives at Westminster.[61]

Chamberlain, from the first speech he gave in the House against Home Rule, made the exclusion clause his main target. This may seem surprising in view of the fact that as late as December 1885 he had regarded exclusion as the sole redeeming grace of Home Rule. But as we have seen, by the time of his resignation, Chamberlain had decided that neither exclusion nor retention would satisfy him. The important question is not why Chamberlain opposed exclusion, but why he made it the crucial issue. For him to do so required a redirection of his tactics. When he resigned from the cabinet, he wanted to defeat the bill outright; but in his speeches after the measure was introduced, he accepted its principle—establishment of an Irish parliament—and concentrated on its details. Arguing that exclusion made the Irish parliament of "equal authority" to West-

---

61. *The Democrat*, April 17, 1886; *The Baptist*, February 26, 1886; *The Echo*, April 9, 1886; *Birmingham Daily Post*, April 9, 1886; T. H. S. Escott, "Affairs," *F.R.* 233 (May 1886), 728–30; and a speech by W. S. Allen, *Hansard* 304 (April 9, 1886), 1222–26.

minster, he contended that Gladstone's bill was a plan for separation. If the Irish were retained in parliament, and if Ulster as well as Southern Ireland got a legislature, then a true federation would exist. In fact, he said, there would be little difference between such an arrangement and his own national councils scheme. Moreover, other changes in the Home Rule bill would naturally follow retention of Irish representatives and provision of an Ulster assembly, so that his and Gladstone's ideas would closely resemble each other.[62] These arguments indicate that Chamberlain had not changed his attitude toward an Irish parliament, but that he found it expedient to attack the Home Rule bill indirectly; the problem is to understand why.

The answer lies in the fact that late in March 1886 Chamberlain began to lose the confidence he had felt about his own situation. The drift of Radical opinion was becoming clear, and he began to doubt that he could defeat Home Rule. This anxiety seemed for the first time, in connection with Home Rule, to raise a conflict between his principles and his self-interest. He told Mrs. Leonard Courtney in mid-March that for once he did not know what public opinion would do.[63] If he managed to defeat the Home Rule bill outright, the Liberal party, including many of his Radical colleagues, would never forgive him. If he opposed it directly and lost, then he would be cast off as a contemptible traitor. His solution was to appear to accept the principle of Home Rule while demanding a change in a major part of the bill. If the government accepted, then he would demand further significant concessions so that enthusiastic advocates of Home Rule, like Morley and Parnell, might have to repudiate the bill themselves. If they swallowed all the concessions and the bill were enacted, then Chamberlain could claim to have saved the union by his amendments. Thus he seized upon the exclusion/retention issue. Retention was an ideal ploy: it was clear, it could be painted as leading away from separation, and it tended to divide the advocates of Home Rule. Chamberlain saw that exclusion was the weak plate in the armor of Home Rule; if he attacked it firmly, he could not lose.

62. *Hansard* 304 (April 9, 1886), 1181–1207; April 16, 1886, 1811–24.
63. Gooch, *Courtney*, 254.

Chamberlain had good reason to be concerned about his ability to defeat the Home Rule bill. During April and early May his closest Radical advisors—Schnadhorst, Labouchere, and Dilke—urged him not to hold aloof from compromise with Gladstone and especially not to make exclusion, the only feature of Home Rule many Liberals liked, his cardinal criticism. Schnadhorst even advised Chamberlain that a majority of Birmingham Liberals, Chamberlain's personal constituency, wanted the bill to succeed.[64] Their warnings were accurate. Chamberlain managed to keep the loyalty of the Birmingham Liberal Association, but not without considerable worry, effort, and a powerful speech.[65] The National Reform Union, an old Radical organization once influential in franchise struggles, adopted a resolution supporting both Irish bills.[66] Most ominously, the National Liberal Federation, largely Chamberlain's creation, revolted against him early in May. This was an astonishing development. The General Committee of the Federation met in London on May 5 and 6. The officers, mostly Chamberlainites, had prepared a resolution advocating retention of the Irish at Westminster. But a number of Radicals prominent in provincial cities other than Birmingham, including James Kitson, president of the Federation, refused to accept any resolution implying opposition to the government. They staged a palace revolt by presenting and carrying resolutions supporting the Home Rule bill as it stood. Chamberlain and six officers of the Federation resigned; all were from Birmingham.[67]

Yet a number of Radicals could not be pleased with Chamberlain's embarrassment, though they might be Home Rulers themselves, for

64. April 15, 21, 1886, Chamberlain Papers, JC 5/63/15, 16; also: Dilke to Chamberlain, May 1, 1886, Chamberlain Papers, JC 5/24/167; and Labouchere to Chamberlain, April 7, 1886, Chamberlain Papers, JC 5/50/51.

65. A. W. W. Dale, *The Life of R. W. Dale* (London, 1898), 455; Garvin, *Chamberlain*, II, 213-14; *Birmingham Daily Post*, April 22, 1886; Chamberlain to Bunce, April 11, 13, 1886, Chamberlain Papers, JC 5/8/84b, 85; Chamberlain to Dilke, April 22, 1886, Dilke Papers, 49,610.

66. *The Times*, April 30, 1884.

67. McGill, "Schnadhorst," 27; Robert Spence Watson, *The National Liberal Federation: From Its Commencement to the General Election of 1906* (London, 1907), 55-57; National Liberal Federation, *Annual Report of the National Liberal Federation, 1886*, 15-16; Arthur Tilney Bassett, *The Life of the Rt. Hon. John Edward Ellis* (London, 1914), 74-77.

they did not wish to see Radicalism divided. Thus among a few top leaders of Radicalism who stood outside the government a desire for unity of the movement led to two major attempts at arranging a compromise between Chamberlain and the Liberal government. The first came before the debate on the second reading of the bill. Since Chamberlain throughout these negotiations refused to give up complete retention of the Irish M.P.'s, the matter came down to whether the government would give in to him.[68] There was considerable resistance both inside and outside the cabinet to full concession to Chamberlain: from John Morley, who thought that Chamberlain wanted the cabinet to "go down on our knees"; and from militant Parnellites, who recognized that Chamberlain under no circumstances could be their friend.[69] Indeed, Chamberlain preferred, as he wrote Hartington, "to fight the matter to the end and abide the result."[70] He informed Hartington further that if the government gave in he would demand other important changes: "It is probable that if Bill gets into Committee it will go to pieces on one of these rocks. If I have to vote for 2nd. Reading I shall make it clear that the concession does not satisfy me except as a step towards the complete recast of the Bill."[71]

To his relief, when Gladstone announced on May 10 the extent of the cabinet's concessions—retention of the Irish on matters of imperial taxation, plus a friendly reception to plans for retention on other imperial affairs—Chamberlain could without embarrassment break off negotiations.[72]

Very quickly thereafter Chamberlain began to strengthen his position by organizing the Radical and moderate Liberal opponents to Home Rule. On May 12 about fifty M.P.'s gathered at his home

68. May 2, 1886, quoted in Hammond, *Gladstone and the Irish Nation*, 491.

69. Morley, quoted in Thorold, *Labouchere*, 300. Also: Morley to Gladstone, April 19, 25, 1886, Gladstone Papers, 44,255; *United Ireland*, April 24, 1886.

70. May 5, 1886, Chamberlain Papers, JC 5/22/116.

71. May 4, 1886, quoted in Garvin, *Chamberlain*, II, 222. See also Chamberlain to Dilke, May 6, 1886, quoted in Gwynn and Tuckwell, *Dilke*, II, 221–22; and his nasty public letter to the Radical M.P., T. H. Bolton, published in *The Times*, May 8, 1886. For Chamberlain's comment on the letter: Chamberlain to Arthur Chamberlain, May 7, 1886, Chamberlain Papers, JC 5/11/6.

72. Chamberlain to Labouchere, May 11, 1886, quoted in Chamberlain, *Political Memoir*, 217.

in South Kensington. These men made up the hard core of his renewed resistance to passage of the second reading. Yet they were
by no means an exclusively Radical group: in fact, of the forty-four
M.P.'s known to have attended the meeting, only twenty-six were
Radicals. The rest were moderate Liberals and even Whigs.[73] They
were supported outside the House by substantial minorities (perhaps in a one-to-two ratio) in both the local Liberal associations and
the local and regional organizations of the Nonconformist denominations, and by a heavy majority of Ulster Protestants.[74] Chamberlain at the outset made retention the key issue. He told the meeting
at his home that complete retention constituted "the symbol and the
flag of the controversy, which was directed to maintaining the supremacy of the Imperial Parliament. . . ."[75] They agreed with him.
Two days later Chamberlain and some of his faction attended an
anti-Home Rule gathering at Hartington's home. Chamberlain urged
cooperation of the two groups in defeating the Home Rule bill.
During the next few days he recruited more M.P.'s for his own faction. By mid-May he again felt confident of his ability to defeat the
bill on the second reading.[76]

Chamberlain, however, found it difficult to hold his alliance together. Many of the Liberal dissidents at the meeting in Hartington's
home were sympathetic toward Gladstone and honestly wanted to

73. Estimates of the number attending the meeting vary: Chamberlain, *Political
Memoir*, 219; *The Times*, May 13, 1886; Newton, *Caine*, 150. A list in the Chamberlain Papers contains only forty-four names: "Meeting *May 12*, 1886," JC 8/6/1. The
same forty-four were named in *The Times*, May 13, 1886. The fact that not all were
Radicals was observed by Edward Hamilton: Hamilton Diaries, May 13, 1886,
48,643; and by the *Daily News*, May 13, 1886.

74. Contemporary estimates of anti–Home Rule feeling among Radicals outside
the House were very imprecise; consequently, the estimate given here is at best
only a guess. The *Birmingham Daily Post* (May 6, 1886) declared that opposition
to Home Rule was greater inside the House than outside. An interesting letter to
the *Daily News* (May 29, 1886) by J. Hirst Hollowell, a Congregationalist minister
from Nottingham, argued that of about sixty Nonconformist ministers in Nottingham, forty-one refused to sign a memorial against Home Rule. Of course, there
is no way of knowing how many of those ministers were Radicals, but the letter
suggests, at least, that the ratio of Home Rulers to anti-Home Rulers among active
Nonconformists in one provincial city was about two to one.

75. Reported in *The Times*, May 13, 1886.

76. Chamberlain to Arthur Chamberlain, May 12, 1886, Chamberlain Papers,
JC 5/11/7.

find a way to rejoin the party.[77] Moreover, Bunce, editor of the *Birmingham Daily Post*, began to waver at the thought of abandoning Gladstone. He had to be whipped back into line by Chamberlain's brother, Arthur.[78] The Parnellites were trying to separate Chamberlain from his following.[79] Radical speakers and writers began to express disillusionment with Chamberlain personally.[80] Even the Birmingham Liberal Association, by refusing to leave the National Liberal Federation, refused to cooperate; and the Federation itself continued to thrive after Chamberlain and his handful of colleagues left it.[81] Finally, at a meeting of the London Liberal and Radical Council, despite appeals for unity by Dilke, the delegates hissed the names of Chamberlain and Hartington.[82]

To make matters more difficult, the cabinet was developing a more attractive concession. This Gladstone announced in a meeting at the Foreign Office of all Liberals who favored the principle of Home Rule: the government would not proceed with the bill after the second reading. In the autumn session they would recast the exclusion clause to allow Irish representation on taxation and imperial affairs.[83] (This was the in-and-out formula introduced again in 1893.) The scheme of withdrawal plus pledges of substantial (though not complete) retention formed the basis of the second attempt to neutralize Chamberlain's opposition. Chamberlain indicated that he would vote against the second reading regardless of promises by the government, but it is highly likely that pressure for party unity would have forced him to accept such a bargain.[84] Chamber-

77. Hamilton Diaries, May 15, 1886, 48,643.

78. J. Chamberlain to Arthur Chamberlain, May 15, 1886; and Arthur Chamberlain to J. Chamberlain, May 16, 1886, Chamberlain Papers, JC 5/11/8, 3.

79. *United Ireland*, May 15, 1886.

80. For example, speeches by Atherley-Jones and Storey, *Hansard* 305 (May 28, 1886), 374–78, 538–39; and the letter from A. J. Mundella to Robert Leader, May 13, 1886, quoted in W. H. G. Armytage, *A. J. Mundella, 1825–97: The Liberal Background to the Labour Movement* (London, 1951), 252.

81. James Kitson to H. Gladstone, May 15, 1886, Viscount Gladstone Papers, 46,028.

82. *The Times*, May 18, 1886.

83. *The Times*, May 28, 1886.

84. Labouchere to Chamberlain, May 25, 26, 1886, Chamberlain Papers, JC 5/50/79, 80; Chamberlain to Labouchere, May 26, 1886, Viscount Gladstone Papers, 46,016.

lain's whip, a burly, back-slapping Radical named W. S. Caine, advised him that thirty of their following might well vote for the second reading. It occurred to Caine that Chamberlain should lead the dissentients in abstaining, for this might keep waverers in the group yet commit them to nothing in the future.[85] That, as it turned out, was the issue on which the fate of the Home Rule bill turned.

On May 31 Chamberlain and Caine summoned their faction to a final meeting. Chamberlain appears to have been prepared to abstain with them if the majority so desired; at least his analyses of the various options seemed objective to the witnesses. But the influence of a letter from John Bright, who had been courted by all sides, proved decisive. In this curious letter Bright declared that he would himself vote against the bill but advised others to abstain.[86] The gathering was more impressed by Bright's action than his advice, and in the end forty-six voted for opposing the bill, four for abstaining, and three for supporting it.[87]

The fateful decision had been made. Bright, reversing himself, later tried to persuade Chamberlain to join him in abstaining, but Chamberlain refused. He wrote Bright that the decision was right and that it was too late to change it in any case.[88] On June 1 Chamberlain announced that, as Gladstone had not promised to reconstruct the entire bill along the lines of a federation, he would oppose the second reading.[89] The House voted on the night of June 7–8. Ninety-three Liberals voted against the bill; it was defeated 341 to 311. The vast majority of Radicals went into the Home Rule lobby, but enough went the other way to defeat the measure. Of 163 Radicals, 131 supported the second reading, four abstained, and only thirty-two opposed, counting the abstentions. A shift of fifteen votes from no to aye would have carried Home Rule past the second reading.[90]

85. Caine to Chamberlain, May 27, 31, 1886, Chamberlain Papers, JC 5/10/2, 3.
86. Bright to Chamberlain, May 31, 1886, quoted in Trevelyan, *Bright*, 454–55.
87. There are several reports of the meeting: *The Times*, June 1, 1886; Chamberlain, *Political Memoir*, 224–25; Newton, *Caine*, 153–55; *Birmingham Daily Post*, June 1, 1886.
88. June 2, 1886, Chamberlain Papers, JC 5/7.
89. *Hansard* 306 (June 1, 1886), 675–700.
90. The division list: *Hansard* 306 (June 7, 1886), 1240–45.

V. The Reason Why

Attention in 1886 naturally fixed itself on the margin of votes that Chamberlain's group provided against Home Rule. This phenomenon has led many historians to the mistaken conclusion that all the Radicals opposed Home Rule; hence it has raised as the primary problem of interpretation a false issue—why did the Radicals throw their weight against Irish self-government? In reality the great majority of Radical leaders inside the House of Commons and in the country as well supported Gladstone. Of the 163 Radical M.P.'s, 80 percent voted for Home Rule. Including those who abstained (who are known to have opposed the bill), only 20 percent opposed it. These figures show that a higher proportion of Radical M.P.'s supported Home Rule than did the members of any other British political faction. No Tory voted for Home Rule. Of the 172 non-Radical Liberal M.P.'s, 65 percent voted for the bill and 35 percent opposed. (Whigs voted 48 percent for and 52 percent against; moderate Liberals, 68 percent for and 32 percent against.)

In the country nearly every substantial organization of Radicals to express an opinion, and almost all Radical journals, supported Home Rule: the National Liberal Federation, the local Liberal and Radical associations, the London Liberal and Radical Union, the Radical clubs, and many regional associations of Nonconformists spoke out for Gladstone. Likewise for Home Rule were the *Daily News, Reynolds's Newspaper, The Congregationalist, The Inquirer,* the *Methodist Times, The Nonconformist and Independent,* the Manchester *Guardian* and most of the provincial Radical press; *The Echo* and *The Democrat* supported the principle of Irish self-rule though not the bill itself. The major national Nonconformist bodies, like the central offices of the various denominations, the Liberation Society, and the United Kingdom Alliance, did not take sides in the Home Rule controversy in order to avoid dividing their memberships. But most of their officers who were politically active supported Home Rule: Henry Richard of the Peace Society and Dissenting Deputies; J. Carvell Williams, chairman of the parliamentary committee of the Liberation Society; Sir Wilfrid Lawson (out of parliament in 1886), president of the United Kingdom Alliance; John

Roberts, Chairman of the Methodist Association of North Wales; Albert Spicer, President of the Congregational Union and President of the London Missionary Society; and Alfred Thomas, President of the Welsh Baptist Union, to name a few. In short, a big majority of the leading Radicals throughout the country supported Home Rule.

This fact leaves two questions to be answered: first, why so many Radical leaders favored Home Rule; and second, why some Radicals broke from their colleagues and opposed it.

Those who opted for Home Rule would probably have explained their action by saying that they did not have any alternative. Parnell had made them attend to Irish problems, and when they did so, Radicals tended to interpret the issues as arising from insecurity of land tenure caused largely by the landlords. Therefore, they had proposed to settle the Irish Question by extreme alterations of the legal relations between landlord and tenant. The Parnellites, however, were only minimally satisfied with the land act of 1881, and continued to press for redress of grievances through their strategy of confrontation. Many Britishers, including numerous middle-class Radicals, turned to coercion to keep order in Ireland. But by 1882 few Radicals thought that coercion had succeeded, or felt that they could tolerate it on a long-term basis. This was a crucial realization for them. As long as the Parnellites kept up the pressure of confrontation, Radicals had to find some solution other than oppression. In addition, the necessities of the political situation connected with the general election of 1885 forced the Radicals to look for a solution that promised to get the Irish Question out of British politics. Increasingly they found Home Rule to be the only way out of their dilemma. Few of them were initially enthusiastic about it; only the debate on the Home Rule bill itself, with all its intrinsic drama and emotional tension, generated deep commitment among many Radicals to Home Rule. Yet by June 1886, many of them were talking about Home Rule as if it were a touchstone of the Radical program.

Few Radicals found it an easy road to Home Rule. They found it difficult to overcome their anti-Catholic feelings and their anxieties about the fate of the empire. But on balancing the advantages promised by Home Rule against the risks, most Radicals found Home

Rule preferable. The factor distinguishing their decision from that of more orthodox Englishmen was their relatively weak identification with the prevailing political and social system of Britain. They perceived the Irish part of that system as a privilege-ridden violation of their achievement-oriented ideal. When the Parnellite strategy required all Britons to set the limits to which they would go to defend that social order, Radicals would not go very far. Naturally, the point at which Radicals came over to the Irish side varied with the individual, particularly with the extent to which he valued British institutions like parliament, the empire, and Protestantism. This observation helps explain why Welsh and working-class Radical M.P.'s, the two parliamentary groups with the least reason to identify with and depend on traditional institutions, supported Home Rule more uniformly than their colleagues: 94 percent of Welsh Radical M.P.'s and 100 percent of working-class M.P.'s. Support for Home Rule among Radicals varied with the geographic and social distance from the English establishment. (See Appendix D.) The Parnellite strategy of confrontation, then, was essential in the conversion of Radicals to Home Rule. Unfortunately for the nationalists, it was also an important factor in driving more orthodox Britons to the wall, hence in bringing about the defeat of Home Rule.

If the imperfect identification of Radicals with the British social order had turned a majority of them to Home Rule, what about the minority who opposed it? Why did they not do as their colleagues did? They were in every important social sense much like the Home Rule Radicals. One cannot say, for instance, that businessmen among Radicals voted one way, and journalists another; or railway directors against, and textile merchants for. No meaningful split according to religious affiliation emerged. Nor did the constituencies of Radicals opposing Home Rule differ noticeably from those of the others. (See Appendix D.) Eric Strauss has suggested that they resisted Home Rule because of economic considerations. Because Parnell had said that he would raise a tariff against British goods, British capitalists, including Radicals, feared that Home Rule would deprive them of an essential market for manufactured goods and eventually develop damaging competition.[91] It is true that Parnell's

91. Strauss, *Irish Nationalism and British Democracy*, 174–75.

talk about a tariff caused a brief flurry among some Radicals, but it was not of great importance. During the debate over Home Rule both in and out of the House, the Radical opponents of Home Rule never showed much concern about an Irish tariff. What they talked about was the inability of the Irish people to make responsible decisions in governing themselves. The Irish would persecute the Irish Protestants, spend state funds extravagantly, bankrupt the Irish nation, destroy private property in land, and ruin the sanctity of contracts. In other words, the Radicals believed that the Irish would squander law and order. The basis of this disbelief in the adequacy of the Irish character came from two closely related sources: the essentially racialist attitude toward Irishmen so extensive in Victorian England; and a virulent hostility to Roman Catholicism especially strong in the Dissenting sects. The commonly held myth of the Irish character—that the Irish were superstitious, romantic, irresponsible, and impulsive—sharply contrasted with the Radical ideal. Some found it impossible to believe that any people, like the Irish, so lacking in admirable qualities could be capable of ruling themselves. They also could not be persuaded that Catholics—allegedly a priest-ridden, tyrannized, foreign-dominated population—could be trusted with the responsibilities of government. If Parnellite tactics had made concessions to nationalism necessary, federation, not Home Rule, was the maximum acceptable plan.

This explanation may be modified when it comes to the case of Joseph Chamberlain, for he was in several ways unique, and more documentation of his motives exists. His attempts to reach accord with the Parnellites in the 1870's and early 1880's indicate that he did not have, at least before 1885, a strongly disparaging view of the Irish character. Moreover, though a spokesman for Nonconformist interests, Chamberlain was not a man wearing religious blinders. While he certainly "played the Orange card" in the debate in 1886, he probably did so to capitalize on what he knew to be a point influential with others, and not to express a personal dislike of Catholicism. The key to understanding Chamberlain's attitude toward the Irish lies in his psychological make-up. This does not mean that Chamberlain's behavior was irrational, while that of other Radicals was not; it means that, according to the existing evidence, Chamberlain's personality differed in degree even from his fellow Radical opponents to Home Rule. Chamberlain was what many modern psychologists call an authoritarian personality. He was an extraordinarily aggressive person—insolent, according to his social superiors; ruthless, according to his defeated opponents. One of the most outstanding features of both his business and political careers was that he rarely just competed with or debated his opponents. Rather, he sought to crush them. As John Morley could testify, once he had disagreed with someone, even a close friend, he cut that person off and tried to destroy him completely. People, singly and in groups, were to him objects to be manipulated and used, then thrown aside. Thus Chamberlain tended to reduce politics to a simplistic pattern in which individuals fell into three groups: the enemies, whom he worked tirelessly to ruin; his friends, whom he sought to dominate; and middle factions, whom he could manipulate for his own purpose. In every respect he needed to control events and people, if only by fitting them firmly into this intelligible and simplistic pattern. When people attempted to thwart him, as Parnell did, or get out of place, as Gladstone and Morley did, then Chamberlain reacted forcefully against them. Thus he found Home Rule unacceptable because it was an intrusion into his mental scenario, and because it was advocated by Parnell, a man who had refused to play the part Chamberlain assigned him. The Irish had to be treated firmly and taught that they would get what the British gave them, not what they won for themselves. If necessary, Chamberlain was willing to coerce them, for unlike most Radicals, he never had developed anything more than a tactical aversion to repression. Other Radicals saw Home Rule as the only alternative to an unacceptable policy; Chamberlain saw it as the fanciful and dangerous demand of men who had proven in their dealings with him that they could not be trusted with self-government.

It may seem strange that such an ardent Radical as Chamberlain could possess so many characteristics of an authoritarian personality. Authoritarian types usually have a very strong sense of identity with prevailing values and institutions, and of course in important areas Chamberlain, like any Radical, did not. But T. W. Adorno, the leading investigator of authoritarian personality types, has found that some men with a definite disposition toward authoritarianism quite accidentally derive anti-authoritarian ideologies from their circumstances.[92] In Chamberlain's case the ideology was stripped away by Home Rule, and his essential rigidity began to emerge. It was no accident that his well-known imperialist tendencies also began to appear during and after the Home Rule crisis. He was, as Nicholas Mansergh has written, one of "Nature's imperialists."[93] But it would be wrong to conclude from this observation that Chamberlain opposed Home Rule because he was an imperialist, in the political sense, before 1886. Like the great majority of Radicals, Chamberlain had supported anti-imperialist policies before 1886. He had opposed the Afghan and Zulu wars and Disraeli's forward policy in Turkey; and though he supported the intervention in Egypt in 1882 and a "smash the Mahdi" policy in the Sudan, he also thought that Britain should evacuate Egypt and the Sudan as quickly as possible. His imperialist tendencies actually developed after 1886, when all the talk about imperial unity brought up by Irish nationalism began to affect him, and when he had been separated from the bulk of the Radical movement and thrown into Unionist company by the Home Rule issue.[94]

The Home Rule scalpel helped show what kind of people Radicals were. Most were shown to be men with a strong sense of law and order but a limited identification with the privileged social system; a few were revealed as tightly constrained by religious blinders and by an extra-strong concern for social discipline; and Chamberlain was shown to be a Radical with an ideology clearly bounded by a powerful authoritarian tendency. More generally, the Home Rule parliament brought to an end the period of confrontation, during which Radicals had been responding to a strategy of pressure and force. The entire experience since 1874 confirmed the notion

92. T. W. Adorno et al., *The Authoritarian Personality* (New York, 1950), Ch. 19.

93. Nicholas Mansergh, *Ireland in the Age of Reform and Revolution* (London, 1940), 108.

94. For a similar view of Chamberlain and imperialism, see William L. Strauss, *Joseph Chamberlain and the Theory of Imperialism* (Washington, D.C., 1942), 18–34. For an opposing view, see John W. Derry, *The Radical Tradition, Tom Paine to Lloyd George* (London, 1967), 329–34.

that the Radical movement was made up of men whose persuasion was thoroughly rooted in the *English* experience. They held principles which, however universal they appeared, were tied to their social origins. It took a great deal to get them to apply those principles to a situation beyond the immediate interests of the Radical social structure. Further, whatever the connotations of the label "radical," the late-Victorian Radical ethos was imbued with the spirit and concerns of middle-class Nonconformity, which dominated the leadership of the movement. If the Radicals had enthusiastically carried the banner of democracy and social equality into Ireland without the pressure of nationalist strategy, they would have perhaps conformed to simpler notions of Radicalism, but not to their own real nature.

CHAPTER SIX

The Impact of Home Rule:
Radicals and Radicalism
1886-95

In 1887 Joseph Chamberlain wrote a letter to *The Baptist* in which he blamed the preoccupation of Liberals and Radicals with Home Rule for delaying social reform. "Thirty-two millions of people," he complained, "must go without much-needed legislation because three millions are disloyal."[1] Early in the 1890's socialists and militant working-class spokesmen sometimes took up this cry to express their discontent with the Liberal party. And in later years the Liberal-Radical commitment to Home Rule has provided one of the main historical explanations for the founding of an independent working-class party; thus the dampening of Radicalism supposedly caused by Home Rule has been regarded as the source of the most important political transformation of recent British history. In the words of G. D. H. Cole:

> With Chamberlain's departure, and with the increasing preoccupation of Gladstone with Home Rule, the Radical impulses of the 'seventies had died away. Some attempt was made to revive them when it had become plain that Liberalism was in serious danger of losing its working-class support. But the attempt was made too late, and the Liberal 'Newcastle Programme' of 1892 was only a very pale shadow of Chamberlain's 'Unauthorized Programme' of 1885.[2]

Despite the neatness and simplicity of this interpretation, another opinion expressed in 1887 suggests that an alternative point of view

1. Quoted in Garvin, *Chamberlain*, II, 292.
2. Cole, *British Working Class Politics*, 128. For a recent statement of much the same interpretation, see D. A. Hamer, "The Irish Question and Liberal Politics, 1886–1894," *Historical Journal* 12 (1969), 511–32; and *Liberal Politics in the Age of Gladstone and Rosebery* (Oxford, 1972), esp. Chs. 5, 6.

should be considered. In that year Gladstone told the National Liberal Federation that Radicalism actually owed much to the advent of the Irish Question: "After this Irish controversy is at an end the advanced Liberals, the Radical portion of the party, will have a vastly increased influence—not in consequence of the proposal of Home Rule, but in consequence of the resistance to that proposal, and all of the influences and powers which that resistance will have brought into action."[3] Even if Gladstone's prediction was only partly right, serious modifications of the standard interpretation of late-nineteenth century politics would be in order. If the spirit of Radicalism were not dampened and its influence not decreased by the commitment to Home Rule, then some other explanation of working-class and socialist discontent with the Liberal party must be found. If the nature of Radicalism after 1886 did not become less reformist, less concerned with its traditional issues, then it might have been the substance of Radicalism itself with which so many working-class leaders became disenchanted. This is not to argue that the involvement with Home Rule left the history of Radicalism unaffected, for it will be seen in subsequent chapters that it contributed heavily to the electoral difficulties of the Radicals. What this alternative point of view does argue is that Home Rule affected Radicalism in complex and contradictory ways which must be carefully sorted out.

I. The Radical Unionists

The most obvious way that the Home Rule controversy affected Radicalism was to split off from the main force of the movement a sizeable splinter of Unionists. As it included Chamberlain, easily the most outstanding Radical in England before 1886, this group inevitably was important. Yet in sheer numbers the Radical Unionists were a small and declining faction from 1886 to 1895. During the Home Rule parliament the Radical Unionists could claim thirty-three M.P.'s. Shortly afterward, Chamberlain enlisted some fifteen thousand members for his organization, the National Radical

3. National Liberal Federation, *Tenth Annual Report, 1887* (London, 1888), 48.

Union.[4] Neither section of unionist Radicalism ever amounted to as much again. The number of Radical Unionist M.P.'s decreased to about twenty after the general election of 1886, and to eleven after 1892. (See Appendix E.) They comprised only about 28 percent of all Liberal Unionists from 1886 to 1892, and about 22 percent from 1892 to 1895. Their number slowly but steadily eroded as discontented Unionists returned to the Gladstonian party: Trevelyan in 1887, Caine in 1890, and Benjamin Hingley in 1893. The losses were not replaced by new recruits—only four new Radical Unionists won seats in the House in 1886 or 1892, two of them being the sons of John Bright and Chamberlain. The National Radical Union, founded for electoral purposes in 1886, faded away in 1888.[5]

Radical Unionism declined because Unionism put Radicals in an awkward and unnatural position. Setting first priority on opposition to Home Rule tended to dull the edge of Radicalism. Chamberlain largely determined the Radical Unionist policy. He said it was to "give loyal support to the Conservatives provided that they do not play the fool either in foreign policy or in reactionary measures at home."[6] In practice, they would try to move the Conservative party toward Radical policies, but whenever the Conservatives might be in danger of defeat, Radical Unionists would support them, regardless of the issue. Chamberlain was fairly successful in swaying the Conservatives toward Radical measures, particularly while Randolph Churchill, the impulsive Tory democrat, carried heavy influence within Conservative cabinet circles.[7] But the situation also entailed Radical Unionist support for the Tories on matters very distasteful to Radicals, such as coercion in Ireland and defense of the House of Lords. Most of the Radical Unionists tolerated such a position only to circumvent Irish self-rule. A few, among them Trevelyan and Caine, eventually found that their allegiance to Rad-

---

4. Chamberlain, *Political Memoir*, 228; Fraser, *Chamberlain*, 106; Garvin, *Chamberlain*, II, 252.

5. Ivor Jennings, *Party Politics* (Cambridge, 1961), II, 202.

6. Chamberlain to Hartington, July 16, 1886, quoted in Holland, *Life of Devonshire*, II, 168–69.

7. Garvin, *Chamberlain*, II, 302–8, 411–12, 417–18; Michael Hurst, *Joseph Chamberlain and Liberal Reunion: The Round Table Conference of 1887* (Toronto, 1967), 343, 361–62.

ical policies outweighed their doubts about Home Rule, and returned to the main Radical force.[8]

II. The Main Body of Radicalism, 1886–95: Personnel

The vast majority of Radicals after 1886 belonged to the Gladstonian Liberal party; thus it was among the Liberal Home Rulers that one finds the men most appropriately called "Radicals." A look at the Radical Home Rule M.P.'s quickly makes several important things clear. First, it becomes increasingly difficult to distinguish a Radical from a Liberal. With the Whig right wing of the party gone, Liberalism generally tended to become more Radical, in the sense that the Liberal party after 1886 generally accepted policies that formerly had been the preserve of the Radicals. Indeed, after the general election of 1892 the growing identification of Liberalism with Radicalism tends to thwart attempts even by fairly sophisticated voting analysis to tell them apart. (See Appendix F.) Second, assuming that the distinction between Liberals and Radicals has some utility (it probably does not after 1895), it is clear that Radicals suffered a considerable absolute loss in parliamentary representation, but a large gain in relation to the parliamentary Liberal party. In the general election of 1886, conducted almost solely on the issue of Home Rule, the number of Radicals winning seats in the House of Commons was, for the first time since 1874, smaller than in the previous parliament. An average of about 145 Radicals held seats in the 1886–92 parliament, about 9 percent fewer than in the Home Rule parliament. The number grew to an average of 200 after 1892; nevertheless, the setback in 1886, largely caused by the commitment to Home Rule, seriously slowed the advance of Radicalism within the House of Commons. (See Table 16, Appendix F.) At the same time, however, the attachment to Home Rule apparently hurt the Liberal party as a whole more than it did Radicalism. After the election of 1886, the Radical M.P.'s amounted to more than 70 per-

8. Trevelyan became disturbed about Chamberlain's attitude toward the Gladstonian Liberals and about the Conservative coercion bill in 1887. Caine, above all a temperance advocate, returned to the Liberal party when the Gladstonians offered more support for his temperance beliefs, and when he felt that Gladstone had modified his Home Rule proposal to remove the danger to imperial unity.

cent of the parliamentary Liberal party, a position maintained after 1892, when the Liberal party fared better at the polls. This made Radicalism by far the most important segment of the Liberal party, and no doubt helps account for the widespread acceptance by Liberals of Radical programs. In this sense, Home Rule contributed greatly to the *advance* of Radicalism. (Appendix F has lists of all Radical M.P.'s for both parliaments.)

The social background of the Radical M.P.'s was generally the same as in the three previous parliaments. Most of them were wealthy middle-class men, some 80 percent getting their incomes from middle-class occupations. (See Table 17, Appendix F.) This is perhaps surprising in that big business was becoming steadily more important, as opposed to the landed aristocracy, in British society; and in that the landed style of life was no longer the main route into political orthodoxy. As James Cornford has shown, the new suburbs were providing avenues into Conservatism for middle-class people in the 1880's and 1890's, a trend which would eventually deprive the Liberal party of one important recruiting ground.[9] But these tendencies had not yet altered the composition of the Radical elite, which still included such men as the world's largest manufacturers of alkalai, tin plates, and mustard (J. T. Brunner, William Williams, and J. J. Colman, respectively). In view of these facts, it is worth speculating that the Radical parliamentary elite would contract in size, but not alter in composition, at least until the early twentieth century, when it was too late.

This speculation is supported by the number of working-class Radical M.P.'s, of whom ten were elected in 1886 and eleven in 1892. This level was the same as in 1885, and a marked increase over 1874 and 1880. However, the number was not *growing*, even though working-class political activity in the latter 1880's and early 1890's was intensifying. Moreover, there emerged in the House a small section of socialists and militant workingmen distinctly to the left of the Radicals. In 1886 R. B. Cunninghame Graham, an eccentric middle-class Fabian, won a seat; and in 1892 so did John Burns, Keir Hardie, J. Havelock Wilson, and Sam Woods, all of whom were

9. "The Transformation of Conservatism in the Late Nineteenth Century," *Victorian Studies* 7 (September 1963), 35–66.

militant working-class spokesmen.[10] Their presence confirmed that as workingmen became politically more powerful, Radicalism would have to compete with a new kind of rival for their support.

Nonconformity continued to be the rock of Radicalism. Nearly 75 percent of the Radical M.P.'s in the parliaments from 1886 to 1895 were Nonconformists. Moreover, a heavy majority of Nonconformists who sat in the House were Radical Home Rulers. These observations suggest that, despite the severity of the dispute over Home Rule within Nonconformity, Radicalism continued to attract large numbers of Dissenters. Precisely how and where Home Rule cut through the Nonconformist community is hard to tell. A small majority of Home Rulers over Unionists in each of the predominantly Nonconformist constituencies could have elected a deceptively large number of Nonconformist M.P.'s who supported Home Rule. Nevertheless, John Morley thought that most Nonconformists did remain loyal to the Liberal party: "The attempt to kindle the torch of religious fear or hate was in Great Britain happily a failure. The mass of liberal presbyterians in Scotland, and of nonconformists in England and Wales, stood firm, though some of their most eminent and able divines resisted the new project [Home Rule], less on religious grounds than on what they took to be the balance of political arguments."[11] Other contemporary observations confirmed Morley's appraisals. The *Methodist Times*, for example, though overstating the case somewhat, asserted that the heavy vote by Methodist M.P.'s for Home Rule in the House (only two opposed it) accurately reflected the feeling of English Methodists. And *The Baptist*, which opposed Home Rule, had to admit that at Baptist association meetings, the preponderance of opinion supported Gladstone.[12]

Morley was also correct in observing that the top Nonconformist ministry was more evenly divided than the rank and file. Two of

10. Burns, Hardie, Wilson, and Woods alike were known as socialists when they first entered parliament. Burns turned out to be an orthodox Radical, and is included in this study with the Radicals. The others are not.

11. Morley, *Gladstone*, III, 323.

12. *Methodist Times*, June 10, 1886; *The Baptist*, June 18, 25, 1886. Newman Hall, in a letter to the *Fortnightly*, admitted that as a Nonconformist opponent of Home Rule, he was in a "small minority." *F.R.* 290 (February 1891), 320–23.

the most important opponents of Home Rule were C. H. Spurgeon and R. W. Dale, who were also among the ablest and most influential Dissenting preachers. Spurgeon, the greatest Baptist orator of his day, was a fanatical Unionist, who felt that Home Rule would sacrifice Ulster and lead to the establishment of the Catholic church in Ireland; consequently, anyone who supported such a policy was a "madman."[13] Dale, an ardent advocate of the Birmingham "Civic Gospel" and a close friend of Chamberlain, was one of the two or three leading Congregationalist ministers in England. Though a staunch Unionist, he was moderate and conciliatory in attitude. During the 1886 parliament Dale had worked for a compromise based on retention of the Irish M.P.'s. Although he continued to advocate reconciliation in the party, Dale gradually lost touch with the bulk of Congregationalist opinion. In 1888 the Congregational Union passed a resolution protesting the Tory government's coercive policy in Ireland, and Dale resigned from the Union on grounds that Nonconformist bodies had no right to mix in politics. In 1892 he refused to participate in founding the National Free Church Council, a federation of Dissenting churches, because he feared it also would become a political agency.[14] Thus Unionism within Nonconformity tended to work against any political activity by official Nonconformist agencies. The emergence of such an attitude was an important change from the existing pattern of late-Victorian politics.[15]

On the Home Rule side, the leading Nonconformist ministers were J. Guinness Rogers and Hugh Price Hughes. Rogers, by birth an Ulsterman related to the Guinness brewing family, was a Congregationalist and perhaps the closest friend of Dale. Like most Nonconformists, however, Rogers idolized Gladstone, even though he

13. *The Times*, May 28, June 3, 1886; J. Guinness Rogers, *The Ulster Problem* (London, 1886), 2.

14. Henry W. Clark, *History of English Nonconformity*, 2 vols. (London, 1913), II, 423–24; Dale, *Dale*, 455–66; R. W. Dale, "The Exclusion of the Irish Members from the Imperial Parliament," *Contemporary Review* 49 (June 1886), 761–71.

15. In his important article, "English Nonconformity and the Decline of Liberalism," John F. Glaser contends that the Home Rule controversy was one of the crucial factors in reducing the political influence of Nonconformity, which contributed heavily to the decline of the Liberal party. *American Historical Review* 63 (January 1958), 352–63.

felt the Grand Old Man had sidetracked the campaign for disestablishment in both 1876 and 1886. He believed that Chamberlain's Unauthorized Programme of 1885 was an attempt to supplant Gladstone as the leader of Liberalism, a feeling that was to him confirmed by the events of 1886. Though he disliked and distrusted Catholicism, Rogers threw his support to Home Rule. He reasoned that Protestant intolerance in Ireland would only strengthen the hands of the Catholic priests. From 1886, therefore, Rogers assumed a leading role in trying to persuade Nonconformists that Home Rule would not harm Irish Protestantism.[16] Hughes was a Methodist of Welsh descent. A fervent evangelical with boundless energy and enthusiasm, he led the Methodist "forward party" which sought to turn the church to urban social problems. The *Methodist Times*, of which Hughes was the first editor, was founded in 1885 as the organ of the forward party. Hughes, like Rogers an avowed Radical, made the paper vigorously political and set it firmly for Home Rule, despite the fact that Methodism was probably more deeply divided over Home Rule than any other Nonconformist denomination.[17]

The general support rendered by Nonconformists to Home Rule is shown by a look at the constituencies from 1886 to 1895. As Henry Pelling points out, there is no evidence of a flight of Nonconformist voters from Liberalism to Unionism in these years.[18] The strongly Nonconformist areas remained Liberal and Radical, except in Cornwall and Birmingham, the former being explained by the proximity to Ireland and the consequent urgency of an imagined Irish threat, the latter by the influence of Chamberlain. The Radicals managed to win more victories even in the election of 1886 in Wales and Scotland, where Nonconformity was exceptionally strong. Their losses came mostly in England and in the big cities, where Non-

---

16. Rogers, *Autobiography*, 55; *The Ulster Problem*; and "Mr. Gladstone and the Irish Bill. A Nonconformist View," *Nineteenth Century* 112 (June 1886), 923–29.

17. *The Nonconformist and Independent*, July 22, 1886. One of the leading Methodists, the Reverend William Arthur, and the journal, *Methodist Recorder*, were opposed to Home Rule.

18. Pelling, *Social Geography of British Elections*, 431–32. Michael Kinnear, *British Voter: An Atlas and Survey*, 125–29, can be seen as supporting this view, though the maps and tables deal with 1922.

conformity was not so influential. As Pelling has written, the larger the city, the weaker the Nonconformity.[19] (See Appendix F.) One effect of Home Rule on Radicalism, it seems clear, was to increase the dependency of Radicalism (hence Liberalism) on the Celtic fringe. Realizing this, Scottish and Welsh Radicals pressed their demands forcefully on the Liberal party after 1886.

In England, nevertheless, there was a significant development in Radical representation after 1886. This occurred in the London metropolitan constituencies, where Radicals since the 1860's had never found much support. In 1885 Radicals won only eighteen of sixty-two metropolitan seats, and in 1886 only twelve. Between 1886 and 1892, however, Radicals in London reacted to the 1886 defeat by strenuous organizational and propaganda work. They formed the core of a strong Progressive party that won control of the London County Council in 1894. In the general election of 1892 London Radicals won twenty seats in the House of Commons, and they had high hopes for even more in the future. Their rising fortunes gave London much greater importance in Radical circles than at any time since the decline of the Philosophic Radicals. As early as 1890 the London Radicals made up one of the key groups of Radicals competing for influence within the Liberal party, a fact that would affect the Liberal commitment to Home Rule, just as did the new-found power of the Celtic fringe.

For all the strength of Radicalism within the Liberal party after 1886, Radicals were hampered by inadequate leadership, and to this extent the loss of Chamberlain was a disaster to the Radical movement. The middle-class Radical prototype from 1886 to 1895 would have resembled that of earlier parliaments—a staunch, earnest, square-faced big businessman or lawyer—but it was precisely this type of person that did not have a leader. Chamberlain formerly had provided the provincial democrats with aggressive leadership, but with him gone, the command fell to less well suited men. Many Radicals expected John Morley to assume Chamberlain's mantle. He was the chief propagandist of the faction even before 1886, and his early and complete devotion to Home Rule gave him an exceptionally strong position after 1886. Unfortunately, Morley's brilliant talents

19. Pelling, *Social Geography of British Elections*, 433.

in editing and writing were accompanied by marked political weaknesses. He did not have the ability to perceive the country's increasingly complex social problems, much less the capacity to construct practical solutions for them. Essentially an intellectual of the 1850's and 1860's, Morley felt less and less at home in the world of the 1880's, and so clung to the one issue he understood and felt secure in—Home Rule. In so doing, he tended to lose contact with the Radical rank and file, particularly with those of the working class. Moreover, Morley was a nervous man, hypersensitive, shy, and vain; he did not strike blunt, hard men as a leader. Though a good platform speaker, often capable of great moral passion and felicitous phrases, Morley was a poor parliamentary debater, too frequently slow, humorless, and off the mark in his responses. In July 1886 Frederic Harrison urged Morley to take the lead and form a party, much as Morley himself had once urged Chamberlain.[20] But the sure sense of the source and uses of power was not there; without it, Morley could never fill Chamberlain's shoes.

No one else rose to fill the void. Sir Charles Dilke, a man of some ability and considerable energy, and one who had enjoyed the respect of all varieties of Radicals, had by 1886 been ruined by his involvement as co-respondent in a sordid divorce trial. The only Radical of any prior standing to enhance his reputation from 1886 to 1892 was Henry Labouchere, a man of wit and charm, and one of the first Radicals to suggest Home Rule, but totally unfitted by background, beliefs, and temperament to lead the Radicals. An unbeliever, anti-cleric, and aristocrat, Labouchere was a maverick even among Radicals. He was a congenital trouble-maker. Like all Radicals, he hated privilege, but unlike them he had no respect for anything else. As a young man he had been sent down from Cambridge for cheating and dismissed from the foreign service for refusing to obey orders. In politics he was best known as a republican and raconteur. After 1886 Labouchere attracted a following of malcontents by his ceaseless energy, by frequent attacks on the House of Lords, and by constant criticism of the expense of maintaining the royal family. He lacked, however, any steady plans or programs. Strangely enough, Gladstone came to have a fairly high regard for

20. July 24, 1886, Harrison Papers, Section A, Box 2.

Labouchere, mainly because both took a passionate interest in strict economy. No other party leader thought of Labouchere as a responsible spokesman.[21]

The most promising young men among the parliamentary Radicals were a small group later known as the Liberal imperialists: H. H. Asquith, R. B. Haldane, Sir Edward Grey, Arthur Acland, Sidney Buxton, Augustine Birrell, and Tom Ellis. This group formed, Morley wrote, a "working alliance, not a school."[22] They sat, conferred, and voted together from 1886 to 1892. Their little alliance included great talent; all but one eventually achieved cabinet rank, and the one, Ellis, was Liberal whip from 1892 to 1895. They generally accepted Home Rule but were not enthusiastic about it. Receptive to new ideas, they were self-consciously progressive and had good relations with the Fabians.[23] The "New Radicals" or "New Liberals"—both terms by which the alliance was known—thought of themselves as constructive politicians, and they detested the influence of Labouchere, whose inclinations were all destructive. In order to counter Labby's strength, Asquith, Haldane, and Grey concerted their activities in parliament with Rosebery, Morley, and H. H. Fowler.[24] Yet the "Articles Club," as the anti-Labouchere alliance was called, was flawed by some confusion of purpose. The Liberal imperialists wanted to check Labouchere because they felt he represented a frivolous, irresponsible kind of Radicalism. Morley and Fowler, on the other hand, had no more constructive ideas than Labouchere; they wanted mainly to stop him from annoying the Liberal front bench. Similarly, the Liberal imperialists in the Articles Club admired Rosebery's concern for empire, yet looked upon Morley, a strong anti-imperialist and Home Ruler, as their mentor and guide. Moreover, the Articles Club, for all the brilliance of its members, did not represent the provincial Nonconformist Radicals; they were too cosmopolitan, too "modern" to lead the bulk of Rad-

21. Biographies of Labouchere: Hesketh Pearson, *Labby* (London, 1937); and Thorold, *Labouchere.*

22. Morley, *Recollections*, I, 323–24.

23. A. M. McBriar, *Fabian Socialism and English Politics, 1884–1918* (Cambridge, 1966), 253–57.

24. Dudley Sommer, *Haldane of Cloan: His Life and Times, 1856–1928* (London, 1960), 76–77; Roy Jenkins, *Asquith* (London, 1964), 45–46.

icalism. It was in this respect that Radicalism suffered most heavily from the Home Rule split: Chamberlain did not take many Radicals out of the Liberal party with him, but he did take his own ability. It was sorely missed.

III. Radical Organizations, 1886–95

The Home Rule crisis had a marked impact on the organizational structure of Radicalism. Before 1886 the main parliamentary and extraparliamentary organizations of Radicals were independent associations, like the Liberation Society and the National Liberal Federation, which were not connected with the central headquarters of Liberalism. After 1886, because Radicals were such an important influence in the party, the main Liberal party institutions were merged with Radical organizations. As a result, party organizations themselves became the chief agencies of and for Radicals; the old Radical associations played a reduced role in Radical affairs. The kaleidoscopic nature of Radical activities was not changed, but now Radical groups competed with each other for official party sanction, rather than acting as pressure groups outside the party. Of the old Radical institutions, only the United Kingdom Alliance, still led by Sir Wilfrid Lawson, retained its former importance. The Peace Society was rarely heard from. And even the Liberation Society seemed to be pushed aside by Welsh and Scottish disestablishers, who were less concerned with general disestablishment than with party approval of their regional demands.

The main parliamentary difference from pre-1886 days was that the whips now functioned largely on behalf of Radical attitudes. Radical M.P.'s were appointed whips in 1886 and 1892—Arnold Morley, son of Samuel Morley, and Tom Ellis, respectively. They used the party whips increasingly for what had been Radical issues. After 1886 the Liberal whips normally could depend on Radical votes to a degree they could not before. Nevertheless, as the merging of Radical and Liberal parliamentary agencies tended to make Radicalism official, the irrepressibly crankish temperament of Radical M.P.'s spawned small parliamentary ginger groups. For example, a few members of the Articles Club, especially Haldane and Grey, prided themselves on action independent of the party whips.[25] Late in the 1880's Labouchere organized his own malcontents into a fairly effective unit, complete with whips, of about seventy votes.[26] Another independent Radical group grew out of national sentiment among some young Welsh M.P.'s who hovered in near revolt against the Liberal party, not because of the refusal of the party to accept Radical policies, but because of the party's concern for Radical claims other than their own. In 1894 four Welshmen—Lloyd George, D. A. Thomas, Frank Edwards, and Herbert Lewis—rejected the party whips for a short time.[27] The discontent of such Radical groups with the party leadership was to contribute much to the Liberals' electoral disaster in 1895.[28]

Outside parliament, the Radicals' main organization, the National Liberal Federation, underwent crucial developments after 1886, all tending to magnify Radical influence within the party. The first change originated in the Liberal defeat in the general election of 1886. Inasmuch as Radicals fared better than moderate Liberals, many moderates as well as Radicals expressed a desire for more control by the Federation instead of the Liberal Central Association.[29] In addition, Birmingham was no longer a congenial home for the Federation. As a result, Schnadhorst moved the Federation to London in October 1886, into offices adjacent to the Central Association. Schnadhorst himself became secretary to the Association while retaining his post with the Federation.[30] These alterations effectively installed Radical views in the party's parliamentary headquarters. The distinction between the functions of the parliamentary and extraparliamentary organizations became much less clear. Both Schnadhorst and Arnold Morley carried out electoral duties, and both advised Gladstone on party policy. In 1887 the combined party headquarters established the Liberal Publication Department to turn

---

25. Richard Burdon Haldane, *An Autobiography* (London, 1929), 101-2.
26. Henry W. Lucy, *A Diary of the Salisbury Parliament, 1886-92* (London, 1892), 215.
27. Kenneth O. Morgan, *Wales in British Politics* (Cardiff, 1963), 141-44.
28. See below, Ch. 8.
29. A sample of Radical opinion is Labouchere to H. Gladstone, July 9, 18, 1886, Viscount Gladstone Papers, 46,016.
30. McGill, "Schnadhorst," 29.

out a stream of party propaganda. It was controlled by Radicals who made up its committee of management: James Bryce, Professor James Stuart, Percy Bunting, and T. Wemyss Reid.[31] Furthermore, Schnadhorst's assistant (and successor), Robert A. Hudson, did many of both the Federation's and the Association's administrative chores. Through Acland and Ellis he kept close contact with the young Liberal imperialists, some of whom under Acland's supervision conducted a series of studies that contributed much to the Newcastle Programme.[32] These steps amounted to a considerable advance of Radicalism within the Liberal party. In 1892 Arnold Morley rightly declared that the Central Association office was "more efficient & more in harmony with recent developments in Liberal thought than it has been in any previous moment of its existence. . . ."[33]

Meanwhile, the Federation greatly expanded its organization outside the offices in Parliament Street. In October 1886 Schnadhorst set out to establish Liberal associations of the democratic type in every part of Great Britain, all to be connected by a network of regional federations or by association with national party headquarters. Federations of Liberal associations were formed in North and South Wales. Sixty-five Liberal associations were founded or newly affiliated with the London office; 340 others were affiliated to the two Welsh federations.[34] By the end of 1887 hardly a locality in England and Wales lacked a Liberal association affiliated with the Federation.

Much the same kind of unifying process took place in Scotland. Before 1886 Scottish Radicals had their own organization, the National Liberal Federation of Scotland, while the Whigs and moderates controlled the Scottish Liberal Association. Rivalry between the two organizations in 1886 contributed to Liberal defeats in normally safe constituencies. Home Rule was the key issue at stake between the two organizations, the Scottish Federation strongly sup-

---

31. National Liberal Federation, *Tenth Annual Report, 1887*, 28–29.
32. J. A. Spender, *Sir Robert Hudson: A Memoir* (London, 1930), 17–21.
33. To Gladstone, April 21, 1892, Gladstone Papers. 44,254.
34. National Liberal Federation, *Tenth Annual Report, 1887*, 11–25; Percy Corder, *The Life of Robert Spence Watson* (London, 1914), 65–69.

porting Home Rule, and the Liberal Association opposing. By permeating the Association, Radicals managed to carry a resolution for Home Rule at a conference of the Association late in 1886. Their victory cleared away the main obstacle to unification of the two organizations. In December 1886 the Federation was merged into the Liberal Association, and Radicals soon won control of the policy-making conferences of the new Association. By October 1887 they had committed the Association executive to disestablishment; by 1892 to a full Radical program.[35]

Radical organization also improved markedly in London in 1886. As early as February the Liberal Central Association was seeking to rationalize metropolitan Liberal organizations, but at the time of the general election of 1886 most London Radicals were divided into two competing associations, the London and Counties Liberal Union, and the London Liberal and Radical Council.[36] Many constituencies had no local associations. Others had very active Radical clubs which remained independent of both the larger associations. After the election, through the efforts of Professor James Stuart and R. K. Causton, a leading metropolitan reformer, the Liberal associations combined to form the London Liberal and Radical Union, with Radicals as officers: John Morley as president, Causton as chairman, Stuart as honorary secretary, and Renwick Seager as secretary. Decidedly Radical in program and membership, the Liberal and Radical Union affiliated with the National Liberal Federation as one of its major subordinate units. For the area surrounding London, party leaders founded the more moderate Home Counties Division.[37] Most of the important Radical clubs, however, refused to be brought into the new organizations. They preferred their own Metropolitan Radical Federation to the predominantly middle-class Liberal and Radical Union; thus the old divide between middle- and working-class Radicals continued to exist, despite their agreement on Home Rule.

London was an outstanding example of Radical organizational

---

35. Kellas, "The Liberal Party in Scotland, 1876–1895," 5–14.
36. For the early efforts at rationalization: *The Times*, February 18, 1886.
37. National Liberal Federation, *Tenth Annual Report, 1887*, 26.

experiences from 1886 to 1895. During this period the most crucial organizational problem that Radicals faced was to respond effectively to growing demands by the working class for working-class parliamentary representation. From the late 1880's the serene assumption by the middle-class Radical elite that they spoke for all workingmen no longer sufficed. The new working-class demand had nothing to do with Home Rule, and little to do with policies of any kind. It was mainly that workingmen in increasing numbers wanted to see their own kind in the House of Commons and in positions of power in party institutions. Schnadhorst and the other Radical leaders took the position that they would welcome more working-class M.P.'s, but that decisions to adopt labor candidates must remain with the local Liberal associations, which continued to be controlled by bourgeois wire-pullers. Schnadhorst felt that he could not deprive the loyal constituency chiefs of their time-honored right to choose candidates.[38] This response was inadequate, for in practice it precluded large-scale working-class representation through Radical institutions. In November 1890 James Tims, secretary of the Metropolitan Radical Federation, formally asked Schnadhorst to have fifty Liberal candidates throughout the country withdrawn, so that labor candidates, with Federation support, could contest the seats. Schnadhorst replied that the Federation could not interfere with the associations; furthermore, that working-class candidates would have to pay their own election expenses.[39] Workingmen knew from this response that very few Liberal candidatures would ever be available to them.

In earlier years Schnadhorst had done good service for Radicals and Liberals, but he showed very poor judgment throughout his dealings with socialists and laborites. He wrote to Gladstone of Sidney Webb, who then was making a name for himself among London Liberals:

38. McBriar, *Fabian Socialism and English Politics*, 234–38; Paul Thompson, *Socialists, Liberals and Labour: The Struggle for London, 1885–1914* (Toronto, 1967), Ch. 5; Pelling, *Origins of the Labour Party*, 59; National Liberal Federation, *Eleventh Annual Meeting, 1888* (London, 1888), 29.

39. National Liberal Federation, *Proceedings of the Fourteenth Annual Meeting, 1891* (London, 1891), 18–20.

He is quite a new man & has little means of knowing the sentiments of London workmen. London to him & others means the few noisy impracticables who meet in a few Clubs, a class whom no programme can ever satisfy—they are the men who keep London Liberals divided and weak. Cooperation with them is almost impossible. There is a wide gulf between the sober, intelligent, hardheaded men of the provinces and these men. Sidney Webb himself is a socialist with little sympathy with us on the Irish question.[40]

This opinion, as well as his decision concerning labor candidates, plainly reflected middle-class attitudes and interests. It clearly revealed the old structural divide within Radicalism between middle class and working class. This, rather than commitment to Home Rule, would eventually deprive Radicalism of working-class support.

IV. RADICAL PROGRAMS, 1886–95

The effect of Home Rule on Radical programs was to help promote them to official party policy. The improved numerical and organizational position of Radicals naturally increased the influence of their policies. But Home Rule did not have much effect on the *nature* of the Radical programs, and it was in this regard that Radicalism failed to respond to new conditions. By 1886 the "Great Depression," whether historians think it substantial or not, was beginning to produce two related phenomena: aggressive, independent working-class activity, and socialist criticism of British society.[41] The pressures generated by these developments caused an important debate within Radical circles, and to a limited extent led them to modify their programs; however, on the whole the Radical response to the new situation was unsatisfactory. The roots of the eventual decline of Radicalism lay in this failure—an inadequate response caused much less by the commitment to Home Rule than by the nature of British Radicalism itself, essentially unchanged since the 1870's.

40. September 10, 1888, Gladstone Papers, 44,295.
41. The best discussion of the important developments of the 1880's is Helen Merrell Lynd, *England in the 1880's: Toward a Social Basis for Freedom* (London, 1945).

The political aspects of the Radical program essentially were modifications of the old Radical goal of democracy, even though the reform acts of 1884 and 1885 had gone a long way toward universal male suffrage. Radicals now advocated such measures as abolition of plural voting ("one man one vote"), simplified electoral qualifications and registration, payment of official electoral expenses from the rates, shorter parliaments, and at least partial payment of M.P.'s.[42] For local affairs they demanded elective county councils and, after these were established in 1889, elective district and parish councils.[43] By all accounts the Radical political issue most hotly debated throughout the country was reform of the power of the House of Lords. Henry Labouchere led a faction devoted to "ending" the Lords entirely, through the formula of "abolition of the hereditary principle" of the upper house. However, most Radicals shied from the difficulties inherent in attacking the Lords outright and spoke either of basing the House of Lords on merit rather than heredity, or of limiting the Lords' veto power. By 1894, when the Lords had rejected a number of Radical bills, the sentiment of Radicals for some kind of reform of the Lords was very strong.[44] This fact would have important consequences for Ireland.

Issues connected with religion continued to provide important points of the Radical program. Disestablishment and temperance were the two most significant. Although Radicals on principle opposed all established churches, the nationalistic fervor of Welsh and Scottish M.P.'s pushed Welsh and Scottish disestablishment to the forefront and left disestablishment in England to the more distant

42. Andrew Reid, ed., *The New Liberal Programme* (London, 1886); *The Speaker*, January 11, 1890. On payment of members: Thomas Burt, "Labour in Parliament," *Contemporary Review* 55 (May 1889), 681–82; *The Speaker*, April 2, 1892; and J. Fletcher Moulton, "What Mr. Gladstone Ought to Do," *F.R.* 314 (February 1893), 265.

43. Labouchere to H. Gladstone, August 27, [1892?], Viscount Gladstone Papers, 46,016; Reid, *New Liberal Programme*.

44. For examples of Radical opinion on the House of Lords: Labouchere to Dilke, July 27, 1893, Dilke Papers, 43,892; Labouchere's motion in the House, *Hansard* 323 (March 9, 1888), 763; E. A. Freeman, "The House of Lords and the County Councils," *F.R.* 257 (May 1888), 599; Alfred Russell Wallace, "How to Preserve the House of Lords," *Contemporary Review* 65 (January 1894), 114–17; *The Speaker*, December 5, 1891; T. Wemyss Reid, "The Leeds Conference," *The Liberal Magazine* (July 1894), 200–202.

future.[45] Led by Stuart Rendel, Welsh Radicals were especially insistent, and by 1891 they had forced the leaders of the Liberal party to put Welsh disestablishment second only to Home Rule in the party platform, much to the vexation of Scottish Radicals. The temperance advocates were even more influential after 1886 than before, having finally settled on a single plan—local option. Their constant pressure finally got the Liberal leaders to accept temperance as part of party policy, and this achievement persuaded at least one Radical, W. S. Caine, to abandon Unionism and return to the Liberal party.[46]

Although popular discontent with the land system of Britain had begun to wane because of the depression in agriculture, the ambience in which Radicals lived led them to keep land reform high in their program. A few still worked for free trade in land through abolition of entail and primogeniture; others concentrated on Chamberlain's idea of allotments through compulsory purchase of land by local authorities.[47] Increasingly, however, Radicals sought to make landowners pay what they regarded as a fair share of social expenses. They wanted owners of real property to pay death duties and other taxes at rates equal to those borne by owners of personal property.[48] And they adopted from Henry George the idea that the value of the "unearned increment" enjoyed by landlords ought to go to local public authorities. In response to urban problems, Radicals after 1886 in growing numbers followed the *Radical Programme* in turning their criticism of the "unearned increment" to cities. They wanted to give city authorities the right to tax the urban unearned increment, to take land for housing, sanitation, and beautification, and to force landlords as well as occupiers to pay the

45. Morgan, *Wales in British Politics*, 77–149; James G. Kellas, "The Liberal Party and the Scottish Church Disestablishment Crisis," *English Historical Review* 79 (January 1964), 31–46.

46. W. S. Caine, "The Attitude of the Advanced Temperance Party," *Contemporary Review* 63 (January 1893), 48–52; Wilfrid Lawson, "The Classes, the Masses, and the Glasses," *Nineteenth Century* 118 (December 1886), 798–801.

47. Arthur Arnold, "The Land Transfer Bill," *F.R.* 247 (July 1887), 113–14; Arnold to Gladstone, January 23, 1886, Gladstone Papers, 44,095; and R. T. Reid to Schnadhorst, September 16, 1891, in Gladstone Papers, 44,295.

48. *The Star*, November 11, 1890; Labouchere to H. Gladstone, March 31, 1888, Viscount Gladstone Papers, 46,016.

rates.[49] This theme formed the basis of the Radical social program.

The London Radicals contributed a number of policies to the Radical program. Their rhetoric seemed too extreme for many of the older and provincial Radicals, no doubt because the London group was influenced by metropolitan socialists and secular working-class Radical clubs. John Morley wrote Chamberlain in 1888: "The anarchic follies of the London Radicals are playing the Tory game to a marvel. Indeed if these men are Radicals, I'm a Tory. We cannot win without accession of strength from the London constituencies, and that strength will never come so long as these blatant democrats persist in frightening the small shopkeeper, for one thing, and in standing aloof from organization for another."[50] Yet Morley need not have been so apprehensive of the London Radicals. Although they introduced into Radicalism a new emphasis on specifically metropolitan problems and a new tone in criticism of rigid *laissez-faire* attitudes, they built their plans on the same kind of municipal intervention and land reform so important to the older elements of the Radical program. Led by Professor James Stuart and J. F. B. Firth, Quaker barrister and president of the London Municipal Reform League, the London Radicals sought to amalgamate the obsolete and complicated system of vestries, districts, and corporations of London into one representative government, this central authority to be used the way Chamberlain had used the Birmingham city council—to improve gas, water, and sanitation services, and to raise standards of working-class housing. They would tax ground owners instead of occupiers, and would through "leasehold enfranchisement" enable occupiers to become owners. For the country at large, the London Radicals advocated improvement of hours and wages of government employees, and abolition of taxes on common items of the breakfast table.[51]

49. A. J. Williams, "A Model Land Law," *F.R.* 244 (April 1887), 569; *The Speaker*, August 9, 1890; and J. Fletcher Moulton, "The Taxation of Ground-Rents," *Contemporary Review* 57 (March 1890), 413–14.

50. February 8, 1888, quoted in Garvin, *Chamberlain*, II, 515.

51. McBriar, *Fabian Socialism and English Politics*, 187–98, 234–42; Thompson, *Socialists, Liberals and Labour*, 90–111; James Stuart, "The London Progressives," *Contemporary Review* 61 (April 1892), 530–31; H. W. Massingham, "The Government and Labour," *Contemporary Review* 64 (December 1893), 770–75.

The New Radicals (or New Liberals), many of whom were also among the London Radicals, were more impressed by the urgency of social questions than were most of their other colleagues. To some extent, this would cause a debate among Radicals over the attention that they should give to Home Rule. But at its basis the debate within Radicalism dealt not with Home Rule, but with the relative merits of new social issues versus the old Radical policies. By the latter 1880's various forms of socialism and general social concern were raising fundamental questions about the nature of industrial society in Britain. To some of the younger Radicals these questions demanded a more positive program than Radicals traditionally had pursued. Haldane, trained in German idealism rather than Benthamite empiricism, was the intellectual leader of this progressive movement. He wrote: "The mere removal of obstacles which used to block the highway of human progress in this country has been pretty well completed. We are face to face with a new kind of social problem. Liberalism has passed from the destructive to the constructive stage in its history."[52]

Implicit in the thought of many of the younger Radicals was a new view of the world. Unlike Radicals of older generations, they did not believe that the unimpeded action of social and economic forces led necessarily to progress; indeed, most of the impediments were gone, they believed, and the social problem was greater than ever. Like all nineteenth-century British Radicals, the New Radicals wanted to establish the conditions in which an individual would have maximum freedom of action. But they now felt that positive action by the state would be necessary to bring about the optimum conditions. Thus they were severely critical of unrestrained capitalism and regarded some of the older Radicals as obsolete individualists; for example, John Morley to a few New Radicals represented the individualist tail of old-fashioned Radicalism; he was the "bondslave of Political Economy."[53]

---

52. "The Liberal Creed," *Contemporary Review* 54 (October 1888), 463.

53. G. W. E. Russell, "The New Liberalism: A Response," *Nineteenth Century* 151 (September 1889), 498. See also L. A. Atherley-Jones, "The New Liberalism," *Nineteenth Century* 150 (August 1889), 192; John Page Hopps, "The Nihilisms and Socialisms of the World," *Contemporary Review* 58 (August 1890), 272–79;

There is no doubt that men like Morley and Bradlaugh, and many others, did not share the New Radicals' sense of urgency about social issues, or look upon new spokesmen of the working class with much understanding. Morley could at best summon up only a patronizing intellectual sympathy for them. From Newcastle he wrote Rosebery: "Last night I battled with my Socialist enemies by the space of 2½ hours—but w^d. not give way. I've a sneaking sympathy for these poor ragged excitables in my Rousseauite bosom, all the same."[54] At worst he regarded the new social thinkers as impudent upstarts: "The Fabians interest and stimulate and suggest—but they are loose, superficial, crude, and impertinent. Does that satisfy you?"[55]

Yet if the old Radicals differed very sharply from the New Radicals in perception of the actual state of society, then in both basic objectives and specific policies they differed very little. All of the Radicals rejected the cooperative ideal underlying socialist programs and reaffirmed their belief in a competitive system. Arthur Arnold, a land reformer who stood at about the middle of the Radical spectrum, explained that Radicals wanted the state to regulate, not replace, the capitalist system: "We seek to establish a well-ordered competition, because we find that in some form competition is the mainspring of production, and that moral and material stoppage and decline follow upon removal of this mainspring from society."[56] As Haldane put it, the state provides a civilized environment for capitalists, and the state has a right to charge "rent" for its services.[57] This sentiment represents only an extension of Chamberlain's old doctrine of "ransom" to property of all kinds. Most Radicals could agree with it, and even more enthusiastically with Haldane's specific proposals: free education, release of charitable endowments through disestablishment, reform of land transfer laws,

---

The Speaker, February 14, 1891. For a defense of the old Radicals, see J. Guinness Rogers, "Nonconformist Forebodings," *Nineteenth Century* 213 (November 1894), 804.

54. February 3, 1889, Rosebery Papers, Box 35.

55. Morley to Haldane, September 28, 1891, Haldane Papers, MS 5903.

56. "Socialism and the Unemployed," *Contemporary Review* 53 (April 1888), 561.

57. "The Liberal Creed," *Contemporary Review* 54 (October 1888), 466.

compulsory powers for local authorities to make improvements and allotments, taxation of the unearned increment, and equalization and graduation of death duties on realty and personalty.[58] This was old Radical wine in New Radical bottles.

The Radicals agreed in rejecting socialism, but in terms of practical policies, they did not agree on where to draw the line. The issue that most often divided Radicals from socialists and militant workingmen was the eight-hour day. In the belief that competition should operate throughout society, Radicals like Morley, Bradlaugh, Mundella, and even Thomas Burt (a former coal miner) rejected proposals for an eight-hour day on the grounds that the state should not interfere with adult labor. They would accept legislative limitation of working hours only if it were proved to them that the health and safety of the workers was at stake. Free and fair bargaining between employers and employees should prevail in industry, and well-run unions could win the conditions at once desired by labor and compatible with the existence of the industry.[59] This was essentially the Radical policy of the 1870's, and it is important to notice that it was shared by some of the New Radicals; Haldane, for example, rejected the eight-hour day and declared that "cowardice and apathy alone" kept workers from winning the hours and wages they wanted.[60] At the same time, however, a majority of Radicals advocated an eight-hour day for miners, because the health and safety of the workers was involved.[61] And a number, mainly from constituencies where the working-class electorate was large, supported the eight-hour day for all industries. The problem for the Radical movement as a whole was that not enough Radicals quickly and enthusiastically took up the proposal for limiting hours. Clearly,

58. *Ibid.*, 462–74; Richard Burdon Haldane, "The Liberal Party and Its Prospects," *Contemporary Review* 53 (January 1888), 156–59.

59. Hamer, *Morley*, 255–70; Charles Bradlaugh, "Regulation by Statute of the Hours of Adult Labour," *F.R.* 279 (March 1890), 440–54; Thomas Burt, "Mr. Chamberlain's Program," *Nineteenth Century* 190 (December 1892), 868; Frederic Harrison, "The New Trades-Unionism," *Nineteenth Century* 153 (November 1889), 721–32.

60. "The Liberal Creed," 468. Also R. B. Haldane, "The Eight Hours Question," *Contemporary Review* 57 (February 1890), 240–55.

61. Arnold Morley to Gladstone, September 24, 1890, Gladstone Papers, 44,254; *The Speaker*, November 15, 1890.

it troubled them; and clearly it was an issue that set at odds the interests of capital and labor. As such, the eight-hour day hit at the structural weakness in Radicalism and foretold the end of the old alliance.

The debate within Radicalism over the Radical program after 1886 shows it was not Home Rule, but the nature of Radicalism itself, that limited the formulation of Radical policies. The movement seemed to be pulling and straining against its own tradition and social structure in a vain attempt to change; but at least the attempt was progressive, not backward. Moreover, as one might expect from the larger proportion of Radicals within the parliamentary Liberal party and their increased influence in party organizations, the Radical program after 1886 enjoyed greater support within Liberal circles than ever before. The Liberal party systematically adopted Radical policies between 1886 and 1892; and insofar as the involvement with Home Rule affected this process, it caused Liberals, in search of support, to accept Radical policies they might otherwise have avoided for years.

There can be no question that the Liberal leaders had their eyes open when they adopted the full load of Radical nostrums. From 1886 on, the officers of the Federation would through regional meetings gather the proposals espoused by advanced Liberals in each area and put them in resolutions passed at the annual Federation conference. Parliamentary leaders attended the conferences and in the prevailing spirit of unity and enthusiasm endorsed the program: in 1887 it was Welsh disestablishment, London municipal amalgamation, abolition of the legislative power of the House of Lords, and equalization of real and personal property taxes;[62] in 1888, the Federation added one man one vote, taxation of ground rents and mining royalties, better housing for the working classes, shorter parliaments, and public payment of election expenses.[63] In 1889 came payment of M.P.'s, "the free breakfast table," Scottish disestablishment, and local option for the sale of liquor.[64] From 1889 through 1893 the

62. National Liberal Federation, *Tenth Annual Report, 1887,* 17–25.
63. National Liberal Federation, *Eleventh Annual Meeting, 1888,* 6–9.
64. National Liberal Federation, *Proceedings of the Twelfth Annual Meeting, 1889* (London, 1890), 6–10.

list of policies remained substantially the same.[65] The 1894 conference added support for an employers' liability bill already passed by the House of Commons.[66] The 1895 meeting changed the order of proposals by moving reform of the House of Lords to a position second only to Home Rule, which took first place every year; otherwise the program was not changed.[67] The National Liberal Federation, it seems plain, had been transformed into an agency for converting the well-established goals of Radicalism into official party policy by the need to associate Home Rule with the desires of the most active and numerous section of the party.

Consider also the leadership of the parliamentary Liberal party. The key men from 1886 to 1895 were Gladstone, Harcourt, John Morley, and Arnold Morley. Of these John and Arnold Morley as Radicals had long advocated the old Radical policies and easily accepted most of the new ones. Harcourt, by birth and temperament more Whig than Radical, through most of his career moved to the left to keep up with party opinion. Caring little for Home Rule, he frequently urged his colleagues to adopt Radical policies to offset the unpopularity of the Irish.[68] At the Federation conference in 1894 Harcourt went so far as to declare himself a "new Radical" and explicitly accept the complete Radical program.[69]

Even Gladstone accepted most of the Radical policies. Inasmuch as he was seventy-seven years old in 1886, Gladstone insisted that Radical proposals would have to be managed and carried by younger men. He did not, however, stand in the way of the party's acceptance of them. He wrote Harcourt in 1886: "I will not break with the 200 (the Federation) or the Radical section of them if I can help it. But I am rather too old to put on a new suit of clothes."[70] Yet put

65. National Liberal Federation, *Proceedings of the Thirteenth Annual Meeting, 1890* (London, n.d.), 10–11; *Proceedings of the Fourteenth Annual Meeting, 1891,* 7–8; *Proceedings of the Fifteenth Annual Meeting, 1893* (London, 1893), 6.

66. National Liberal Federation, *Proceedings of the Sixteenth Annual Meeting, 1894* (London, 1894), 5.

67. National Liberal Federation, *Proceedings of the Seventeenth Annual Meeting, 1895* (London, 1895), 5–7.

68. Harcourt to Gladstone, July 16, 1892, quoted in Gardiner, *Harcourt*, II, 179.

69. National Liberal Federation, *Proceedings of the Sixteenth Annual Meeting, 1894,* 72.

70. November 16, 1886, quoted in Gardiner, *Harcourt*, II, 12.

on a new suit of clothes he did. After coaching by Arnold Morley, the Grand Old Man accepted the Radical program as it stood at the Federation conference of 1887.[71] During 1888 he introduced into the House of Commons a motion to equalize death duties on real and personal property, and spoke and voted for payment of members.[72] In November 1888 he strongly advocated one man one vote.[73] In 1890 he adopted Scottish disestablishment.[74] And in 1891, by endorsing the Newcastle Programme, Gladstone accepted a strong Radical scheme of proposals.[75] This is not the record of a man chaining Radicals to a moderate Liberal policy.

It is clear, then, that the Radicals gained influence within the Liberal party as a result of Home Rule. It may seem strange, by modern standards, that such moderate and unadventuresome people were regarded by themselves and others in the late 1880's and early 1890's as Radicals; but the evidence clearly shows that they were. Radicalism had not changed in essentials since the 1860's and 1870's. However, neither had Radicalism been dampened. And, despite the setback in 1886 and the loss of Chamberlain, Home Rule on balance contributed to Radical power. The years from 1886 to 1895 undeniably were a period when Radicals began to lose the allegiance of some working-class and socialist leaders. The point to remember is that it was not the Radicals' involvement with Home Rule which caused them to turn a deaf ear to the new voices. Rather, it is that to listen would have required Radicals to violate the basic preconceptions and power arrangements within their own movement. Radicals would have had to alter their ultimate goals and ignore the interests of main elements in their alliance to accept the outlook and programs of people with a completely different orientation and class identity. Few political movements have ever made such a fundamental adjustment. Home Rule had vitally affected the *history*, but not the *nature*, of British Radicalism. None of these ob-

71. Arnold Morley to Gladstone, October 4, 8, 15, 1887, Gladstone Papers, 44,253; National Liberal Federation, *Tenth Annual Report, 1887,* 67–75.

72. Hamilton Diaries, April 25, July 11, 1888, 48,648, 48,649.

73. Hamilton Diaries, November 6, 1888, 48,649.

74. Morgan, *Wales in British Politics,* 82–90.

75. National Liberal Federation, *Proceedings of the Fourteenth Annual Meeting, 1891,* 100–115.

servations is meant to argue that Radicals after 1886 did not debate their commitment to Home Rule, or the rank it should have in the Radical program, or the alliance with the Parnellites. Indeed, an agrarian policy of the nationalists called the Plan of Campaign would seriously test the Radical sense of political morality. These were important issues—ones that largely formed the history of Radicalism from 1886 to 1895, the period of cooperation with Irish nationalism.

CHAPTER SEVEN

The Struggle for Home Rule
1886-92

The commitment of the Liberal party to Home Rule opened a period of good will between the heart of that party, Radicalism, and Irish nationalism. The politics of cooperation replaced the politics of confrontation. The activities of Gladstone and the Liberal leadership in the new situation are a fairly well known story; what is not so well known is that Radicals, particularly the parliamentary elite, were an extraordinarily important factor in the new equation. Besides Gladstone's continuing determination to stay active, the most significant conditions of Liberal politics after 1886 were, first, the predominance of Radicalism within the Liberal party, and second, the commitment of all but a handful of Radicals to the alliance with Irish nationalism. For Ireland the question would be whether in the long run the predominance of Radicals and the theme of cooperation would serve nationalism as well as confrontation had. Would the Radicals maintain their attachment to Home Rule when the nationalists no longer exerted the pressure so important in the preceding decade? For Radicals, this same question also had significant implications. Would they open their program and ideology enough to integrate Irish self-rule into the Radical persuasion? Would they be able to reconcile their new commitment to Home Rule with the continuing desire to implement their domestic program?

I. THE GENERAL ELECTION OF 1886 AND THE CRUSADE FOR HOME RULE

At first the answer to these questions seemed affirmative. The general election of 1886, which immediately followed the defeat of the Home Rule bill, was very bitterly fought. Though the Gladstonians suffered a severe defeat (316 Conservatives and 78 Liberal Unionists, against 191 Liberals and 85 Irish nationalists), the electoral effort contributed to the determination of all Liberals,* including Radicals, to support the claims of Irish nationalism. Only in Wales, where local issues of land and disestablishment were important, did any subject but Home Rule play a significant part. The Radical Home Rulers followed Gladstone in refusing to tie themselves to the details of the 1886 bill, but their advocacy of Irish self-rule was nonetheless vigorous. Temporarily putting aside their interest in domestic reforms, most Radicals went so far as to contend that Home Rule and Radicalism were one and the same. As in the Home Rule parliament, they argued simply that there were no choices except Home Rule and coercion, and no Radical would tolerate the latter.[1]

The struggle between the Liberal Unionists and Radicals was particularly severe. Liberal Unionists contested about eighty seats against Radicals, and were successful in nearly twenty. In all of these contests there were battles for control over local machinery, appeals by both sides to the same traditionally Liberal groups, and mutual accusations of disloyalty and betrayal. Liberal Unionist candidates utilized arguments especially embarrassing to Radicals—that the Gladstonians had tried to bribe Irish landlords with the policy of land purchase, that they wanted to sacrifice Irish Protestants, and that they would not support for Ulster the same kind of claims to self-determination they recognized for the rest of Ireland. No less bitterly, Radicals accused the Liberal Unionists of splitting Liberalism for the sake of a repressive policy, and Chamberlain in particular of taking up Unionism for reasons of purely personal ambition.[2]

The extreme hostility generated by the general election hardened the lines of the Home Rule dispute and raised mountainous obstacles

---

* Hereafter "Liberal" is used to mean "Gladstonian Liberal."

1. For example, the speech by Randal Cremer at Shoreditch, *The Times*, June 29, 1886; and *The Nonconformist and Independent*, June 17, 1886.

2. *The Nonconformist and Independent*, June 17, 1886; *Congregationalist*, July 1886.

to reunion within the Liberal party. The advantages of reunion were obvious, but many Radicals felt so embittered by the election that they desired to confront, not conciliate, the Liberal Unionists. Labouchere, among others, urged Gladstone to stay in office, bring in a "big Radical programme," and force the Liberal Unionists to show their colors.[3] Gladstone toyed with the idea, but with the advice of Morley, decided that the Tories, who would inevitably form a government and assume responsibility for Ireland, should have as much time as possible before winter brought its usual difficulties to Ireland to develop their policy.[4] Many Radicals were disappointed; to them the road back to power seemed long indeed.[5]

For a few Radicals, the quickest way to regain control of the House of Commons was to sandwich Home Rule between Radical policies: the electorate, which clearly did not like Home Rule, would still vote for Radicals if they avoided Irish issues.[6] The idea of connecting Home Rule to a Radical program was an obvious tactic, but for most Radicals it was not to be a matter of playing down the commitment to Irish self-rule. In 1886 and the next few years, a majority of Radicals opted for a bold and direct effort to persuade Britain to accept Home Rule. In a belligerent frame of mind after the general election, they concluded that Home Rule had done remarkably well in the constituencies, and that the conversion of a relatively small number of voters by the time of the next general election would suffice to carry Home Rule to victory. Besides, the irrefutable demand by more than 80 percent of Ireland's M.P.'s still compelled support for Home Rule.[7] Thus the Radicals entered into a crusade lasting several years to demonstrate the sub-

3. Labouchere to H. Gladstone, July 9, 1886, Viscount Gladstone Papers, 46,016; T. Wemyss Reid to H. Gladstone, July 13, 1886, Viscount Gladstone Papers, 46,041.

4. Hamilton Diaries, July 14, 16, 1886, 48,644; Morley to Gladstone, July 19, 1886, Gladstone Papers, 44,255.

5. Labouchere to H. Gladstone, July 28, 1886, Viscount Gladstone Papers, 46,016.

6. Labouchere to H. Gladstone, July 28, 1886, Viscount Gladstone Papers, 46,016; Andrew Reid, ed., *The New Liberal Programme*, 172–73.

7. Arthur Arnold, "The Answer to Mr. Gladstone," *F.R.* 226 (August 1886), 244–48; J. Guinness Rogers, "The Fray—and Afterwards," *Contemporary Review* 50 (August 1886), 169–84; E. A. Freeman, "Prospects of Home Rule," *F.R.* 237 (September 1886), 317–30.

stantial support Home Rule already possessed even in England and to familiarize the rest of the electorate with the arguments for Irish self-rule. Of course, Gladstone provided the heavy artillery in the Home Rule campaign. But the Grand Old Man could not have won many battles without the Radicals as his army. Periodically the Liberal party managers persuaded him to issue forth from Hawarden Castle and fire a few salvoes at the Unionist fortress, but the skirmishers and the siege troops came from Radicalism.

The crusade began even as the final election results were coming in. In July 1886 Gladstone asked James Bryce, already a well-known historian, to supervise the preparation and publication of a substantial historical and philosophical case for Home Rule.[8] Bryce quickly accepted the task and conferred with John Morley, Shaw Lefevre, Sir Charles Russell (the noted Irish Liberal attorney), E. R. Russell (Radical M.P. and editor of the *Liverpool Daily Post*), Barry O'Brien (an Irish nationalist historian and publicist, later the biographer of Parnell), and Malcolm MacColl (Canon of Ripon and friend of Gladstone). The result of their planning was two books, one a dull, straightforward narrative history of Ireland, the other a volume containing eleven articles and entitled the *Home Rule Handbook*.[9] The *Handbook*, published in time for the 1887 conference of the National Liberal Federation, eventually sold perhaps 15,000 copies. Even as a work of propaganda it was not of very great quality, but it did contain two impressive contributions: Bryce's accurate and dispassionate history of the Liberal party's slow and reluctant movement toward Home Rule, and Morley's eminently practical discussion of the relations between England and Ireland. The *Handbook* was the most important single Liberal publication in the decade after 1886, but it was not by a long way the only piece of official Liberal literature for Home Rule. As chairman of the supervisory committee of the Liberal Publication Department, Bryce

---

8. Gladstone to Bryce, July 8, 1886, Bryce Papers, MS 10.

9. James Bryce, ed., *Handbook of Home Rule*, 2nd ed. (London, 1887); *Two Centuries of Irish History, 1691–1870* (London, 1888). The counterpart to these publications was more tightly argued: A. V. Dicey, *England's Case against Home Rule* (London, 1886). For the *Handbook*'s sales: Bryce to Gladstone, November 5, 1887, Bryce Papers, MS 11.

arranged that about half of all party publications between 1886 and 1892 dealt with Home Rule.[10] A substantial number of these were aimed at persuading the English workingmen that Home Rule would have beneficial effects for their specific interests.[11] These leaflets and pamphlets represented the Liberal and Radical concern not to ignore Home Rule, but to link it to existing Radical goals.

The National Liberal Federation played a very important role in the official party crusade. Some Liberals after the defeat in 1886 wanted the Federation to moderate its stand on Home Rule and the alliance with Irish nationalism. However, at the annual conference of 1886 in Leeds, a great majority of the delegates, the bulk of these being ardent Radicals, wanted to put forth a hard line for Home Rule. Their policy easily carried the day, and as its first substantive resolution the Federation declared that Gladstone's Irish policy should be pursued until successful, and that any Irish settlement would have to meet the "views and wishes" of the Irish representatives.[12] By this action the Federation defiantly opted for a policy of extensive rather than limited Home Rule, deliberately supported Gladstone as against Chamberlain and Hartington, and pledged to keep the Parnellite alliance. During the following year the Federation staged an impressive series of demonstrations designed both to whip up enthusiasm for Home Rule and to associate the Irish policy with standard Radical issues. There were nine of these regional conferences in England and Wales. At each one a carefully coached speaker chosen by the central party offices spoke for Home Rule and the reforms especially desired by Liberals and Radicals of that area. In November 1886, for example, Asquith was the main speaker at a conference in Leicester of the Liberal associations of the Midland counties. He took as his subjects Home Rule and reform of the electoral registration laws. In Rhyl, Mundella spoke to the Liberals of

10. See the publications by the Liberal Publications Department, *Pamphlets and Leaflets, 1887–1892*. The Bryce Papers include many of these, but an even more complete set is in the George Howell Collection in the Bishopsgate Institute.

11. Examples are: Liberal Publications Department, "Home Rule and English Labour and Trade" (London, n.d.), Leaflet no. 1516; and "Working men and the Liberal Party" (London, n.d.), Leaflet no. 1534.

12. National Liberal Federation, *Ninth Annual Report, 1886*, 7; Hamilton Diaries, November 2, 5, 1886, 48,645.

North Wales about Home Rule plus disestablishment of the Church in Wales and a Welsh "three F" bill.[13] In raising the morale of Radicals, as well as in promoting Radical policies to official Liberal party rank, these demonstrations achieved much success. In recognition of this fact, Gladstone made his observation at the Federation conference in 1887 that Radicalism would emerge greatly strengthened from the campaign for Home Rule.

Yet for many Radicals the official party crusade for Home Rule was not enough. A number of Radical M.P.'s in February 1886 had founded the British Home Rule Association to publicize the argument for Home Rule while the bill was still before the House of Commons. It staged some fifty demonstrations and distributed 250,000 pamphlets, including 35,000 copies of a speech by Joseph Cowen. At the end of the general election of 1886 members of the National Liberal Club in London (primarily a social organization of provincial Radicals) formed the United Kingdom Home Rule League. Led by Professor Thorold Rogers, a noted Radical political economist, the League distributed nearly 100,000 leaflets, pamphlets, and handbills. In December 1886 these organizations joined a committee of pro–Home Rule M.P.'s led by Professor James Stuart in founding the Home Rule Union. Directed by a number of rather extreme Radicals—James Stansfeld, Thorold Rogers, B. J. S. Coleridge, C. A. V. Conybeare, Charles Bradlaugh, E. H. Pickersgill, L. A. Atherley-Jones (son of the Chartist Ernest Jones), and Handel Cossham—the Union embarked on an educational campaign patterned after the Anti–Corn Law League. E. J. C. Morton, a young Radical barrister who won a seat in the Commons in 1892, devised a course of lectures to be presented throughout Britain. Subcommittees in many constituencies were formed which could obtain the lecture material from the central headquarters and present the course themselves, or get one of a number of paid lecturers to deliver the course, complete with syllabuses. In the first months alone the Union had presented 120 lectures, most of them in London and southwest England, where James Stuart was very active. The

13. Watson, *The National Liberal Federation from Its Commencement to the General Elections of 1906*, 65–69; National Liberal Federation, *Tenth Annual Report, 1887*, 17–25.

Union also distributed pamphlets and leaflets. In 1887 it obtained financial aid from the headquarters of the Liberal party. To solidify relations with the Parnellites, the Union organized and helped finance visits to Ireland by British M.P.'s.[14]

The crusade for Home Rule won impressive results. It demonstrated to the Irish nationalists that Gladstone was far from alone in support of Home Rule, that the bulk of Radicals were enthusiastic in the Irish cause, and that as Radicalism advanced, so would the chances of Home Rule. In Britain the effects of the campaign were more tangible. It reassured Liberals and Radicals that advocacy of Home Rule would not entail political isolation and sure defeat. It familiarized the British public with the concept of Irish self-rule as something less than revolution. And it countered the argument of the Liberal Unionists that Liberal involvement with Home Rule would necessarily put off Radical reforms indefinitely. By-election results quickly began to go favorably for the Home Rulers. By 1892 the Unionist majority had been reduced from 115 to 67; most of the accessions to the Liberal side were Radical M.P.'s.

Probably the most important immediate effect of the crusade for Home Rule had to do with possibilities for reunion of the Liberal party. In one sense, the attempt to reunite the party—known as the Round Table Conference—was a function of the crusade for Home Rule itself; that is, the Gladstonians moved toward reunion only when they had built their own confidence to the point at which they could engage in discussions with the Liberal Unionists without feeling that they were surrendering to Chamberlain. The Round Table Conference, therefore, took place in conditions not conducive to compromise by Gladstonians. As far as Radicals were concerned, the main object of any reunion would be to get Liberal and Radical Unionists to give up their opposition to Home Rule, though many of them were willing to devise a formula to allow the enemy to give in gracefully. The Whigs were not to be included, for Morley alone among the Radicals wanted to bring them back

14. Home Rule Union, *Report of the Home Rule Union, 1886* (London, 1887); Home Rule Union, *Lecture Scheme of the Home Rule Union* (London, n.d.); *The Times*, December 10, 1886, February 25, 1887, February 11, 1888.

into the party.[15] As for Chamberlain, the Radicals were angry with his behavior, and confident enough of their own position to feel that the Liberal party could get along without him. Radicals would agree to discussions with him to receive his surrender or to keep up conciliatory appearances, but not otherwise.[16]

On the Liberal Unionist side there was also little desire for compromise. Hartington never showed any desire for reunion. His main objective was to keep close ties to Chamberlain so that Liberal Unionism could sustain itself as a viable popular force.[17] Chamberlain did not intend to give up his position of June 1886, but he did have difficulties in keeping the allegiance of a significant number of moderate Liberal and Radical Unionists. He felt that he could wait until Gladstone had passed from the scene without giving in to Home Rule, if he could restrain the Conservative government from acting illiberally and above all maintain a strong base of support among Birmingham Radicals.[18] It was the increasing trouble he met in doing both of these things that resulted in the Round Table Conference. The precipitating event was the resignation from the cabinet of Lord Randolph Churchill, who was Chamberlain's hope for liberality in the Conservative party. When some of the Birmingham Radical Unionists became restless, Chamberlain dropped an obvious hint about reunion in a speech on December 23. Although neither Gladstone nor the Radicals intended to give up anything of significance in their policy, the Liberal leaders agreed to meet Chamberlain.[19]

15. Labouchere to H. Gladstone, August 3, 1886, Viscount Gladstone Papers, 46,016. This account of the Round Table Conference throughout relies heavily on Michael Hurst's exhaustive study, *Joseph Chamberlain and Liberal Reunion*.

16. See the speech by Labouchere, *The Times*, November 25, 1886, and his letter to a correspondent, *The Times*, December 8, 1886; T. Wemyss Reid to H. Gladstone, August 5, 1886, Viscount Gladstone Papers, 46,041; Morley to Gladstone, September 3, 1886, Gladstone Papers, 44,255; and A. Morley to Gladstone, December 17, 1886, Gladstone Papers, 44,253.

17. Hartington to Salisbury, July 24, 1886, quoted in Holland, *Life of Devonshire*, II, 170–71.

18. Hurst, *Chamberlain and Liberal Reunion*, Ch. 1; Dilke Diary, October 1, December 17, 1886, 43,927.

19. Hurst, *Chamberlain and Liberal Reunion*, 79–81, 97–110; A. Morley to Gladstone, December 24, 1886, Gladstone Papers, 44,253; *Daily News*, December 24, 1886; J. Morley to Gladstone, December 24, 1886, Gladstone Papers, 44,255.

The Round Table conferees—Chamberlain, Trevelyan, Morley, Harcourt, and Farrer Herschell (a moderate Liberal barrister)—met three times early in 1887. The first two meetings were quite friendly and seemed to make good progress toward reunion, but the third was a disaster. The reason for the collapse, as Michael Hurst has shown, is that neither side would surrender on the important points.[20] Between the second and third meetings, various excitable Radicals, most notably Henry Labouchere, made it clear that they would accept Chamberlain back into the party only after he admitted to a grave mistake.[21] The third session focused on the big issues—separate treatment for Ulster, control over the Irish judiciary, and exclusion of the Irish M.P.'s from Westminster—and got nowhere. Chamberlain responded to his opponents' hostility with his letter to *The Baptist*, already referred to, in which he argued that all Liberal reforms would be postponed as long as the party adhered to Home Rule.[22] This hit the Liberals, and especially the Radical section, where it hurt. After an acrimonious exchange of letters by Chamberlain and Harcourt, one of the few Gladstonians genuinely to favor reunion, the Round Table ended.

The Round Table Conference had caused a great stir but had come to nothing. The only significant result was Trevelyan's dismay over Chamberlain's behavior. He concluded that Chamberlain had not met the Gladstonians fairly, and in April 1887, when the Conservatives had introduced a coercion bill, he returned to the party.[23] But Chamberlain's personal behavior was not really the cause of the

20. Hurst, *Chamberlain and Liberal Reunion*.

21. *The Times*, January 15, 21, 1887.

22. Hurst says that F. H. Stockwell, editor of *The Baptist*, asked Chamberlain to reply to a public letter written by Gladstone, in which the Grand Old Man had said that the Liberal Unionists were delaying passage of vital reforms by their resistance to Home Rule. (*Chamberlain and Liberal Reunion*, 277–79.) Apparently Hurst took his information from Chamberlain's *Political Memoir*. *The Baptist* itself does not support Hurst's account. The editor published on February 18 a leading article urging Gladstone to take up Welsh disestablishment immediately; on February 25, *The Baptist* included a reply from Gladstone, and the article by Chamberlain. There is no evidence that either Gladstone or Chamberlain had seen the other's letter. See the explanation in *The Baptist*, March 11, 1887. See also Chamberlain to Bunce, January 25, 1887, quoted in Fraser, *Chamberlain*, 134.

23. Trevelyan to Halley Stewart, printed in full in the *Daily News*, June 29, 1887. Also: Hamilton Diaries, March 25, 1887, 48,646.

Round Table's failure. The two sides in the Home Rule controversy had invested too much emotion and pride for them to compromise. In fact, for the history of Radicalism the meaning of the Round Table episode lies in the Radicals' unflinching attitude. By early 1887 the crusade for Home Rule was well under way, and Radicals were committing large amounts of time and energy and intellect to Home Rule—so much that they could turn aside the blandishments of their former leader.

II. THE PLAN OF CAMPAIGN AND COERCION

In the meantime the agrarian problem in Ireland—that seemingly inexhaustible source of trouble—was reasserting itself. In 1885 and 1886 the prices of Irish produce fell sharply. By one estimate, corn prices dropped 30 or 40 percent; those of other crops and cattle by 20 or 30 percent.[24] The Land Commission responded by setting judicial rents in 1886 20 percent lower than the previous year. The vast majority of tenants, however, could not qualify for rent reductions by the Commission. In England landlords generally abated rents because of the collapse in prices, but in Ireland many (though not all) demanded the full amount. Hundreds of evictions of helpless tenants followed, with the prospect of even more in the winter of 1886–87. The Conservative Chief Secretary, Sir Michael Hicks Beach, developed a hearty dislike for Irish landlords and brought what pressure he could on them to reduce rents; in a few cases he refused to support evictions with the constabulary or the army. But he was unable to persuade the cabinet to amend the land law.[25]

Parnell came forward with a moderate plan. With the advice of Morley and Harcourt, the nationalist leader introduced a bill into the House in September 1886 that would have admitted leaseholders to the land act of 1881 and would have suspended evictions of tenants who paid half the arrears and rent.[26] The Radicals unani-

---

24. Eversley, *Gladstone and Ireland*, 316.

25. L. P. Curtis, Jr., *Coercion and Conciliation in Ireland, 1880–1892: A Study in Conservative Unionism* (Princeton, 1963), 120–37.

26. Initially Parnell wanted to introduce a more extreme bill, but Harcourt and Morley persuaded him to come forward with the moderate one. Morley to Glad-

mously supported Parnell's bill. They argued as Parnell himself did—that agricultural prices had fallen so low, eviction and agrarian crimes would inevitably follow unless the government took immediate action.[27] But the government refused the bill; eviction and disturbances did follow.

Meanwhile, the tenantry had already begun to devise its own scheme of averting eviction. In Galway the tenantry on the estates of Lord Clanricarde had requested abatement of their rents, which were among the highest in Ireland. Clanricarde, generally regarded by contemporaries as the worst of Irish landlords, instructed his agent to refuse. Tenants on his Woodford estate thereupon agreed among themselves to pay no rent until Clanricarde consented to a reduction. Evictions followed, during which some tenants defended their fortified cottages with ingenious weapons, including boiling water. After the defeat of Parnell's tenant relief bill, several leaders of the National League—most notably Timothy Harrington, John Dillon, and William O'Brien—urged the tenants at Woodford and elsewhere to apply systematically the idea of combination to reduce rents. They promulgated their scheme, known as the Plan of Campaign, in *United Ireland* in October 1886. According to the plan, the tenants would collectively offer the landlord a reduced rent; if he refused, they would pay their rents into a fund which would be used to support those evicted on the estate. Dillon and O'Brien spread the idea of the plan throughout the depressed areas of Ireland. In 1886–87 tenants on eighty-four estates followed the idea, and sixty of these exacted abatements from the landlords. In many cases tenants accompanied the plan with intimidation, boycotting, and violence against other tenants who refused to cooperate or who rented the land of evicted men.[28]

As a conspiracy against payment of rent, the Plan of Campaign broke the letter of the law. Moreover, it clearly inspired other crimes. But in spirit it resembled a trades union strike, which was protected by law. Moderate Liberals condemned the plan. Gladstone refused

---

stone, September 4, 10, 1886, Gladstone Papers, 44,255; *Hansard* 309 (September 20, 1886), 984–1000.

27. *Hansard* 309 (September 21, 1886), 1133–44, 1165–70, 1247–51.

28. Eversley, *Gladstone and Ireland*, 324–25; Lyons, *Dillon*, Ch. 4.

to give "the slightest countenance to illegality." "We too suffer under the power of the landlords," he wrote Morley, "but we cannot adopt this as a method of breaking it."[29] Among the Radicals, who had long condemned landlords and supported the right of workers to combine for collective bargaining, there was more diversity of opinion. At one extreme there were those like Samuel Storey, who felt as a Nonconformist that the plan was immoral as well as illegal.[30] Morley also disapproved of the plan, on grounds that it would alienate English opinion.[31] At the other extreme, libertarians like Labouchere, Coleridge, and Conybeare believed that the plan was both legally and morally justifiable. They preached civil disobedience for the tenantry: the laws of land tenure in Ireland were unjust; therefore they should not be obeyed.[32] Most Radicals stood between these extremes. They regretted the intimidation that seemed to accompany the plan, but they thought it natural and understandable for the tenants to combine against unreasonable landlords. To them the plan was legally wrong but morally right. For one old Radical, Samuel Laing, the plan in this way even resembled the American underground railway.[33]

The plight of the tenantry and the Plan of Campaign generated a remarkable wave of sympathy among Radicals for the Irish people. The Conservative government's reaction to the plan only strengthened this tendency. Early in 1887 the government introduced a stringent coercion bill into parliament. Probably the most severe in the long line of repressive acts by which Britain ruled Ireland in the nineteenth century, the new bill would give the Irish executive the power to stop public meetings at will, allow the state prosecutors extensive change of venue powers, provide that cases involving major crimes be tried before "special" juries (men known to be

29. December 8, 1886, Gladstone Papers, 44,255.

30. *Hansard* 310 (February 10, 1887), 1162–75.

31. Morley to Gladstone, December 7, 1886, Gladstone Papers, 44,255.

32. Speeches by Labouchere in *Hansard* 310 (January 31, 1887), 351–60, and in *The Times*, December 18, 22, 1886; speech by Coleridge in *Hansard* 310 (February 9, 1887), 1025–31; and a speech by Conybeare in *The Times*, March 7, 1887.

33. Campbell-Bannerman to Gladstone, December 8, 1886, Gladstone Papers, 44,117; Laing, "The Plan of Campaign," *Contemporary Review* 51 (April 1887), 577–84.

favorable to the government), and grant stipendiary magistrates summary authority over lesser offenses. Unlike earlier coercive statutes, it was to be a permanent part of Irish law. Here was what Salisbury called "twenty years of resolute government" with a vengeance.

Liberals and Radicals fought the bill almost as desperately as did the nationalists themselves. They argued incessantly that the land-lords, not the tenants, caused the turmoil in Ireland; that coercion would only increase disorder; that the bill would establish a tyranny in Ireland; and that it was designed simply to wring from the tenants unjust and impossible rents.[34] Radical associations held demonstrations in most big cities. In London there was a gathering in Hyde Park of 40,000 to 50,000 people, representing Liberal associations, Radical clubs, temperance societies, socialist groups, and labor unions.[35] The National Liberal Federation called a special conference at Wolverhampton to protest the measure. As a display of unity among very different kinds of Radical organizations, the resistance to coercion was impressive; but as an attempt to stop the passage of the bill, it was a failure—on July 8, 1887, the measure won a third reading. But the struggle was only beginning.

Not only did the government pass a severely restrictive measure, but they also enforced it with stunning vigor. Arthur Balfour, nephew of Lord Salisbury, replaced Hicks Beach as Chief Secretary early in 1887. Much to everyone's surprise, the indolent and feline Balfour turned out to be an energetic and forceful administrator. Though he tried to accompany coercion with conciliatory gestures, he raised himself to a politician of the first rank by stern and unbending execution of the crimes act—earning for himself in the process the macabre title of "Bloody Balfour." He sought to restore confidence in the landlords and the Castle administration by giving unquestioning support to property rights and to the decisions of his police and magistrates. He prosecuted leading nationalists like Dillon and O'Brien. He outlawed the National League. He stopped the publication of newspapers that carried accounts of the League's meetings. He supported eviction procedures with large numbers of troops,

34. For example, *Hansard* 313 (April 5, 1887), 577–78.
35. *Daily News* and *The Times*, April 12, 1887.

some equipped with battering rams. The object of all this was to shore up faith in law and order, but the evicted tenants felt with some justice that under Balfour there was more order than law.[36]

Gladstone and the Radicals resisted Balfour's administration of the coercion law at every step, moderate Liberals taking a less active role. The Radicals especially made the case of the nationalists their own, and their old concern for authority seemed entirely gone. They staged hundreds of demonstrations in Britain and passed countless resolutions.[37] Some of them joined the National League. When Balfour proclaimed the League illegal, about fifty Radical M.P.'s plus a few others formally declared their confidence in the legality and constitutionality of the League and its activities.[38] Most strikingly, Radicals of the Home Rule Union and other organizations sent numerous deputations to visit Ireland and appear at nationalist rallies. In 1887 and 1888 Ireland swarmed with Radicals. In the autumn and winter of 1887 ten different delegations numbering some forty Radical M.P.'s toured the country. One M.P., H. J. Wilson, made nine trips from 1887 through 1889. Whenever the Plan of Campaign clashed with the government, Radicals inevitably appeared. In September 1887 Labouchere, J. E. Ellis (a Quaker colliery owner), and J. T. Brunner (the alkalai manufacturer) saw at Mitchelstown riots in which five men were killed by police gunfire.[39] In Tipperary in 1891 John Morley witnessed a police assault on a crowd at the trial of Dillon and O'Brien.[40] Others were followed by the police and experienced baton charges first hand.[41] Some of these men were extremists like Conybeare and Labouchere, but most of them were respectable businessmen like Joshua Rowntree, Alfred Illingworth, and Briggs Priestley. Together they represented both

36. For differing views of Balfour's term as Chief Secretary, see Curtis, *Coercion and Concilliation*, and Lyons, *Dillon*, Ch. 4.

37. For example: resolutions passed at the National Liberal Federation conference in 1887; *Tenth Annual Report, 1887*, 8; and the account of a demonstration in Trafalgar Square in *The Times*, August 29, 1887.

38. *Freeman's Journal*, August 23, 26, 1887.

39. *The Times*, September 12, 1887; Thorold, *Labouchere*, 331–35.

40. *The Times*, March 26, 31, 1891; *Hansard* 350 (February 6, 1891), 691–711.

41. H. J. Wilson to his wife and family, undated (early April 1888); April 4, 1888; March 14, 1889; all in Wilson Papers, Sheffield Central Library, MD 2564-16, 17, 38.

a remarkable outpouring of sympathy by Radicalism for Ireland, and the substitution of civil liberty for social discipline in Ireland as a prime Radical objective.

Balfour and other Unionists thought that the Radicals who came to Ireland contributed to disorder by inspiring the tenantry to crime.[42] To a limited extent, the accusation was true. Radicals certainly encouraged Irishmen to demonstrate their right to hold orderly public meetings, even when those meetings had been prohibited by legal authorities. In a few cases Radicals did in fact advise the Irish, if not to commit outrages, at least to resist coercion and eviction and to sustain the Plan of Campaign. In County Limerick, for example, Professor James Stuart urged the tenants to continue their combination against the landlords, to refuse to pay more than fair rents, and to boycott anyone who took a farm from which a tenant had been evicted.[43] At Woodford, on the Clanricarde estates, James Rowlands, an advanced New Radical M.P. from London, and Wilfrid Blunt, the Tory Home Ruler and poet, deliberately participated in a "proclaimed" demonstration. (For his sins, Blunt was knocked down and arrested by the police.[44]) However, in general the Radical visitors clearly advised their Irish audiences to avoid violence. They stressed the importance to the future of Home Rule of forsaking crime, and they hoped that their presence would show the Irish that they had genuine British allies and so keep them from acts of desperation.[45]

Two of the Radicals who visited Ireland merit special attention. The first of these was Charles Augustus Vansittart Conybeare, graduate of Christ Church, Oxford, barrister, and M.P. for a Cornwall constituency. Naturally an intemperate man, Conybeare was one of the first Radical M.P.'s to make the Irish tour, and he was always

42. Irish Loyal and Patriotic Union, *The Latest Invasion of Ireland* (London, 1888).
43. *The Times*, September 28, 1887.
44. *The Times*, October 24, 1887.
45. Home Rule Union, *Report of the Deputation to Ireland* (London, 1887), 5–20; circular from Alfred Illingworth to other Liberal M.P.'s, October 31, 1887, Wilson Papers, Sheffield Central Library, MD 2564-37; *The Times*, September 17, 20, October 17, 1887, for speeches and letters by E. H. Pickersgill, James Rowlands, and Philip Stanhope.

the most vociferous and irrational critic of coercion. (He told a Welsh audience that Balfour was "a cowardly bully and an unmanly poltroon.")[46] On all of his many trips to Ireland, he urged the tenants to defend themselves from eviction in any way they could. He supported his words with action. In August 1889 he and Henry Harrison, then an undergraduate at Balliol and later a defender of Parnell's honor, helped some tenants resist eviction. These people had fortified their cottages and had turned away even a police battering ram. By the time Conybeare arrived on the scene, the police were trying to starve out the tenants. He and Harrison, circling the cottages like Indians round a wagon train, managed to throw food into some of the cottages. The two were arrested and tried before a stipendiary magistrate. Despite Conybeare's impassioned self-defense, the magistrate found him guilty and sentenced him to three months in prison. Here Conybeare made himself a nuisance by complaining of both the cold in his cell and the heat in the exercise yard. Undaunted by imprisonment, he lifted a cry for the Plan of Campaign as he was leaving the prison, and for his trouble was detained an extra eight hours. He returned to London a hero among Radicals. Of course, it was a silly performance, but symbolic of the extent to which some Radicals took the Irish cause as their own.[47]

The other Radical of special note was Shaw Lefevre, an entirely different kind of man from Conybeare. Dispassionate, phlegmatic, and industrious, Shaw Lefevre had no intention of inciting anyone to violence. Yet he considered the Plan of Campaign a reasonable response by the tenantry to their miserable situation. During several of his investigations on various Plan of Campaign estates, he found that the tenants actually wanted a settlement. On three of the most important estates—those of Clanricarde, Massareene, and Vandaleur—one of the key obstacles to a solution was reinstatement of those already evicted. To Shaw Lefevre this seemed a relatively insignificant point, and he worked hard to persuade the landlords that the tenants should not have to renounce either the Plan of Campaign or their evicted brethren prior to settlement by arbitration.

46. *The Times*, November 9, 1887.

47. For the adventures of Conybeare, see *The Times*, April 26, 27, 30, May 2, 3, 7, August 20, 24, October 5, 7, 1889.

His efforts foundered on this difficulty, for he underestimated the strength of the landlords' belief that the plan was an illegal conspiracy. But his work was not all in vain. His tireless search for facts and his knowledge of the intricate details of land law enabled him to write two valuable accounts of Irish conditions: *Incidents of Coercion* (1888) and *Combination and Coercion* (1890). These small volumes helped publicize the unreasonableness of the most unyielding landlords and show the close connection between the Plan of Campaign and the government's coercive policy. More than any other Radical, Shaw Lefevre helped Englishmen understand the agrarian origins of Irish disorder.[48]

The number of Radicals visiting Ireland remained high through 1889, but it fell off rapidly in 1890. The reason for the decline is debatable. L. P. Curtis, Jr., has suggested that the imprisonment of Blunt and Conybeare discouraged Radicals from challenging the Irish executive.[49] No doubt this was true for some Radicals. But Blunt was arrested in 1887, and the number of British Home Rulers crossing to Ireland remained high for two more years. Conybeare was lionized by Radicals when he returned from prison, and some of the most important Radical delegations went to Ireland after his arrest. The visits probably declined partly because it was difficult to maintain such intense activity indefinitely. Mainly, however, it was because most of the tours were made in the autumn and winter of each year, in order to induce the tenantry to keep to nonviolent agitation during the hard winter months. By the autumn of 1890 Parnell's involvement in the O'Shea divorce trial had burst into the news, resulting in fierce fraternal strife among Irish nationalists, and in considerably dampened enthusiasm among Radicals.

What did the Radical struggle against coercion and the visits to Ireland accomplish? With their secure majority the Tory government defeated every motion of censure, every resolution, every attempt to block passage of the bill. The government with remarkable placidity carried out the crimes act and attacked the Plan of Campaign in spite of all the nationalists, Liberals, and Radicals could

48. G. J. Shaw Lefevre, *Incidents of Coercion: A Journal of Visits to Ireland in 1882 and 1888*, 3rd ed. (London, 1889); *Combination and Coercion* (London, 1890).
49. Curtis, *Coercion and Conciliation*, 255.

do. Nevertheless, the fight against coercion by the Radicals did have some significant results. It had a moderating effect within Dublin Castle. Especially in the legal department, Castle bureaucrats avoided where possible confrontation with the nationalists and their allies. The Parnellites felt that the presence of British M.P.'s tended to restrain the police at public meetings.[50] More important, the Radical efforts solidified the alliance between Liberals and Parnellites. The Irish were genuinely impressed by the behavior of the Radicals, and they gave up at least for a time the idea that the only concessions to be gained from Britain would come from Irish pressure. For a fleeting moment, many Irish patriots saw in Liberal and Radical opinion hope for real unity between the two countries.[51]

III. Difficulties of the Alliance with Nationalism

The alliance between the Liberal party and the Parnellites worked remarkably well from 1887 to 1890. Naturally, there were tensions within the entente, but the full commitment of Radicals to the Irish cause helped submerge differences between Liberalism and nationalism. Parnell also helped smooth over rough spots. His contribution was shown very clearly in connection with the land question. Parnell, as always, believed land purchase would provide the best solution to the perennial Irish land problem. Radicals who had been hurt in 1886 by Gladstone's land purchase bill were more determined than ever not to come to the landlords' aid by buying them out with state funds. The Conservatives, however, had found that the Ashbourne act (1885) had worked well, and in the autumn of 1886 proposed to extend its operations with another dose of British credit. Most Radicals immediately leaped to the attack, on grounds that the act was a risk to British funds and that it was very inconvenient to replace the landlords with the state.[52] Their reaction put Morley

50. H. J. Wilson to his family, April 7, 1888, Wilson Papers, Sheffield Central Library, MD 2564-13; Curtis, *Coercion and Conciliation*, 191-97.

51. For expressions of Irish feelings about the Radical visitors: *Freeman's Journal*, August 24, September 7, 9, 15, 1887; and Justin McCarthy, *An Irishman's Story* (New York, 1904), 308-10; O'Brien, *Parnell and His Party*, 226.

52. G. J. Shaw Lefevre, "The Liberal Split," *Nineteenth Century* 116 (October 1886), 592-608; *Hansard* 330 (November 20, 1886), 1698-1703, 1708-9, 1711-13.

and Gladstone in a quandary, for these two still believed that an Irish parliament could not function until the landlords had been bought out.[53] Parnell helped them out of the difficulty. He and his party argued, despite the advantages of the Tory proposal, that as purchase agreements would depend on rental rates, purchases made at the current inflated rents would overcompensate landlords. Thus, Radicals, Parnellites, and Gladstone together could support an amendment declaring that purchase should be postponed until problems of arrears and rents had been settled.[54] In essence, this was a policy of improving the land act of 1881, which had long been the object of the Radicals. Parnell accepted it in place of purchase as a temporary way to get some worthwhile reforms, yet satisfy the Radicals without repudiating Morley and Gladstone.[55]

Irish university education could have provided an even more divisive issue. In August 1889 the Tories let it be known that they liked the idea of a state-supported Catholic university in Ireland. The mere suggestion was like a red flag to Nonconformist Radical bulls. Morley wrote to Gladstone that on this subject Parnell naturally would take what he could get, but some of "our Radical friends will become restive."[56] Gladstone was sufficiently concerned to write Parnell a letter—one of the few times he did so. He asked Parnell to remember the Nonconformists: "They have strong Protestant prejudices, which, on the Irish Church question, and again (with some exceptions in England) on Home Rule they have nobly overcome."[57] No one knows what Parnell would have done; fortunately for the alliance, anti-Catholic prejudices within the Conservative party ended the threat before it became a practical issue.[58]

The zenith of Liberal-Parnellite unity came in relation to the Parnell Commission. In April 1887, on the day of the vote on the second

53. Gardiner, *Harcourt*, II, 8. Haldane and Grey also supported land purchase: *Hansard* 330 (November 20, 1888), 1668–75.

54. *Hansard* 330 (November 20, 1888), 1743–54, 1756–60.

55. Morley to Gladstone, October 28, 1888, Gladstone Papers, 44,255; Morley to Gladstone, April 2, 14, 1890, Gladstone Papers, 44,256; Gardiner, *Harcourt*, II, 65.

56. August 30, 1889, Gladstone Papers, 44,256.

57. August 30, 1889, quoted in Hammond, *Gladstone and the Irish Nation*, 645.

58. O'Brien, *Parnell and His Party*, 237.

reading of the coercion bill, *The Times* published one of a series of articles attempting to link Parnell with violent crime in Ireland. This article even carried a facsimile letter, supposedly written by Parnell, which declared that Undersecretary Burke had got what he deserved at Phoenix Park, and implied that Parnell at least had prior knowledge of the assassination. Parnell absolutely denied the authenticity of the letter, but many Englishmen—including Chamberlain—believed it to be valid.[59] The Radicals never wavered in their support for Parnell. Having completely altered their attitude toward the origin and nature of Irish crimes, they held fast to their new belief that the Parnellites had constitutional methods and goals. They gave Parnell whatever help they could.[60] When the government introduced a bill to establish a commission to investigate, not just the letters implicating Parnell, but the entire agrarian movement, Radicals vigorously opposed it. They abandoned their opposition only on Parnell's request.[61] Naturally they exulted when cross examination by Parnell's defense counsel exposed the forger of the letters, one Richard Pigott, a disreputable Irish journalist.[62] The situation looked as if the Radical attachment to Home Rule would pay big dividends. Had a general election taken place early in 1890, Liberal and Radical enthusiasm probably would have won a large majority for Home Rule.

The Conservatives, of course, had no intention whatever of dissolving at such a disadvantageous moment. The septennial act would not force them to hold a general election until the middle of 1893; until then they could wait. Time turned out to be their greatest ally, because a movement within Radicalism was gradually working to Unionist advantage—a slowly growing discontent among some Radicals with the attention being devoted by the Liberal party to Irish

---

59. Garvin, *Chamberlain*, II, 384.

60. Morley advised Parnell not to take *The Times* to court, on grounds that Parnell could not win before an English jury and a victory before an Irish jury would be regarded as meaningless. He also advised Parnell not to accept the Tory offer for a commission to investigate Parnellism. Morley, *Gladstone*, III, 393; Gardiner, *Harcourt*, II, 70.

61. Morley, *Gladstone*, III, 400.

62. *The Speaker*, February 8, 1890; National Liberal Federation, *Proceedings of the Thirteenth Annual Meeting, 1890*, 21.

affairs. It was not that Radicals were beginning to oppose Home Rule or regret the Irish alliance, but that some were becoming impatient with Ireland's demands on their time and energy. In this sense the temper of some Radicals very much resembled that of 1882 and 1883, when there had been a strong desire to concentrate on those things that were the backbone of the Radical program. There were two other factors that contributed to this malaise. One was the recognition by many Radicals (among them some ardent Home Rulers) that Home Rule alone would not be an attractive program for the electors. The other was the growing concern of some Radicals for the increasing attention being given by the public to social problems. It was in this regard that the new urban orientation among the New Liberals and London Radicals affected the Irish policy of Radicalism and the Liberal party. By the late 1880's the focusing of public opinion on social problems was plain for all to see. Many Radicals feared that they would lose their share of the electorate unless they too concentrated on issues directly concerning the working class. Such a shift of attention would require diversion of energy from Home Rule. Here cooperation between Liberals and Home Rulers worked against Irish nationalism. Without the pressure of confrontation tactics by the Parnellites, the full Radical devotion to Home Rule tended to fray at the seams, and the nationalists had no way to stop the process.

It would, however, be a serious mistake to say that the issue of emphasizing Radical measures at the expense of Home Rule neatly divided the more modern, socially concerned Radicals from the more old-fashioned. The Radicals who were concerned about the attention given to Home Rule included a wide variety of people. Labouchere was probably the most insistent exponent of the view that Home Rule had little electoral power, yet he had himself been one of the earliest Radical Home Rulers, and in 1886 and 1887 he had advocated a hard line for Home Rule and against Chamberlain. Moreover, he was far from being a progressive social reformer. To him, the social program was only a way to win votes.[63] Other, more typical Radicals like the Scottish and Welsh Nonconformists and

63. Labouchere to H. Gladstone, March 31, 1888, Viscount Gladstone Papers, 46,016.

the Liberation Society in general had also been among the firmest proponents of Home Rule, yet by 1890 many of them were reemphasizing the priority of disestablishment.[64] Even the Radicals who wanted the party to look to the needs of labor included a very diverse range of men: from individualists like Bradlaugh to positivists like Frederic Harrison and New Liberals like Haldane. Their concern was to harness the energy generated by social awareness and labor militancy to Radicalism, and they were afraid that Home Rule might not suffice. As Andrew Reid put it, Home Rule must stay at the top of the Liberal program, because until Ireland had self-rule there would be no English legislation; yet Home Rule must not be the only policy: *"The English labourer is a hungry man, and Irish liberty may not fill his belly."*[65]

For all the cogency of these views, a large number of Radicals remained committed to keeping Home Rule the first and foremost in the Liberal platform. John Morley was the most influential of this group. Morley felt comfortable with Home Rule, an issue he understood superbly well. Keenly aware that Home Rule had made him a politician of top rank, he sensed that other issues, regardless of how favorably their advocates may have felt about Ireland, might shoulder it aside in the next general election. Thus Home Rule for him would be the sole issue between Liberalism and Conservatism.[66] Other Radicals, though not so personally involved with Ireland and not so determined to concentrate on Home Rule alone, recalled the practical problems of legislating on any issue while Irish nationalists were dissatisfied. J. Guinness Rogers, for instance, wrote that all Radicals realized social questions were coming on strong, but he reminded them that until Home Rule was enacted, Ireland would block the way to all reform.[67]

64. Morgan, *Wales and British Politics*, 90–91; *The Times*, October 9, 1889.

65. Reid, *New Liberal Programme*, 172–73. Also: Haldane, "The Liberal Creed," *Contemporary Review* 54 (October 1888), 463–65; L. A. Atherley-Jones, "The New Liberalism," *Nineteenth Century* 150 (August 1889), 189–92; Frederic Harrison to Morley, undated, Harrison Papers, Section A, Box 3; *The Times*, February 8, 1890; *The Star*, November 11, 1890.

66. Hamer, *Morley*, Chs. 13, 14, 16, 17; Morley to Haldane, January 29, 1888, Haldane Papers, MS 5903.

67. Rogers, "The Middle Class and the New Liberalism," *Nineteenth Century* 152 (October 1889), 710, 717.

By 1890, then, Radicals generally fell into two categories: those who believed that, without emphasis on domestic reforms, Home Rulers could not win; and those who thought that, without a clear victory for Home Rule, no other Radical policies could be enacted. The issue between these views was still undecided when the bombshell of the O'Shea-Parnell divorce trial burst on the arena. Late in 1890 Captain O'Shea sued his wife for divorce, citing Parnell as co-respondent. The trial began in November 1890 amid a flurry of Liberal fears that the revelations in court would sully Parnell's honor.[68] From a conversation with Parnell, Morley concluded that the trial would yield no adverse decree, but the court soon shattered this illusion.[69] Not only did O'Shea win the divorce, but Parnell made no defense against his most sordid charges. To the public, Parnell appeared the worst kind of man, a low and calculating destroyer of a comrade's marriage.[70]

It is difficult to imagine an incident more likely to disturb the Parnellite-Liberal alliance, depending as it did on Nonconformist Radicals. The news of the Parnell-O'Shea affair reached the press just as the National Liberal Federation was gathering in Sheffield for the annual conference. John Morley's first thought after the divorce was that the nationalists must stay united, and as they seemed prepared to keep Parnell as leader, Liberal spokesmen should say nothing. Gladstone agreed, although he feared the reaction of "our Nonconformist friends."[71] His apprehension was well founded. Nonconformists at Sheffield and around the country made evident their disgust with Parnell. H. J. Wilson reported to some correspondents that the delegates at the Federation conference were unanimous in feeling that Parnell had to be dropped. Morley found that Nonconformist preachers and Federation laymen alike would abandon Home Rule if Parnell kept the leadership.[72] Parnell's im-

68. Morley to Gladstone, November 3, 1890, Gladstone Papers, 44,256.

69. Morley, *Recollections*, I, 253-54.

70. Jules Abels, *The Parnell Tragedy* (London, 1966); Henry Harrison, *Parnell, Joseph Chamberlain and Mr. Garvin* (London, 1938) and *Parnell Vindicated* (New York, 1931), give the opposing sides of the Parnell-O'Shea affair.

71. Gladstone to Morley, November 19, 1890; Morley to Gladstone, November 17, 22, 1890, Gladstone Papers, 44,256; Morley, *Recollections*, I, 256.

72. Wilson to twenty-eight correspondents, November 22, 1890, Wilson Papers,

moral behavior could do to Nonconformist opinion what even agrarian crime could not. Inasmuch as he recognized his dependence on the Nonconformist Radicals in the party, Gladstone felt that he had to inform Parnell of Liberal opinion. He and four other party leaders decided to send a letter to Parnell stressing the embarrassment to the Irish cause in the minds of Liberal Home Rulers, and added that continuation of Parnell's leadership would render his own leadership of the Liberal party, "based as it has been mainly upon the presentation of the Irish cause, almost a nullity."[73]

When Gladstone's letter reached the newspapers, it seemed to force the Irish nationalists to choose between Gladstone and Parnell, between the Liberal alliance and their own Uncrowned King. Not to be deposed easily, Parnell struck back at his erstwhile allies with a manifesto of his own, charging that the Gladstonians meant to hobble new Home Rule proposals with severe restrictions and that they had tried to buy his approval with a seat in the cabinet.[74] None of these accusations was true. When Justin McCarthy saw a draft of Parnell's manifesto, he objected to every word of it, as did many of the nationalist M.P.'s. When the Irish parliamentary party met again to debate the continuation of Parnell's leadership, they split asunder. Including the members at the moment in America, the alignment of forces ultimately was: McCarthy, Healy, Sexton, Dillon, and O'Brien leading about two-thirds of the party against Parnell, John Redmond, Timothy Harrington, and the rest. McCarthy's wing held fast to the Liberal alliance, while Parnell and his faction utterly renounced it.[75]

For Liberals the golden days of their alliance with nationalism were over. In the gloom of fading electoral chances they had to decide what to do about the party program. The initial reaction of

Sheffield Central Library, MD 2574-2; Morley, *Recollections*, I, 257; John F. Glaser, "Parnell's Fall and the Nonconformist Conscience," *Irish Historical Studies* (12) 119–38, is a full story of this episode.

73. Morley, *Recollections*, I, 259–61; Gardiner, *Harcourt*, II, 83–86.

74. Morley, *Gladstone*, III, 445–46.

75. For the nationalist split, see F. S. L. Lyons, *The Fall of Parnell, 1890–91* (Toronto, 1960), and *The Irish Parliamentary Party, 1890–1910* (London, 1951); and Emmet Larkin, "The Roman Catholic Hierarchy and the Fall of Parnell," *Victorian Studies* 4 (June 1961), 315–36.

many Liberals, including some Radicals, was that Home Rule would have to retire to an inconspicuous place at the rear of the platform. Those who had expressed doubts about the electoral value of Home Rule now had new influence. Haldane told Edward Hamilton that social and labor questions would be forced to the front.[76] Harcourt and a few others wanted to drop Home Rule altogether. Even Gladstone consulted Arnold Morley as to other policies they could advocate.[77] John Morley, however, fought to keep Home Rule in first position. He wrote Gladstone to remind him of the damage Parnell could do to Liberals and anti-Parnellite nationalists if the party threw over Home Rule.[78] Harcourt and Morley clashed so fiercely on the issue that for a time Morley refused to speak to Harcourt at all.[79]

As time passed and passions cooled, a compromise emerged. The Liberal party did not abandon Home Rule. Further, its retention was due not only to Morley's struggle, but also to the refusal by the Radical rank and file to give up something to which they had committed so much energy and passion. Even as early as January 1891 Arnold Morley reported to Gladstone that for every letter advocating abandonment of Home Rule, he received a hundred contending that "what has happened cannot & ought not to affect the policy with regard to Ireland."[80] *The Speaker*, a voice of New Radicalism, declared that Home Rule would be first in the party, Parnell or no Parnell.[81] Nevertheless, those who had urged other issues to the forefront also won some concessions. As Morley later wrote, after Parnell's fall "every politician knew that it would be necessary to balance home rule by reforms expected in England and Scotland."[82] The desire of Radicals to broaden the appeal of their program was one source of the Newcastle Programme's fame. The full program

76. Hamilton Diaries, December 14, 1890, 48,654.

77. A. Morley to Gladstone, December 30, 1890, Gladstone Papers, 44,254.

78. December 31, 1890, January 2, 1891, Gladstone Papers, 44,256.

79. Gardiner, *Harcourt*, II, 95–99; Morley to Gladstone, January 19, 1891, Gladstone Papers, 44,256.

80. January 5, 1891, Gladstone Papers, 44,254.

81. *The Speaker*, March 14, 1891; also *Daily News*, November 18, 1890; *The Star*, November 18, 1890; J. Guinness Rogers, "Nonconformists in Political Life," *Contemporary Review* 61 (April 1892), 502–5.

82. Morley, *Gladstone*, III, 462.

had been elaborated as early as 1888, but at Newcastle the attention clearly was on non-Irish issues.[83]

IV. THE ELECTION OF 1892

Considering the nearly hopeless situation at the end of 1890, the Liberals and Radicals recovered relatively well during the next year. In this sense the Newcastle Programme did its work admirably. When Lord Salisbury advised the Queen to dissolve parliament in June 1892, Home Rulers thought that at last their moment had come. Yet the nightmare of 1890 meant that for most Radicals the election issue was not simply Home Rule, but the full Newcastle platform. Unquestionably, Home Rule still stood at the top of the Radical program, and no Radical tried to ignore it. Even *The Speaker* cautioned against those who would divert attention from Home Rule in the name of labor and social reform.[84] But at the same time Radicals, following the lead of Gladstone himself, gave extensive attention to domestic issues.[85] More than any other Radical, John Morley stressed Home Rule and argued that no reforms could be enacted until Ireland passed from the political scene. Yet he too advocated all of the Newcastle Programme.[86] The single-minded enthusiasm of Radicals for Home Rule, so evident in 1886–88, clearly had evaporated; and the Irish nationalist majority, trapped now by the Liberal alliance, could do nothing about it.

This turn of events was also preparing a great trap for the Radical Home Rulers—the House of Lords. As the living symbols of a kind of society most detested by the Radicals, the Lords looked upon growing Radical power with alarm. They considered the Radical-nationalist alliance as the work of the devil. In 1886 the Duke of Marlborough had made his comment that the Radicals and Irishmen had joined forces because both were desirous of "spoliating the

83. National Liberal Federation, *Fourteenth Annual Conference, 1891.*
84. May 7, 1892.
85. More than half of Gladstone's election address was devoted to British reforms: *The Times*, June 24, 1892.
86. *The Times*, June 15, 20, 1892; also Frederic Harrison advised Morley not to stick to Ireland alone: June 4, 1892, Harrison Papers, Section A, Box 3.

classes in the interests of the proletariat. . . ."[87] In the Lords, then, the Radicals faced a potentially explosive issue. Their course of action should have been clear. By 1892 most Radicals advocated abolition of the legislative power of the Lords and realized that the upper House would reject any Home Rule measure. Obviously they needed to prepare for a struggle. They failed to do so—and for an interesting reason. Following the lead of Gladstone, the Radicals argued simply that the Lords could not constitutionally force a dissolution. They warned the Lords that the upper House could not defy the House of Commons; but during the general election they never said what they would do, other than stage demonstrations, if the Lords *did* defy them. They seem to have assumed that they could overwhelm the Lords with a show of popular feeling and with a flood of Radical programs.[88] But the Lords had passed the point of being overawed by demonstrations; moreover, the proliferation of Radical programs only diffused Radical power and gave the Lords an excuse to claim that the election was not being conducted on Home Rule at all. The Radicals could find no way out of this snare.

When the final polls were in, Radicals and Liberals could only be disappointed at the results. They won a majority, but a small one of only forty, and that dependent on the nationalists: there would be 274 Liberals (including labor) and 81 Home Rulers, against 269 Tories and 46 Liberal Unionists. Everyone realized that Home Rule had not carried England. Moreover, as Gladstone wrote Spencer, the majority was too small to force Home Rule on the Lords.[89] Most Liberals and Radicals agreed that, without Radical domestic policies, there would have been no majority at all.[90] Home Rule, they rightly thought, had not been a winning issue after all. In this regard Radicals took particular note of the fact that John Morley had been returned in Newcastle only in second place behind a Tory. Morley was practically alone in disputing this analysis. He thought

---

87. "Political Crossroads," *F.R.* 40 (August 1886), 137–51.

88. *The Times*, November 28, 1891; *The Speaker*, December 5, 1891; July 2, 1892; *The Star*, June 23, 1892.

89. July 13, 1892, Gladstone Papers, 44,314.

90. Hamilton Diaries, July 24, 1892, 48,658; *Daily News*, July 21, 1892.

the Radical program had hurt the chances of Home Rule: "The truth is, we have moved much too fast and too far towards the Extreme Left in every subject at once—and quiet sensible folks don't like it."[91] Harcourt expressed what most Liberals felt when he wrote Spencer that Morley would have been correct if he had confined his remarks to Ireland.[92] The narrow margin of victory and the consequent decline in Radical morale convinced many Radicals that another general election within a few years would be impossible. The party would have to hang on and pass as many measures as possible in order to rebuild party strength.[93] Implicit in this strategy was a decision to proceed with Radical policies no matter what happened to Home Rule. This was a bitter conclusion indeed to so many years of fighting for Ireland, but it was a significant statement of the abiding interests of late-Victorian Radicalism.

91. July 14, 1892, quoted in Hamer, *Morley*, 280.
92. Harcourt to Spencer, July 18, 1892, quoted *ibid.*, 280.
93. *Daily News*, July 21, 1892; *The Speaker*, August 6, 1892.

CHAPTER EIGHT

The Second Home Rule Parliament
1892-95

The story of Radicalism became submerged in the troubles of the Liberal party from 1892 to 1895. Born in disappointment and discontent, the Liberal government of those years died in frustration and defeat. It was troubled by various debilitating ailments for its entire course—Gladstone's age and infirmity; the vanity, narrowness, and jealousy of the top three subordinates, Rosebery, Harcourt, and Morley; and the insecurity of the small Liberal majority. Accentuating all these troubles was the unruliness of Radicals and Irishmen alike. The majority of Irish nationalists remained remarkably loyal, even docile, throughout the term of the government, but a virulent minority—the Parnellites—provided a constant stream of embarrassments for the Liberals. Ireland itself continued to supply the usual knotty issues, only the most important of which was Home Rule. Try as the Liberals might, they could not escape the Irish web. As men with many causes, the Radicals found the Irish tangle especially bothersome. Each Radical group wanted desperately to push its own issue, but Ireland and the Irish alliance seemed always to be in the way. This made for a curious situation: the Radicals were committed to Ireland, and they professed allegiance to the anti-Parnellite nationalists, yet the Irish were not able to keep the Radicals steadily to the wheel. From the viewpoint of neither the Radicals nor the nationalists did the politics of cooperation prove satisfying.

I. THE SECOND HOME RULE BILL

Despite all the crusading for Irish self-rule that had gone on since 1886, the drafting and passage of the second Home Rule bill pro-

vided Liberals with a seemingly endless series of problems. No one
doubted that Home Rule would be the first business of the new
government, but the cabinet was very slow in producing its proposal. Not the least of the reasons was the dilatoriness of the Grand
Old Man. Discouraged by the small Liberal and Home Rule majority, beset by old age, Gladstone was very slow in preparing the
new bill. Many Liberals—the Radicals had no monopoly on the
feeling—soon became restless, and Morley had to write Rosebery:
"You really must be a stoic. We are all in a very mighty tight place,
I can tell you—with a P.M. of 83."[1] The Irish themselves were
difficult, because Morley, as Chief Secretary and as the government's
messenger, had two competing factions of nationalists to deal with,
each afraid to accept limitations of Irish autonomy for fear of re-
ceiving damaging criticisms from the other. This fact put Morley
squarely in the sights of Harcourt, who, while ostentatiously refusing to share responsibility for the measure, did everything he
could to reduce the power granted to the Irish legislature.[2] As a
sensitive and diffident man, Morley found Harcourt's "invariable
insolence" unbearable, as well as enormously obstructive.[3]

Under these conditions it is a wonder that the bill was drafted at
all, and in the event, the final product was not very satisfactory.
The two big problems which came up during the drafting stage
had to do with financial arrangements and retention of the Irish
representatives. Few Radicals cared much about matters of Irish
taxation, and the financial clauses were fought out inside the cabinet, with Morley the advocate of granting full powers of taxation
to the Irish parliament, and Harcourt the opponent. The main results of this squabbling were an unhappy compromise and the reduction of relations between Harcourt and Morley to a state of sullen
snarling.[4] The matter of retaining the Irish M.P.'s was of consider-

1. December 15, 1892, Rosebery Papers, Box 35. Also: Hamilton Diaries, November 2, 1892, 48,659; Algernon West, *Private Diaries of the Rt. Hon. Sir Algernon
West*, G.C.B., ed. Horace G. Hutchinson (London, 1922), 71.

2. Harcourt declared to Hamilton that it would be better to leave the Irish
rather than the English unsatisfied on Home Rule, for this would at least get rid
of the Irish Question, because the Irish would have to defeat it themselves. Hamilton
Diaries, November 4, 1892, 48,659.

3. West, *Private Diaries*, 71.

4. For the Gladstone-Morley plan, see Gladstone to Morley, November 11,

able importance to the Radicals, although their councils on the issue were almost as divided as ever. In general the drift of Radical opinion since 1886 was toward fairly complete retention, but Labouchere and a few others argued that the Irish should not be given the right to control their own affairs and interfere in British business as well.[5] The cabinet's solution, the "in-and-out" clause, whereby Ireland would have eighty M.P.'s at Westminster for imperial affairs only, got a mixed reception from Radicals. A small number of Radical M.P.'s held out for complete exclusion on grounds that no other formula would give the Irish genuine self-rule.[6] However, under heavy pressure from several quarters, the cabinet had to accept retention of the eighty Irish M.P.'s for all purposes. This formula suited the majority of Radicals, but it disappointed many of the very Radical M.P.'s who had long been the most enthusiastic advocates of Home Rule. Their grievance undoubtedly helped discourage the government from forcing Home Rule on the Lords.[7]

Three other enervating disputes arose during the committee stage of the bill. The first had to do with the government's proposal of a bicameral legislature, the upper house to be elected by voters of a high property qualification. Many Radicals deplored this provision

---

1892, Gladstone Papers, 44,257. For Harcourt's views: Hamilton Diaries, November 4, December 19, 1892, and January 14, 21, 23, 24, 1893, 48,659; Harcourt to Morley, January 18, 1893, quoted in Gardiner, *Harcourt*, II, 220. For Harcourt-Morley relations: Morley to Harcourt, February 13, 1893, quoted in Gardiner, *Harcourt*, II, 221-22.

5. Labouchere to Edward Marjoribanks, August 28, 1892, included with Marjoribanks to Gladstone, September 3, 1892, Gladstone Papers, 44,332.

6. Examples of those who wished simply to get Ireland out of the way: *Hansard*, 4th ser., 8 (February 16, 1893), 1663-64; 10 (April 6, 1893), 1741; 14 (July 13, 1893), 1534-35; R. Wallace, "The Ninth Clause," *Nineteenth Century* 197 (July 1893), 10-18; National Liberal Federation, *Proceedings of the Sixteenth Annual Meeting, 1894*, 14-16; *The Star*, February 14, 1893. Some speeches for complete exclusion, by Atherley-Jones, Rathbone, and Wallace: *Hansard*, 4th ser., 11 (April 13, 1893), 512-13; 14 (July 12, 1893), 1425-27; (July 13, 1893), 1485-95.

7. Radical speakers for complete retention included Thomas Shaw, John Leng, and John Wilson: *Hansard*, 4th ser., 11 (April 13, 1893), 261-64; (April 19, 1893), 682-87; 15 (August 9, 1893), 1680. The *Daily News* also was reluctant to keep the Irish out if they wanted to stay: February 14, 1893. The cabinet's response: Hamilton Diaries, July 6, 1893, 48,660.

because they felt it introduced an aristocratic principle into the measure, and about forty of them joined a few Parnellites in trying to erase the proposal.[8] The second conflict occurred in connection with an amendment proposed by Henry James, a Liberal Unionist, to specify clearly the supremacy of the parliament at Westminster. As might have been expected, Harcourt supported the amendment, while John Morley opposed it. The Irish nationalists very strongly objected to the proposed alteration, and when the cabinet accepted it, Morley felt that his reputation in Ireland had been severely damaged.[9] The confidence of the nationalist leaders in the Irish executive was even more acutely tested by the third dispute, which concerned the financial clauses. Due to a mistake in the calculations by Treasury officials, the cabinet had to recast the economic provisions of the bill. The dispute between Morley and Harcourt burst out again at the last minute. This time Morley, who was indispensable as Chief Secretary, warned Gladstone that he could not govern Ireland without the confidence of the Irish leaders, and that limitation of the Irish legislature's taxing authority would destroy precisely that confidence.[10] Morley's play of his trump card worked, for the cabinet agreed to substitute the old plan of 1886, wherein Ireland would collect her own taxes and contribute a fixed sum to the British exchequer. Yet this arrangement, like the others, only added to the fragmentation and malaise of the Home Rule forces in parliament.

All of the difficulties attending the drafting of the second Home Rule bill worked to erode the enthusiasm of Radical M.P.'s for the Irish cause. The unusually slow progress of the bill in the House of Commons added to their unrest. Balfour, leader of the Conservative parliamentary party, contested the measure at every possible point, and in the committee stage, which took sixty-three sittings, fought it clause by clause. During this tedious time, most of which was spent in controversies that had been debated innumerable times since 1886, Radicals became extremely impatient. Increasingly they

---

8. *Hansard*, 4th ser., 12 (May 9, 10, 1893), 525–39, 550–607.

9. Gardiner, *Harcourt*, II, 224; West, *Private Diaries*, 159; Morley to Gladstone, May 10, 15, 16, 17, 1893, Gladstone Papers, 44,257.

10. June 19, 1893, Gladstone Papers, 44,257. Also: West, *Private Diaries*, 167–68; Hamilton Diaries, May 17, 31, June 1, 7, 11, 1893, 48,660.

felt that Home Rule was detracting attention from the Newcastle Programme, which they regarded as the platform upon which they had been elected. They resented, for example, the fact that the government had to give up hopes of passing in 1893 a death-duties budget.[11] The Welsh Radicals resented the delay to the Welsh Church suspensory bill, a step toward disestablishment.[12] As early as the debate on the second reading of the Home Rule bill, restless Radicals began to ask when the government would move on to other measures.[13] Finally, on June 29, Gladstone began to try to speed things up by moving the guillotine closure for the various clauses of the bill. Two months later, on September 1, the House gave the bill its third reading. After all their grumbling the Radicals remained loyal to the government, which won a majority of thirty-four.[14] Home Rule at last had struggled through the House of Commons.

One week later, after four nights of perfunctory debate, the Lords rejected the bill, 419 to 41.

II. Home Rule, the Lords, and the Succession to Gladstone

By their rejection of the second Home Rule bill, the Lords not only thwarted Gladstone's great mission, but also destroyed seven years of work by Radicals and flaunted aristocratic privilege in the face of men who for years had vowed to end the power of the upper House. Inasmuch as the Radicals held a dominant position within the Liberal party by 1893, they could have led Liberalism on a campaign to force Home Rule on the Lords or break the strength of the Lords in general. Surprisingly, they did neither. They had only two ways of reversing the decision of the upper House. One was defiant re-passage of the Home Rule bill, supported by mass agitation in the country. Perhaps with a little tactical violence—railings pulled down in Hyde Park, riotous demonstrations before the

11. Hamilton Diaries, March 10, 1893, 44,660.
12. Morgan, *Wales in British Politics*, 136–39.
13. Remarks by Labouchere, Atherley-Jones, Morton, and Woods: *Hansard*, 4th ser., 11 (April 13, 1893), 211; (April 19, 1893), 558; 14 (June 28, 1893), 241–42. Also Frederic Harrison to Morley, April 19, 1893, Harrison Papers, Section A, Box 3.
14. *Hansard*, 4th ser., 16 (September 1, 1893), 1839.

House of Lords, and a few broken windows on Park Lane—they might have overawed the recalcitrant nobles. The other method lay in a dissolution on the combined issues of Home Rule and aristocratic privilege, on the hope of returning with a majority so large that the Lords might not dare to defy it. But the troubled and discontented state of Radical opinion made both techniques impossible.

Radicals immediately and clearly ruled out reintroduction of the bill. Convinced that their mandate in 1892 depended on the whole of the Newcastle Programme, nearly all of them felt strongly that the government should not take up another session with Home Rule. Further, the Radicals believed that a battle with the Lords was imminent, and that passage of a number of Radical measures would strengthen the hands of the anti-aristocratic forces.[15] Early in 1893 Labouchere advocated creation of enough peers to pass Home Rule, but when it became obvious that the cabinet would not fight the Queen on this idea, he too began to press for a "British" rather than a Home Rule session.[16] With various Radical groups like the temperance advocates and the Scottish and Welsh nationalists expressing anger at having been put off, the government quickly agreed not to reintroduce Home Rule in 1894. Asquith declared at Leeds that if the party brought in Home Rule again, "I think we should be acting falsely to our obligations to the democracy of Great Britain."[17]

The same reasoning by Radicals told heavily against schemes of dissolution or campaigning against the Lords. In their belief that domestic programs alone had carried the party to victory in 1892, however disappointing it might have been, Radicals had little desire to consult the constituencies on the single issue of Home Rule so soon after the general election.[18] Moreover, the Radicals now found themselves trapped by their own assertion that the Lords had no power to force a dissolution. The executive committee of the Na-

15. *Daily News*, September 11, 1893; J. F. Moulton, "What Mr. Gladstone Ought to Do," *F.R.* 314 (February 1893), 265–66; National Liberal Federation, *Proceedings of the Fifteenth Annual Meeting, 1893*, 52.

16. *The Times*, June 8, July 15, August 14, 1893.

17. *The Times*, October 31, 1893.

18. Moulton, "What Mr. Gladstone Ought to Do," 266; *The Star*, September 9, 11, 1893.

tional Liberal Federation declared that "we entirely reject the pretension of the Peers to the right to force a dissolution, and we confidently expect the government to go forward with those Reforms for which the country waits."[19] This brave talk led to much sabre-rattling against the Lords, but precluded a genuine campaign against them. Evidently the Radicals assumed—probably correctly —that the electorate would not become sufficiently enraged with the Lords unless the issue thrown out by them was itself regarded as crucial; and Home Rule, by 1893, was not.[20] Even Labouchere, who was panting for a go with the peers, tried to separate Home Rule from abolition of the aristocratic privilege.[21] And John Morley, more deeply involved with Ireland than any other Radical, told Gladstone that a dissolution against the Lords was impossible because the most popular Radical issue, one man one vote, had not yet come before the upper House.[22]

With such attitudes prevalent among the largest portion of the party, there was little even the most enthusiastic Home Rulers could do, especially as there was no counter-pressure from the Irish nationalist majority. Only Gladstone among the cabinet members seriously considered attacking the Lords for their rejection of Home Rule. Shortly before the peers had acted, he told Algernon West that their rejection of Home Rule would raise two great questions: "Is the majority to rule or the minority? Is the House of Lords to prevail or the House of Commons?"[23] But when his cabinet colleagues failed to show any desire for an enterprise against the peers, Gladstone made no effort to push Home Rule. Discouraged, weary, suffering from the effect of eighty-four years on his sight and hearing, Gladstone naturally began to think about retirement. It must have seemed to him and to many others that he had outlived his political usefulness. In addition, he had since December

19. National Liberal Federation, *Proceedings of the Sixteenth Annual Meeting, 1894*, 20. Also *Daily News*, September 13, 1893.

20. One of the few Radicals who did think the electorate would be up in arms about the rejection of Home Rule was Sir Wilfrid Lawson: G. W. E. Russell, *Sir Wilfrid Lawson: A Memoir* (London, 1909), 216.

21. Labouchere to Dilke, October 8, 11, 1893, Dilke Papers, 43,892.

22. Morley, *Recollections*, II, 7.

23. West, *Private Diaries*, 191.

1893 seriously clashed with the majority of the cabinet over Lord Spencer's proposed increases in the naval estimates. Unable to persuade them of his cherished economic principles, Gladstone had all the more reason to look fondly to the pleasant vistas of retirement.[24]

Most of the cabinet were quite as ready to see the Old Man retire as they were to drop his great issue. They were impatient with him and impatient with his policy. The cabinet member who might have been expected to want Gladstone to stay on was John Morley, for Morley agreed with him on the naval issue and Ireland alike. Yet Morley played a double game. He wrote Gladstone to urge him not to retire, on grounds that his going would disillusion the Irish and make them retreat into their usual "sullen resentment."[25] But to other members of the government Morley indicated that he felt the time had come for Gladstone to go.[26] In later years Morley wrote that consideration of the welfare of Ireland was the "polestar" of his policy regarding Gladstone's retirement.[27] However, when Gladstone, in a final burst of energy, decided to attack the Lords by allowing them to mutilate the Radical policies already in progress, then by dissolving immediately against them, Morley joined the cabinet in resisting him. That was the last blow to him and the second Home Rule bill. The Grand Old Man retired on March 3, 1894.[28]

At that point the great issue impinging on the fate of Irish self-rule became the succession to Gladstone. This had been a subject of extensive public and private speculation for years, and by the time of the resignation the leading members of the cabinet already had begun intricate maneuverings for the position.[29] The claims of both Radicalism and Ireland logically should have been crucial con-

24. Peter Stansky, *Ambitions and Strategies: The Struggle for Leadership of the Liberal Party in the 1890s* (Oxford, 1964), 19–78.

25. February 2, 1894, Gladstone Papers, 44,257.

26. Morley, *Recollections*, II, 4, 8.

27. *Ibid.*, 8. A recent interpretation which generally supports Morley's view is Stephen G. Koss, "Morley in the Middle," *English Historical Review* 82 (July 1967), 553–61.

28. Stansky, *Ambitions and Strategies*, 37–41; West, *Private Diaries*, 268–75; Hamilton Diaries, February 8, 11, 1894, 48,662.

29. There are two excellent recent accounts of these maneuverings: Stansky, *Ambitions and Strategies*; Robert Rhodes James, *Rosebery* (New York, 1963).

siderations in the process of choosing a leader, for Radicals made up the bulk of party strength, and the party was committed to an alliance with the Irish nationalists as well as to Home Rule itself. In reality these were practically insignificant factors. The influence of the large Radical majority was nullified by the fact that neither the parliamentary nor extra-parliamentary Liberal party was considered in the decision. The choice rested entirely with three men—Harcourt, Rosebery, and Morley—none of whom was a spokesman for the Radical rank and file. The Radicals contributed to this situation because their councils were divided and self-defeating. A few old-fashioned Radicals preferred Harcourt to the other contenders because he was the strongest House of Commons man.[30] But as an offspring of a prestigious Anglican Whig family, Harcourt had neither a large personal following among parliamentary Radicals nor influence in any of the great extra-parliamentary Radical organizations. Labouchere's faction eventually became Harcourt's main source of strength, but mainly because they found him the only alternative to a premier from the House of Lords. Though a peer, Rosebery probably attracted a larger and more devoted personal following among Radicals than did Harcourt. The "Liberal imperialists" felt that he would be more sympathetic to modern Radicalism than Harcourt, and that Harcourt would be personally insufferable as prime minister.[31] Yet the enigmatic and sophisticated Rosebery had little in common with the hard-driving men of the provinces who formed the bulk of Radicalism. Most of them by nature resisted the idea of having a premier from the House of Lords. On March 1, 1894, Labouchere and Samuel Storey led a delegation of Radicals to speak to Edward Marjoribanks, the Liberal chief whip, against the selection of Rosebery. But Marjoribanks, who was not a Radical, attached little importance to the group, though they claimed to represent fifty Radical M.P.'s. In the meantime Haldane was busily organizing a pro-Rosebery section to

30. Hamilton Diaries, February 26, March 1, 1894, 48,662, 48,663.

31. Stansky, *Ambitions and Strategies*, 68–69; West, *Private Diaries*, 174; H. W. Massingham, "The Old Premier and the New," *Contemporary Review* 65 (April 1894), 463–65.

counter Labouchere.[32] Radical attempts to stop the selection of Rosebery came to nothing.

It is significant that considerations about Ireland played no part in the Radicals' opposition to Rosebery, nor in the Liberal imperialists' support for him. If anything, Rosebery was more sympathetic toward Irish claims than Harcourt, but neither contender was an enthusiastic Home Ruler. Morley was something of an exception to the Radical rule. For him Ireland continued to be of primary importance, and he felt that, in choosing the successor to Gladstone, members of the cabinet "were under a special moral obligation to the Irish." According to his own account, he felt that Rosebery would be more sympathetic to Ireland than Harcourt, who had strongly urged policies other than Home Rule on the party and then made a nuisance of himself in the drafting of the bill.[33] Yet other, less commendable, though perfectly understandable, factors helped determine Morley's position in the days of decision. For one thing, his personal feelings about Rosebery and Harcourt were important to him. In the years since 1886 Morley had fallen under the spell of Rosebery's charm, for the moody earl was a brilliant conversationalist, a graceful host, and a sensitive friend. But Harcourt, being a rough, impetuous man, had frequently bruised Morley's rather feminine sensitivity and his severe, solemn, sincerity. By 1894 Morley had declared that he would never serve under Harcourt.[34] In addition, Morley was ambitious. He seems to have thought that he would fare better in the cabinet reorganization if Rosebery got the premiership instead of Harcourt—in fact, that he might even be made foreign secretary.[35]

Whatever his goal, Morley certainly misplayed what could have been a strong hand. Any Liberal prime minister in 1894 and 1895, particularly one who, like Rosebery or Harcourt, intended to ignore Ireland, would have needed Morley's help in maintaining a favor-

32. Hamilton Diaries, March 3, 1894, 48,663; Stansky, *Ambitions and Strategies*, 80; Gardiner, *Harcourt*, II, 270.

33. Morley, *Recollections*, II, 11–13.

34. Stansky, *Ambitions and Strategies*, 55.

35. *Ibid.*, 60, 80; James, *Rosebery*, 302, 310; Morley, *Recollections*, II, 19–20.

able relationship with the Irish nationalists. In addition, Morley was the most prestigious exponent of Radicalism and could have used this position to great advantage for both himself and Ireland. But Morley was too uncertain of his objectives, too hesitant to say clearly what he wanted, to be an effective force. Late in the maneuverings, Harcourt's son Loulou offered Morley the exchequer in any cabinet Harcourt might form, and Morley began to show interest in supporting Harcourt. But the change of heart came too late to do any good. As Rosebery's position became stronger, Morley leaned increasingly to Harcourt's dictum that if a noble became prime minister, then a commoner must hold the foreign office. But here, too, Morley had no influence; for, as Harcourt had warned him, once Rosebery had the premiership in hand, he ceased attending to Morley's opinion.[36]

In the end, neither Radicalism nor Ireland nor Morley fared well in the new cabinet arrangements. Lord Rosebery became prime minister and Lord Kimberley the foreign secretary in a government resting, ironically enough, on an essentially Radical party. Rosebery was not required to make any pledge to the primacy of Home Rule or to the Irish alliance, though Morley tried belatedly to get one from him.[37] In his first official speech to the parliamentary Liberal party, Rosebery said that "every tie of honour and policy" tied him to Home Rule, but he made no promise to reintroduce a Home Rule bill or to go to the constituencies on the issue.[38] Nor did Morley get a promotion. Rosebery persuaded him to stay on as Chief Secretary in evidence of the government's sympathy toward Ireland. Morley could not refuse this flattering request, but sulked about his fate and made Rosebery promise not to ask him to take part in any non-Irish debate or speaking engagement. "I will lock myself fast in the Irish back-kitchen," he said.[39] However petty Morley's attitude may have been, his assumption was correct: in Rosebery's official household, Ireland would be only a back kitchen.

The intent of the new government to ignore Home Rule quickly

---

36. Stansky, *Ambitions and Strategies*, 90–91.
37. Morley to Rosebery, March 11, 1894, Rosebery Papers, Box 36.
38. Stansky, *Ambitions and Strategies*, 100.
39. Morley, *Recollections*, II, 19.

became apparent. On the same afternoon of Rosebery's statement to the parliamentary party, the Queen's speech was read, and it made no mention of Home Rule at all. To make matters worse, in the debate on the Address, Salisbury reminded the Liberals of their earlier commitment to Home Rule and challenged them to go to the electorate on it. Rosebery responded with a defense of the government's policy that the House of Lords could not force a dissolution. He continued: "The noble Marquess made one remark on the subject of Home Rule with which I confess myself in entire accord. He said that before Irish Home Rule is conceded by the Imperial Parliament England, as the predominant member of the partnership of the Three Kingdoms, will have to be convinced of its justice and equity."[40] To Irishmen, the implication was plain. England still should decide what was best for Ireland.

Rosebery's gaffe embarrassed Morley before his nationalist allies and gave Labouchere and his Radical friends a golden opportunity to express their disgust with a noble prime minister. Morley pelted Rosebery with scoldings and warnings: "For Heaven's sake, blurt out what you please about any country in the whole world, civilised or barbarous, except Ireland. Irish affairs are the very last field for that practice."[41] But Morley did not think of resigning, and he loyally defended Rosebery in the House of Commons, explaining that the prime minister had only meant, as a practical view, that Englishmen would have to be converted before Ireland would get Home Rule.[42] These words may have satisfied the anti-Parnellite nationalists, but John Redmond, speaking for the Parnellites, put his finger on the truth: Rosebery's slip showed that the Liberal party was shelving Home Rule, and that the Newcastle Programme was forcing Ireland aside.[43] Later the same day Labouchere took his revenge on Rosebery. Arguing that Rosebery's blunder proved the impossibility of the cabinet arrangements, he moved in the Commons that the power of the Lords over legislation ought to be

40. *Hansard*, 4th ser., 22 (March 12, 1894), 32.
41. Quoted in Morley, *Recollections*, II, 21; Morley to Rosebery, March 16, 1894 (two letters), Rosebery Papers, Box 36.
42. *Hansard*, 4th ser., 22 (March 13, 1894), 176–78.
43. *Ibid.*, 180–84.

abolished. And though he had himself often urged that Radical issues should replace Home Rule in the Liberal party platform, Labouchere now contended that the Liberal party should adhere to Gladstone's policy of maintaining Ireland's right to self-government regardless of what England thought. This clever maneuver attracted an odd assortment of Radicals—some who were angry about having a prime minister from the Lords, others who were upset by the cavalier treatment of Home Rule, plus Parnellites and Healyites who wanted to demonstrate the wisdom of their renunciation of the Liberal alliance. Labouchere's motion carried by two votes, and the government had to abandon its Address to the Queen, substituting for it a simple, innocuous statement.[44] The Gladstone era had ended with many Radicals in revolt and the commitment to the Irish reduced to a meaningless phrase.

III. JOHN MORLEY IN IRELAND

Every step in the Liberals' turn away from Ireland made John Morley's task as Chief Secretary more difficult—and it was difficult enough for any man to begin with. As a Radical and a Home Ruler Morley essentially did not believe an Englishman could rule the Irish. He knew that Dublin Castle was alienated from the sympathy of the majority of Irishmen, and as a scholar of Irish history he had long recognized that legitimate Irish agitation was bound to be accompanied by serious disturbances. His fatalism might well have led to inactivity. Moreover, from 1887 to 1892 he had criticized Tory rule as blindly supporting the behavior of the constabulary and the police. As a result, Unionists tended to doubt that he could win enough support from law enforcement agencies to maintain public order. The less rational Unionists had long considered Radicals like Morley to be the agents of revolution. And if these problems were not enough, even the Irish nationalists caused trouble. The Parnellites had turned on the Liberals for their role in deposing Parnell in 1890. Yet from the anti-Parnellites themselves Morley received little solid support. The anti-Parnellites by 1892 had fallen into two groups—the Dillonites and the Healyites—and the Healyites were

44. *Ibid.*, 194–208. Also: Lyons, *Dillon*, 161–62.

218

not very happy about the Liberal alliance (they abandoned the alliance after Rosebery's blundering speech in 1894). Morley found it impossible to ascertain a united nationalist policy on any issue of importance, and also discovered that none of the three factions of nationalists could cooperate fully with him for fear of denunciation from the others.[45]

Nevertheless, Morley had on his side considerable advantages. He honestly intended to rule for the good of the Irish, and many Irishmen regarded him as a friend to Ireland second only to Gladstone. They welcomed him as an amicable agent in the hated Dublin Castle system.[46] Moreover, Morley, for all his democratic theories, enjoyed the exercise of power. He had made it clear to Hamilton in 1892 that he, not the Viceroy, would be the governor of Ireland.[47] His fatalism did not lead to enervation, but to a willingness to use the power of his office to rule firmly, knowing that distasteful decisions were a grim necessity until Ireland had Home Rule. This fatalism, in other words, gave him a flexibility missing in a more rigid Radical like Trevelyan, and allowed him to govern while deliberately setting Radicalism aside. To everyone's surprise, Morley was a failure at obtaining legislation for Ireland, but he was an energetic and successful administrator.

Upon arriving in Dublin for the first time, Morley and the new Viceroy, Lord Houghton, were immediately approached by James O'Connor with a plea from the Evicted Tenants' Association.[48] This was an appropriate introduction to the problems of office, for Morley found that the evicted tenants, victims of the struggle between the landlords and the Plan of Campaign, provided his most important and intractable legislative problem. Under pressure from the Dillonites, Morley agreed to a royal commission to investigate ways of settling the question.[49] The difficulty was to have the commission proceed in such a way as to attract support from landlords as well as tenants. Inasmuch as he had long ago decided that the Plan of Cam-

---

45. Morley, *Recollections*, I, 331; William O'Brien, "Mr. Morley's Task in Ireland," *F.R.* 311 (November 1892), 585–94.
46. *Freeman's Journal*, August 16, 17, 1892.
47. July 22, 1892, Hamilton Diaries, 48,658.
48. *The Times*, August 23, 1892.
49. Morley to Gladstone, September 1, 1892, Gladstone Papers, 44,256.

paign was justified, if illegal, Morley did not want the commissioners to investigate the whole question of landlords versus tenants. He wanted them only to make proposals for reinstating those evicted.[50] This idea received support from the anti-Parnellites and the British Radicals, but not from Unionists, who saw it as sanctioning the Plan of Campaign. Unionists also felt that Morley had packed the commission by appointing only one representative of the landlords, and that one withdrew from the commission shortly after it began its investigations. Even the nationalists thought the commission was made up of weak men.[51] Despite these difficulties, the commission, directed by its sole strong appointee, Justice James C. Matthew, produced a report condemning the landlords and recommending compulsory reinstatement of tenants in cases approved by a board of arbitration.[52] This represented a middle view between the nationalists and the landlords; as such, it disappointed both sides.[53]

There was little Morley could do but introduce a bill based on the recommendation of the commission. This he did on April 19, 1894.[54] The anti-Parnellites in the House defended the measure, but the Parnellites declared that its compulsory features were inadequate.[55] To the Unionist landlords, these same compulsory features were anathema. Colonel Saunderson, an Ulster Unionist of great wrath but short historical vision, called the bill "the most extraordinary legislative monstrosity ever introduced in this or any other Parliament on the whole face of the earth."[56] Faced with several hundred such Unionists in the House of Lords, Morley had to compromise. In late July and early August 1894 he worked to obtain agreement to a plan of voluntary rather than compulsory reinstatement of the tenants. However, at the moment a compromise seemed

50. Morley's letter of instruction to the commissioners was quoted in *The Times*, October 15, 1892.

51. Lyons, *Dillon*, 157.

52. Eversley, *Gladstone and Ireland*, 314. ·

53. Lyons, *Dillon*, 157.

54. *Hansard*, 4th ser., 23 (April 19, 1894), 865–77.

55. For example, see the speeches by Harrington (Parnellite) and Dillon (anti-Parnellite), *ibid.*, 889–93, 898–905.

56. *Hansard*, 4th ser., 27 (July 19, 1894), 436.

settled, he mismanaged his parliamentary forces and allowed some nationalists to get out of hand in their denunciation of landlords. The attempt at compromise failed, and the bill had to be pushed through the Commons by frequent use of the guillotine closure. Inevitably, the Lords threw it out.[57]

By the autumn of 1894 Morley was determined to redeem himself with a major land bill. With the cabinet in no mood to reintroduce the evicted tenants bill, Morley proposed instead to amend the 1881 land act to strengthen the position of the tenants. In April 1894 he had persuaded the Commons to establish a select committee to study the results of the previous Irish land tenure acts. Here again Morley ran into trouble, for a number of Unionists withdrew from the select committee when Morley would allow no landlords, only officials from the land departments, to testify. Nevertheless, the committee was useful in showing that in Ireland most improvements on the land were made by the tenantry. This conclusion formed the basis of Morley's bill, whereby tenants were to be exempted from paying rent on their own improvements.[58] Oddly enough, with the nationalists speaking in rival factions, Morley's strongest support in drafting the measure came from T. W. Russell, an Ulster landlord.[59] Despite intemperate opposition from Edward Carson, later the leader of Ulster Unionism, the bill won a second reading without a division in April 1895. But the bill went no further, as the government fell soon afterward. Morley wrote that "both Report and Bill were in a few months packed safe away in the crowded, dusty, and unhonoured pigeonholes allotted decade after decade to Irish land."[60]

Frustrated on Home Rule, the evicted tenants bill, and the big land bill, Morley was distinctly a failure in the legislative half of his position. Yet his Liberal colleagues could scarcely complain, for

57. Morley, *Recollections*, I, 349–50; Hamilton Diaries, August 5, 9, 15, 22, 24, 1894, 48,664.

58. *Hansard*, 4th ser., 31 (March 4, 1895), 295–320; Hamilton Diaries, November 26, 1894, 48,665; Morley, *Recollections*, I, 350–51.

59. T. W. Russell, "Mr. Morley and the Irish Land Bill," *F.R.* 339 (March 1895), 348–51.

60. Morley, *Recollections*, I, 351–52.

they afforded him very little help and in fact were very reluctant to give him parliamentary time for his proposals.[61] Further, he was an administrative success, at least in that he helped keep Ireland relatively tranquil for a few years. Morley conceived his administrative task in Ireland to be one of restoring the confidence of the majority of the Irish people to the Irish executive. Because he looked to Home Rule as the only way to substantial institutional reform for Ireland, he thought of this problem as merely one of changing the closed and repressive attitude of the existing Dublin Castle system. Thus he introduced no significant alteration in the structure of the system, but he did make important changes in administrative policy. He tried to make himself more open to nationalist opinion than past Chief Secretaries had been; he even had the former revolutionary, Michael Davitt, to luncheon in the Chief Secretary's lodge. With no small difficulty, he replaced Balfour's permanent undersecretary, Sir Joseph West Ridgeway, because he thought Ridgeway's presence would subvert his attempts to moderate the behavior of the police.[62] And he took many of the decisions made in the Castle, including routine administrative matters, into his own hands. He ruled the Castle like a minor despot. Before his departure, Ridgeway felt compelled to complain that Morley was a martinet: he made the staff keep regular hours of work and give up fox-hunting in the afternoons, and he exercised strict personal supervision over their labor.[63] The effort to control the bureaucracy paid handsome dividends. In January 1894 Morley reported to Gladstone with justified pride: "The tranquility is profound for the time; but it is only secured by incessant vigilance on my part—not so much over the people as over the officials, who mean well, but have bad habits."[64]

Maintenance of law and order was Morley's most difficult ad-

61. Morley frequently had to beg for attention to Ireland. For instance, see his letters to Rosebery on November 18, 1894, January 24, 25, 1895, all in Rosebery Papers, Box 36.

62. West, *Private Diaries*, 106–7, 210; Morley to Gladstone, September 22, 1892, Gladstone Papers, 44,256; Morley to Rosebery, September 18, 1892, Rosebery Papers, Box 35.

63. Curtis, *Coercion and Conciliation*, 412.

64. January 25, 1894, Gladstone Papers, 44,257.

ministrative problem. He went to Ireland determined to install a policy of conciliation but at the same time to enforce normal law. In September 1892, with Gladstone's approval, Morley revoked the proclamations that had put the infamous crimes act into effect.[65] This was a popular move with the Irish, but they, and many Radicals as well, also wanted the government to seek formal repeal of the act.[66] Morley gave his sympathy and support to nationalist bills to repeal the law, but as the government was unwilling to spend more parliamentary time on Ireland, he did not force the issue.[67] The hated law remained on the books, though only as a dead letter. Morley also tried to bring the legal machinery into harmony with the feelings of Irishmen by appointing a large number of Catholics to the magistracy—554 of 637 appointed during his tenure.[68] And in many ways he tried to reduce the traditional harshness of the law in Ireland. He gave amnesty to four men convicted of murdering a policeman at Gweedore some three years before.[69] He refused Unionist demands to revive the secret inquiries formerly employed by Balfour, even in Clare, where lawlessness was widespread.[70] He ordered the constabulary not to provide assistance to sheriffs who wanted to execute writs and seizures at night against tenants.[71] All of these policies were meant to generate an atmosphere of peace in Ireland, and to induce the Irish to hold patiently to the Liberal alliance.

Nevertheless, Morley sought with his characteristic attitude of fatalism to enforce the normal law. He rejected nationalist appeals for amnesty of convicted dynamiters, on grounds that such men were not political prisoners but criminals.[72] (His refusal apparently

---

65. Morley to Gladstone, September 10, 1892, Gladstone Papers, 44,256; *The Times*, September 15, 1892.

66. For nationalist opinion, see the following note. For Radical attitudes, see *The Speaker*, September 17, 1892.

67. *Hansard*, 4th ser., 23 (April 18, 1894), 778–88; 33 (May 8, 1895), 738–50.

68. Morley, *Recollections*, I, 339–40.

69. *The Times*, December 26, 1892.

70. *Hansard*, 4th ser., 9 (March 2, 1893), 852–58.

71. *The Times*, February 3, 1893.

72. Morley to Gladstone, October 30, 1892, Gladstone Papers, 44,257; *The Times*, October 30, 1894.

inspired a terrorist dynamite attack on Dublin Castle in which a policeman was blown to bits.) [73] Morley also continued to give police support for evictions. The eviction rate continued at a level comparable to the Balfour years: in 1893, for example, 6,526 ejectment notices were served, and 574 tenants actually evicted.[74] In an effort to avoid violence Morley tried to restrain public demonstrations against "land grabbing" by keeping them at least one mile away from the tenancy that had been taken by the land grabber. He stuck to his policy of "Morley's Mile" even when it became unpopular with the nationalists.[75]

Morley's administrative policies seem to have contributed significantly to the reduction of agrarian crimes in Ireland, though it is certainly true that other factors, including the attitude of the nationalists themselves, were also important. The figures on Irish crime are difficult to evaluate, but the evidence generally supports Morley's claim of January 1895 that Ireland was quieter than at any time since 1876.[76] Even Balfour admitted that Ireland had settled considerably, though he asserted that the country was quiet only because the nationalists chose to make it so.[77] Morley did not entirely disagree with Balfour's interpretation of the cause of the relative tranquility; indeed, he reminded Rosebery that the quiet in Ireland came from the confidence of the Irish people in the policy of the government.[78] In view of the fact that Home Rule had been defeated and shelved, and land legislation had made little progress, the contribution of Morley's administration in Ireland toward the retention of Irish confidence becomes very clear.

The effectiveness of Morley's rule did not by any means make it

73. Morley to Gladstone, December 25, 1892, Gladstone Papers, 44,257; *The Times*, December 26, 1892.

74. *Hansard*, 4th ser., 22 (March 20, 1894), 697.

75. *The Times*, June 21, 1894.

76. From a speech at Newcastle, reported in *The Times*, January 31, 1895. See also Morley's report to Rosebery, December 7, 1894, Rosebery Papers, Box 36; and the figures on Irish crime submitted to the inspector-general of the Royal Irish Constabulary: Sessional Papers, 1893–94, C. 7014, vol. 74, pt. 2, pp. 415–26; 1894, C. 7332, vol. 72, pp. 43–54; 1895, C. 7689, vol. 82, pp. 101–12; 1895, C. 7716, vol. 82, pp. 121–23; 1895, C. 7849, vol. 82, pp. 125–27.

77. *Hansard*, 4th ser., 22 (March 12, 1894), 53–54.

78. December 7, 1894, Rosebery Papers, Box 36.

popular. Both Unionists and nationalists found fault with the Chief Secretary. In various resolutions of censure, Unionist M.P.'s claimed that Morley was abandoning loyal Irishmen to criminal elements and was condoning criminal acts.[79] *The Times* and H. O. Arnold-Forster, two formidable critics of Liberal policy, accused Morley of encouraging intimidation of landlords and law-abiding tenants.[80] Though Morley survived these attacks, they contributed to his desire in 1894 to leave the Irish office. He got small comfort from the Irish nationalists. Both Parnellites and anti-Parnellites denounced him for continuing to support evictions.[81] After the government let the Lords' rejection of the Home Rule bill go uncontested, the Parnellites became very severe in their criticism. They accused Morley of encouraging evictions, of packing juries, of suppressing public meetings, and of heartlessness in refusing to release convicted dynamiters and in failing to realize the extent of agrarian distress in the winter of 1894–5.[82] Morley's unwillingness to use the power of Dublin Castle against landlords and Ulstermen, his inability to help the evicted tenants, and his determination to prosecute terrorists contributed to an estrangement even from many anti-Parnellites.[83]

Under these circumstances, as Morley himself admitted, success "in any full sense" for his tenure of office could not be expected. It can be counted as remarkable that in 1895 a number of men from all British and Irish parties agreed that his administration had sponsored peace and calm in Ireland.[84] It is also remarkable that Radicalism *per se* entered so little into his policies. Morley did not try to apply any distinctly Radical principles in Ireland. He did not attempt to break the power of the landlords or promote democracy through institutional reforms. He made no attempt to get to the root of the fundamental Irish objections to the Dublin Castle system.

---

79. *Hansard*, 4th ser., 9 (March 2, 1893), 840–47; (March 23, 1893), 914–23; 10 (March 27, 1893), 1205–25.

80. *The Times*, October 19, 1892; June 21, 1894.

81. *The Times*, December 26, 1893.

82. *The Times*, November 14, 1894; *Hansard*, 4th ser., 22 (March 13, 1894), 241–44; 30 (February 12, 1895), 601–4.

83. For example, see Lyons, *Dillon*, 157; Morley, *Recollections*, I, 356.

84. T. W. Russell, "Morley and the Irish Land Bill," 347; Hamilton Diaries, June 28, 1895, 48,667.

Indeed, he survived partly because he put Radical expectations away. These facts symbolize the stalemate in which the Radicals after 1893 found themselves. For them as for Morley, Home Rule was the only solution to the Irish problem, yet Home Rule had been put out of reach by the House of Lords and the pressure of other, largely Radical, claims. In this situation Morley was forced to approach the Irish Question as his predecessors had done—neither as a Radical nor as an Irishman, but as an Englishman.

IV. THE HOUSE OF LORDS AND THE ELECTION OF 1895

While Morley was balancing on the fine line between conciliation of Irish nationalism and maintenance of public order, Radicals in Britain were continuing to turn their attention away from Ireland. Though they never repudiated Home Rule outright, they elevated other issues to the top of the Radical program. In so doing they continued the process of substituting Radical for Irish policies implicit in their decision not to fight the House of Lords over the second Home Rule bill. Ironically, in 1894 and 1895 the issue of reforming the House of Lords itself was important in supplanting Home Rule. Labouchere's successful amendment to the Address in March 1894 revealed that many Radicals had become enthusiastic about destroying the power of the Lords. Their hostility to the peers continued to grow during the following months. In May 1894 delegates from 347 English and Welsh Liberal and Radical associations met in Leeds to establish the policy of the National Liberal Federation toward the upper House. Though the Leeds conference rejected an extreme proposal by Lawson and Labouchere to abolish the Lords immediately, it did pass a resolution calling for neutralization of the Lords' veto power over measures passed twice through the House of Commons.[85] Most Radicals applauded this action, on grounds that Liberal domestic legislation had to be saved and that reform of the Lords ought to be the battle cry for the next general election.[86] Even

85. National Liberal Federation, *Proceedings of the Seventeenth Annual Meeting, 1895*, 25–27.

86. *Daily News*, June 21, 1894; *The Star*, June 21, 1894; T. Wemyss Reid, "Leeds Conference," *Liberal Magazine* (July 1894), 201–2; Henry Labouchere, letters to *The Times*, September 27, December 1, 1894.

the Home Rule Union turned to denunciation of the peers. In their annual meeting of May 1894 the Union expressed pleasure with the progress of Home Rule and vowed to fight the Lords to the bitter end for it, but did not demand either reintroduction of the measure or an immediate dissolution.[87] The House of Lords had seized the attention of even the most enthusiastic Radical Home Rulers.

Quite understandably, the Irish nationalists became disturbed with the obvious decline of Liberal interest in Home Rule. The feeling arose in some quarters of the National League that Irishmen should once more assert their independence from both British parties.[88] This attitude tended to strengthen the Parnellites, who argued that the Liberal interest in attacking the House of Lords might postpone passage of Home Rule for a generation.[89] The anti-Parnellites publicly supported the Liberal party's efforts to limit the power of the Lords, but in private they recognized their vulnerability to the charge that they were allowing the Liberals to drop Home Rule.[90] To reinforce the McCarthyites (the pro-Liberal anti-Parnellites) against such attacks, Morley, in the session of 1894, promised them that the government would keep Home Rule "the first and principle policy" in the Speech from the Throne for the 1895 session.[91] Even earlier in 1894 Morley had promised McCarthy that the government would reintroduce the evicted tenants bill and bring in a more general land bill as well. He also had agreed with McCarthy that the session of 1895 would be the last for the existing parliament.[92] By all of these agreements Morley had meant to reassure the McCarthyites that the government would to all appearances commit itself firmly to Ireland, then quickly dissolve. Presumably, then, the anti-Parnellite forces could make a strong appeal against the Parnellites in Ireland during the general election.

In reality, however, the promises made by Morley only provided

87. *The Times*, May 12, 1894.

88. See *The Times*, August 16, 1894, for a report of a meeting of the National League, at which Dr. Joseph Kenny advanced this view.

89. John Redmond, "What Has Happened to Home Rule?" *Nineteenth Century* 213 (November 1894), 665–67.

90. Morley to Rosebery, March 11, 16, 1894, Rosebery Papers, Box 36.

91. Stansky, *Ambitions and Strategies*, 147–48.

92. Memorandum by Morley, July 10, 1894, Rosebery Papers, Box 96.

the occasion for the final struggle between Home Rule and Radicalism for priority in the Liberal program. When the cabinet began to draw up its plans for the Queen's speech in January 1895, Morley reminded his colleagues of the pledges to which he thought they were bound.[93] But by that time the claims of various Radical groups, especially the Welsh nationalists, had become irresistible. In mid-January at Cardiff the annual conference of the National Liberal Federation resolved that Welsh disestablishment should be the first measure brought before the House of Commons.[94] With such strong support the cabinet decided to announce that it would proceed first with a Welsh disestablishment bill, and to make no public pledges about satisfying the Irish representatives on Irish self-rule. At a cabinet meeting on January 25 Morley frantically protested the repudiation of his pledge to the Irish on Home Rule, and he threatened resignation a number of times. But he could make no headway against his colleagues, for even Rosebery and Harcourt, in a rare moment of harmony, united against him.[95] The Speech from the Throne made no mention whatever of Home Rule.

The Parnellites were determined to make the Liberal abandonment of Home Rule as clear as possible. In the debate on the Address John Redmond moved an amendment calling for immediate reference of Home Rule to the constituencies. This maneuver threatened to break the Liberal–anti-Parnellite alliance and to split the Liberals as well. Though in an embarrassing position, Morley gamely contended that Home Rule still occupied first place in the party platform, and that this fact would be proved in the next general election; meanwhile, he said, passage of English and Scottish proposals would put the ministry in a better position to pass Home Rule. The Radical M.P.'s saved the day for the ministry by agreeing that the time for dissolution had not yet come. To them, the pressing issue was now the power of the House of Lords; thus the Liberals should retain office, fill up the cup of popular resentment by forcing the Lords to reject Radical proposals, and then dissolve on the issue

93. Morley to Rosebery, January 24, 1895, Rosebery Papers, Box 36.
94. National Liberal Federation, *Proceedings of the Seventeenth Annual Meeting, 1895,* 6.
95. Stansky, *Ambitions and Strategies,* 148.

of the Lords.[96] Thus Redmond's amendment did not split the Liberal party, but it did show very plainly that Home Rule had become an almost insignificant issue to Liberals and Radicals alike.

The Liberal government managed to stagger on, despite sagging morale and tiny majorities, until June 21, 1895, when they were defeated on a motion of censure concerning shortages in cordite for the army. This setback need not have forced a resignation. But, weary from internal strife and from discontent within the parliamentary party, the cabinet seized the opportunity to escape. They hoped that their resignation would force the Conservatives to form policies which would unify Liberalism. This strategy did not work, for Lord Salisbury assumed office only long enough to dissolve parliament. Thereupon the Unionists made the Liberal commitment to Home Rule, though in actuality moribund, their whipping-boy for the general election.[97]

The Conservative tactics neatly precluded Liberal unity. Morley kept Home Rule to the forefront of his own policies, and he insisted to his constituents in Newcastle that the party agreed with him.[98] But none of the other Liberal or Radical leaders supported his argument. Lord Rosebery urged that the main issue be the House of Lords; he made no significant reference to Home Rule. Harcourt, though obviously at odds with Rosebery, was happy to be free of Ireland at last. He made local veto of the liquor trade the key to his campaign in Derby. Acland and Asquith spoke mainly on social reforms. Radical candidates studiously avoided any reference to Ireland. R. K. Causton talked about London's problems. Labouchere campaigned on abolition of the Lords. Sidney Buxton refused to answer a direct question as to whether he supported Home Rule. None of the leading Radical journals paid any but lip service to Ireland.[99] Yet the results of the election further contributed to the demise of Home Rule as a viable issue within the Liberal party. The Unionists won a huge majority (152) and proved that the Lords had

96. *Hansard*, 4th ser., 30 (February 11, 1895), 465–77, 480–89, 518–20; (February 25, 1895), 877–87, 892–93, 905–7; (February 18, 1895), 983–93, 1001–8, and 1032–37.

97. Stansky, *Ambitions and Strategies*, 167–74.

98. *The Times*, July 5, 10, 1895.

99. For the Radical campaigns, see *The Times*, July 1–15, 1895; for the attitudes of Radical journals: *The Star*, July 10, 1895; and the *Methodist Times*, July 18, 1895.

been right to throw out Gladstone's bill. Moreover, many of Ireland's truest Radical friends were defeated: Arnold Morley, Shaw Lefevre, Hopwood, Hibbert, Everett, Barran, Conybeare, and, most serious of all losses for Home Rule, John Morley. Having lost the struggle for precedence within the Liberal party, the Home Rulers seemed to be repudiated by their constituencies.

Radicals of different persuasions produced very different interpretations of the severe Liberal defeat. A few, like J. Guinness Rogers, an old-fashioned Nonconformist Radical, speculated that the country was not as progressive as most Liberal observers had thought, and that "filling the cup" had been a mistake. He believed that Home Rule had played only a subordinate role in the election, but had to admit that Liberals generally had become less enthusiastic about Home Rule and less committed to satisfying the Irish nationalist party.[100] H. W. Massingham, like most of the New Radicals, thought that Rosebery and Harcourt had not showed enough sympathy for the poor. For the future he advocated clear, socially oriented policies and made no mention of continuing the struggle for Home Rule.[101] The *Daily News* speculated that the cause of defeat was a general lack of enthusiasm in the party, brought about by the failure of Liberals to attend to familiar issues such as the power of the House of Lords and voter registration.[102] The one thing that most Radicals could agree on was that Home Rule had been a hindrance rather than a help in the election, and that it must receive less attention in the coming years. Morley's defeat was taken as particularly indicative of the inutility of Home Rule—even though in fact the main cause of his loss was his unwillingness to promise Newcastle workingmen that he would support an eight-hours bill. As a prediction of Radical attitudes, a comment by *The Times* on Morley's defeat was accurate: "The blow is final, and as such, we believe, it will soon be accepted by the more sagacious members of the Radical party."[103] Open repudiation by the Radicals of Home

100. J. Guinness Rogers, "The General Election. I. What Does It All Mean?" *Nineteenth Century* 222 (August 1895), 177–85.

101. H. W. Massingham, "The Debacle—and After," *Contemporary Review* 68 (August 1895), 301–3.

102. *Daily News*, July 30, 1895.

103. *The Times*, July 19, 1895.

Rule was not forthcoming, because it was not necessary. The politics of cooperation by the nationalist majority allowed Radicals simply to ignore the issue. It would take the recovery of powerful parliamentary leverage by the Home Rule party to force Radicals to recall their deep and active commitment to justice for Ireland.

V. Conclusion

Radical involvement with Home Rule and Irish nationalism ended with a whimper and not a bang. The Radicals did not take up the Irish cause again until 1909, when parliamentary embarrassments resulting from the Lloyd George budget and the recalcitrance of the House of Lords gave the Home Rule party new influence over the Liberal party and restored something of a situation of confrontation, or at least made the nationalist alliance operative. By then it was too late for Home Rule, for though the Home Rule party remained popular in Ireland, Ulster Unionist opposition had solidified; hindsight teaches that little time was left before the Great War. For a decade after 1895 cooperation failed to win its primary goal for the Irish.

The history of Radicalism after 1895 is lost in the troubles of the Liberal party, itself a historical problem that has occupied a large and growing number of historians. The solution to the question "What happened to the Liberal party?" may well lie in understanding the nature of the late-Victorian Radical movement. In the early twentieth century Radicals were scarcely to be distinguished from the rest of the Liberals, for the Radical policies of the 1870's and 1880's had become the Liberal orthodoxy of the 1890's and early 1900's. The term "Liberal" tended to absorb "Radical" and put an end to Radicalism as a distinct movement on the left wing of Liberalism. One long-term explanation for the decline of the Liberal party is that, even after taking on a full load of Radical policies and preoccupations, it could not hold the allegiance of the working class. This it had to do in order to survive, for an increasing proportion of middle-class people, particularly in the expanding suburbs, had been moving into the Conservative camp in the years after about 1880. The Liberal party depended more than ever on working-class support, for which the best hope was Radicalism, with its tradition of appeal to working people. But Radicalism proved to be relatively impervious to working-class desires and failed in the competition with the the new Labour party for the votes of workingmen.

It is precisely in the context of the nature and history of Radicalism that the story of Radical involvement with Ireland has its meaning. Partly, the significance of the story lies in structural matters (in, for example, the fact that the Irish Question split the Radical movement in 1886, but the importance of that division, as this study demonstrates, has been exaggerated). More of significance arises from the divisions and disputes opened in the Radical body by Parnellite pressure from the mid-1870's on. These divisions contributed to the ineffectiveness of Radicalism by aggravating the inherent tendency of the movement to splinter. Of special consequence was the impulse toward working-class self-consciousness given by Irish issues in the latter 1870's and early 1880's: the very different attitudes toward coercion, and the concomitant distinctions in analysis of the root problem in Ireland, helped the working-class Radicals form institutions and ideologies necessary for their independence from the middle-class Radicals. At the same time, the Home Rule crisis precipitated both a solidification and a promotion to official status of middle-class Radical agencies. In the latter half of the 1880's, when the Irish Question provided the occasion for Radicalism to be injected into the programs and power structure of the Liberal party, working-class Radicals found it harder than ever to play an important role in Radical leadership. It is striking that individual workingmen influenced Liberal or Radical thinking very little in the major political crises from 1886 through 1895, even though working-class Radicals as a whole formed earlier and more complete attachment to Home Rule than any other segment of the movement. The Irish Question, one may conclude, helped show that the organizational structure of Radicalism was of, for, and by middle-class Radicals.

Of equal interest are the revelations made by the Irish Question concerning the main stream of Radical ideology. These features can be seen in both the period of confrontation and the period of cooperation, for the two forms of Irish strategy were like the controlled variable in a laboratory experiment. The Radicals were above all British, formed in (a response to) an industrializing society. Radicals found it extremely difficult to translate their principles into the Irish context, because they frequently did not understand the Irish predicament and because they did not mean by stock terms like democracy and religious liberty precisely what the Irish nationalists did. The Radicals had an elaborate program but a limited target area, which did not include an agrarian Catholic society. Their attitude toward the land problem is a good illustration. They were ready to join the nationalists in protecting Irish tenants from the arbitrary authority of landlords, for Radical ideology held that landed privilege and power were the greatest of all enemies of progress; but they were not willing to support a genuinely workable land purchase scheme, because that would risk British funds and would be a violation of sacrosanct economic principles.

The fullest revelation of the meaning of their ideas is to be found in their response to Home Rule. The principles of democracy and of doing the greatest good for the greatest number in theory are easily capable of including a proposition like Home Rule for Ireland. Yet the Radicals did not respond positively to Irish nationalist reasoning alone, even when the Home Rulers argued in terms of Radical precepts. The behavior of middle-class Radicals showed that a concern for parliamentary propriety and social discipline was an important, if usually unspoken, aspect of their ideology. However, they did respond favorably when forced by confrontation to weigh the costs of coercion against those of conciliation. They were in this sense more receptive to a demand for power from a group outside the British political elite than were more orthodox politicians. Still, the commitment of a substantial majority of Radicals to Home Rule was due more to a realization that Ireland was beyond Radical understanding and capabilities than to an application of Radical precepts to Ireland. Home Rule never became an integral part of Radicalism, even though enthusiasm for the Irish cause reached remarkable heights between 1886 and 1890, when a sense of justice touched the Radical tendency to emphasize the moral dimension of politics. The significant feature of their commitment was how rapidly this fervor wilted under the natural inclination of the Radicals to return to their essential interests: the redress of specific Nonconformist, regional, bourgeois grievances. It was the nature of Radicalism to be vitally concerned with such issues, and not with the application of democratic principles to a problem area raised by an external force like Irish nationalism. The historical origins of Radicalism provided limits as well as positive content to the late-Victorian Radical movement, and not even the long and extraordinarily acute crisis raised by the Parnellites could alter their basic program or ideals.

These conclusions as much as say that the personnel of the Radical elite were not changed by the Irish Question. As already emphasized, the Irish Question slowed the advance of Radicalism in the country but impelled it to preeminence within the Liberal party. It gave Radicals the opportunity to exercise power in Liberal institutions, but it did not make them a different kind of people. It neither changed the men who regarded themselves as Radicals (except for a few who became Unionists) nor caused the Radical elite to be recruited from a broader or different base. The Radical movement throughout the period was dominated by men with grievances of a special kind, those arising from the Nonconformist, commercial, industrial, professional, and provincial segments of British society. These were men of considerable drive and force—but, as the Irish Question revealed, they often were also narrow and inflexible, seemingly incapable of sympathy for a plainly outraged and suffering people. Radicals characteristically liked humanity in the abstract, but not, except when their own interests were involved, people in the concrete. Their self-image was one of unique spokesmen for groups outside the traditional structure of power in Britain, for all underprivileged in a privileged world. Yet their behavior in the case of Irish nationalism makes it clear that it was their own particular out-group, their own special region, they cared about. They were not always in favor of change, nor did they continually try "to get to the root of things." They thought of themselves as the repository of progressive and reformist impulses, open always to change and modernization. But they were themselves slow to move on Ireland and inclined to demand that the Irish nationalists conform to Radical concepts both of political style and of political priorities. This was the ethos in which Radical principles were embedded—the dimensions of the Radical persuasion.

Method of Selecting Radical Members of Parliament

Before discussing what British Radicals thought, said, and did about Ireland, it was necessary to find out who they were; that involved distinguishing the Radical from the non-Radical Members of Parliament. The most reliable way to accomplish this would have been to sort out all M.P.'s who were regarded by themselves and others as Radicals. Such a method would have the advantage of avoiding all arbitrary decisions in the process of selection, except for the few M.P.'s about whom there was some dispute even in their day. Presumably written records exist that would turn up even the most obscure Radicals. But the task of going through so many hundreds of newspapers and private collections necessary to find the commonly used labels of the less well-known M.P.'s is huge—too great, in fact, for the returns.

Another method might involve public speeches and election addresses. By this method, if an M.P. advocated a program that was Radical, then he could be regarded as a Radical. The trouble with this process is that Radicals, being politicians, often did not say in public exactly what they thought, at least not in sufficiently clear terms to allow distinctions between Radicals and non-Radicals. Like the tracing of the label "Radical," this method can be useful but not completely satisfactory.

A third process would use analysis of voting patterns in the House of Commons. The assumption here is that if the term "Radical" had any meaning at all, then Radical M.P.'s would vote similarly (though not necessarily by arrangement) in the House. The problems here are two: defining a pattern of votes that can be regarded as Radical, and determining what degree of conformity to that voting pattern should be regarded as qualifying an M.P. as Radical. Obviously this method involves some arbitrary decisions and ignores all the reasons of chance (like sickness and constituency pressure) that help determine a member's vote. Still, it can be very helpful if used cautiously.

The method used throughout this study involved elements of all three processes. The first step was to establish as far as possible from contemporary "literary" sources the number of Radicals in the House of Commons. For example, a party whip may have estimated to his chief that a certain number of Radicals won seats in a general election. Such estimates are not entirely reliable, as we do not know what constituted the criteria of selection or how carefully the list of members was examined, but they can be used to set approximate numbers to look for. Thus contemporary estimates are helpful as checks on the other methods. The second step was simply to assemble, from as much biographical research on Liberal M.P.'s and candidates as several years' work would allow, a list of all those known as Radicals. References to an M.P. as "Radical" in two independent and reliable contemporary sources have been regarded as sufficient to put a member on the list of Radicals.

The third step was to use a computer to analyze voting in the House of Commons. The computer program utilized is the EIDISC program developed by Donald Morrison and William Klecka of Northwestern University.* The unique quality of this program is that it recognizes differences in the power of divisions in the House to discriminate between groups. When supplied with a group of known Radicals and a group of known non-Radicals (like Gladstone), the EIDISC program enables the computer to assess the discriminating power of the various divisions. By a stepwise procedure, the computer then determines as far as it can the membership probability of each unclassified Liberal M.P. for each of the two groups, Radical and non-Radical. With this information the problem of selecting Radical M.P.'s was eased, though not eliminated. In no case in this study have the findings of the computer been regarded as final, but only as a guide to more investigation of selected individuals. Moreover, the program cannot deal with Members who did not sit in the House through the entirety of a parliament, and decisions about them had to be made by inspecting partial voting records. Finally, the computer cannot eliminate the arbitrariness of decisions concerning certain M.P.'s; it can only present data in a somewhat more manageable form. Thus the computer was not able to group all unclassified M.P.'s with assurance; some M.P.'s simply got middling scores on their voting, and no statistical juggling can disguise that fact. Here the statistical analysis undoubtedly was reflecting reality. The members of the parliamentary Liberal party in terms of political position

* The quantitative procedure is described in detail in T. W. Heyck and William Klecka, "British Radical M.P.'s, 1874-95: New Evidence from Discriminant Analysis," *The Journal of Interdisciplinary History* 4 (Autumn 1973), 161–84. In this article the computer program is called STPDIS, which is a modification of EIDISC.

ranged in a continuous spectrum from very Radical to very conservative. There were many moderates in the middle, some of whom may or may not have been regarded as Radical. These have been listed separately from the M.P.'s about whom there can be little doubt, and they have not been considered in describing Radical attitudes toward Ireland.

The divisions used in the voting analysis for the 1874–80 and 1880–85 parliaments follow. They were selected on the basis of their conformity to Radical principles and policies described in the first chapter. Theoretically, the computer could assess the discriminating power of every vote in any parliament, but as most divisions concerned matters not peculiar to Radicalism, they would not contribute toward the ability of the program to discriminate between Radicals and non-Radicals. Therefore, only these 'Radical'' issues were used. Even here the EIDISC program found a number of the issues made no addition to its power of discriminating and so did not use them.

Divisions Used in Selecting Radical M.P.'s, 1874–80

(All references are to *Hansard*, 3rd ser. Where *Hansard* gives only division totals, division lists from the *Parliamentary Papers* have been used.)

1. Bill to extend the hours of polling. 218 (March 25, 1874), 290.
2. Motion to reduce Royal grants. 218 (April 17, 1874), 769.
3. Motion to abolish the 25th Clause. 219 (June 10, 1874), 1304.
4. Prohibitory liquor bill. 220 (June 17, 1874), 2.
5. Compulsory education bill. 224 (June 9, 1875), 1562.
6. Triennial parliaments bill. 225 (June 17, 1875), 138.
7. Allotments extension bill. 225 (July 14, 1875), 1449.
8. Motion to reduce Royal expenses. 225 (July 15, 1875), 1509.
9. Resolution to extend the franchise. 225 (July 15, 1875), 1533.
10. Elementary education act amendment bill. 228 (April 5, 1876), 1251.
11. Resolution to extend the franchise in the counties. 229 (May 30, 1876), 1442.
12. Amendment for public control over education. 230 (July 10, 1876), 1186.
13. Resolution for municipal ownership of taverns. 232 (March 13, 1877), 1861.
14. Resolution to demand Turkish guarantees of reform. 233 (March 23, 1877), 395.
15. Resolution to restrict Crown prerogative in foreign policy. 246 (May 13, 1879), 242.

16. Resolution for quintennial parliaments. 250 (February 24, 1880), 1316.
17. Resolution for local option in liquor prohibition. 251 (March 5, 1880), 441.

Of these divisions, the EIDISC program used, in order of discriminating power, numbers 13, 5, 14, 16, 2, 1, 3, 15, 11, 4, 12.

Divisions Used in Selecting Radicals, 1880–85

1. Resolution for local option in liquor prohibition. 253 (June 8, 1880), 340.
2. Resolution opposing the Transvaal war. 257 (January 21, 1881), 1109.
3. Resolution for parliamentary control over foreign policy. 260 (April 29, 1881), 1424.
4. Resolution for local option in liquor prohibition. 262 (June 14, 1881), 524.
5. Bill to put parliamentary election expenses on the rates. 266 (February 9, 1882), 331.
6. Opposition to exclusion of Bradlaugh. 266 (February 22, 1882), 1344.
7. Motion to control agents of the Crown in foreign affairs. 277 (April 3, 1883), 1333.
8. Bill to create Scottish parish boards. 278 (April 18, 1883), 529.
9. Resolution for local option in liquor prohibition. 278 (April 27, 1883), 1280.
10. Resolution to admit Bradlaugh. 281 (July 9, 1883), 801.
11. Motion opposing Bradlaugh's exclusion. 284 (February 11, 1884), 480.
12. Resolution to remove bishops from the House of Lords. 286 (March 21, 1884), 501.
13. Bill to open cemeteries to all denominations. 289 (June 25, 1884), 1305.
14. Resolution to curtail the power of the House of Lords. 294 (November 21, 1884), 141.
15. Opposition to the Sudan war. 294 (February 27, 1885), 1724.
16. Resolution to reform death duties on land held in mortmain. 299 (July 23, 1885), 1679.

Of these divisions, the EIDISC program used, in order of discriminating power, numbers 12, 11, 3, 4, 13.

British Radical Members of Parliament, 1874–85

1874–80

English

1. W. S. Allen
2. J. Barran*
3. T. Blake*
4. W. E. Briggs*
5. Jacob Bright*
6. John Bright*
7. S. B. Bristowe
8. A. Brogden
9. A. H. Brown
10. T. Burt*
11. R. M. Carter*
12. J. Chamberlain*
13. Sir H. A. H. Cholmeley†
14. J. J. Colman*
15. L. H. Courtney*
16. J. Cowen*
17. J. K. Cross*
18. Sir C. Dilke*
19. G. Dixon*
20. J. Dodds
21. T. Earp*
22. H. Fawcett*
23. R. Ferguson
24. W. Fletcher*
25. Sir C. Forster

26. L. Fry
27. Sir J. Goldsmid
28. E. T. Gourley*
29. C. Harrison
30. Sir H. Havelock*
31. J. T. Hibbert
32. T. R. Hill
33. J. Holms*
34. C. H. Hopwood*
35. J. D. Hutchinson*
36. W. J. Ingram
37. W. H. James†
38. D. J. Jenkins
39. A. Laverton
40. Sir J. C. Lawrence
41. Sir W. Lawson*
42. E. A. Leatham*
43. A. McArthur
44. W. McArthur*
45. A. Macdonald*
46. S. Morley*
47. A. J. Mundella*
48. P. H. Muntz*
49. G. Palmer
50. F. Pennington*
51. S. Plimsoll*

* Denotes those referred to as Radicals in reliable contemporary sources.
† Denotes those from Whig families.

52. T. B. Potter*
53. P. Rylands*
54. H. B. Samuelson
55. G. J. Shaw Lefevre*
56. H. B. Sheridan
57. J. Simon
58. T. E. Smith*
59. J. Stansfeld*
60. J. C. Stevenson
61. P. A. Taylor*
62. C. P. Villiers*†
63. G. W. Whalley
64. J. Whitwell
65. C. H. Wilson
66. A. W. Young

Scottish
67. G. Anderson*
68. Sir G. Balfour
69. J. W. Barclay*
70. W. E. Baxter*

71. C. Cameron*
72. Sir G. Campbell*
73. Sir H. Campbell-Bannerman*
74. A. Grant
75. J. F. Harrison*
76. W. Holms*
77. J. E. Jenkins*
78. J. F. Leith
79. D. McLaren*
80. R. Reid*
81. G. O. Trevelyan*†

Welsh
82. D. Davies*†
83. R. Davies
84. L. L. Dillwyn*
85. P. E. Eyton*
86. M. Lloyd*
87. G. O. Morgan*
88. H. Richard*
89. J. Roberts*

1880–85

English
1. W. Agnew
2. D. Ainsworth
3. W. S. Allen
4. B. Armitage
5. A. Arnold*
6. J. Barran*
7. W. C. Borlase
8. C. Bradlaugh*
9. W. E. Briggs*
10. Jacob Bright*
11. John Bright*
12. H. Broadhurst*
13. A. H. Brown
14. J. Bryce*
15. T. Burt*
16. S. C. Buxton*

17. W. S. Caine*
18. R. K. Causton*
19. J. Chamberlain*
20. J. F. Cheetham
21. J. Collings*
22. J. J. Colman*
23. L. H. Courtney*
24. J. Cowen*
25. J. K. Cross*
26. A. W. Dilke*
27. C. Dilke*
28. T. Earp*
29. P. Edwards*
30. H. Fawcett*
31. R. Ferguson
32. J. F. B. Firth*
33. Sir C. Forster

34. H. H. Fowler
35. W. Fowler
36. L. Fry
37. T. Fry
38. E. T. Gourley*
39. Sir H. Havelock-Allan*
40. J. T. Hibbert
41. T. R. Hill
42. I. Holden
43. J. R. Holland
44. J. Holms*
45. C. H. Hopwood*
46. J. D. Hutchinson*
47. A. Illingworth*
48. W. H. James†
49. J. Joicey*
50. H. Labouchere*
51. Sir W. Lawson*
52. R. Leake
53. E. A. Leatham*
54. H. Lee
55. A. McArthur
56. Sir W. McArthur*
57. A. Macdonald*
58. R. B. Mackie
59. C. B. B. McLaren*
60. P. S. MacLiver
61. Hugh Mason*
62. A. Morley*
63. J. Morley*
64. S. Morley*
65. A. J. Mundella*
66. P. H. Muntz
67. G. Palmer
68. J. H. Palmer*
69. F. Pennington*
70. J. A. Picton*
71. T. B. Potter*
72. T. Roe
73. J. E. T. Rogers*
74. G. W. E. Russell*†

75. J. Ruston*
76. H. B. Samuelson
77. P. Rylands*
78. T. Shaw*
79. G. J. Shaw Lefevre
80. H. B. Sheridan
81. J. Simon
82. J. Slagg
83. T. E. Smith*
84. L. Stanley*†
85. J. Stansfeld*
86. J. C. Stevenson
87. S. Storey*
88. Prof. J. Stuart*
89. W. Summers
90. P. A. Taylor*
91. J. P. Thomasson
92. T. C. Thompson*
93. J. H. Tillett
94. W. Willis
95. E. W. B. Willyams
96. C. H. Wilson
97. W. Woodall

Scottish
98. G. Anderson*
99. G. Armitstead
100. J. W. Barclay*
101. W. E. Baxter*
102. J. C. Bolton
103. T. R. Buchanan*
104. C. Cameron
105. Sir G. Campbell*
106. H. Campbell-Bannerman*
107. Dr. R. Farquharson
108. A. Grant
109. F. Henderson
110. W. Holms*
111. D. McLaren*
112. J. D. Peddie*
113. A. Craig Sellar

114. G. O. Trevelyan*†
115. J. Webster
116. Sir D. Wedderburn
117. S. Williamson

Welsh
118. D. Davies*†
119. R. Davies
120. L. L. Dillwyn*
121. C. H. James

122. Sir J. J. Jenkins
123. M. Lloyd*
124. G. O. Morgan*
125. W. H. R. Powell*
126. S. Rendel*
127. H. Richard*
128. J. Roberts*
129. S. Smith
130. S. C. E. Williams*

The following M.P.'s possibly were Radical, but the evidence is ambiguous:

1874–80

1. Sir T. Bazley
2. J. C. Clarke
3. C. C. Clifford
4. J. Cowan
5. S. Holland
6. C. Fraser Macintosh[1]
7. W. E. Price

8. P. Ralli
9. J. Ramsay
10. W. Rathbone
11. C. Seely
12. S. H. Waterlow
13. I. Wilson

1880–85

1. R. B. Bruce
2. J. C. Clarke
3. C. C. Clifford
4. J. Cowan
5. W. Davies
6. A. D. Elliot
7. S. Holland
8. J. Howard

9. C. Fraser Macintosh[1]
10. P. Ralli
11. J. Ramsay
12. W. Rathbone
13. C. Seely
14. Sir S. Waterlow
15. I. Wilson

1. C. Fraser Macintosh often was called a Radical, and on certain issues he was. For example, regarding land questions, Fraser Macintosh was an ally of the crofters; yet he opposed the disestablishment of the Church of Scotland. He was a Jacobite rather than a Jacobin, so his Radical tendencies arose from anti-Whig beliefs of an unusual kind.

Appendices

BRITISH RADICALS, 1874–85: TABLES

Table 1. Occupations of Radical M.P.'s, 1874–85

OCCUPATION	1874–80	1880–85
Commerce and industry	48	64
Law	21	26
Professions	0	3
Writing and journalism	5	11
Teaching	0	4
Civil service	1	0
Workers	2	3
Armed forces	2	1
Land	5	8
Others	1	1
Unknown	4	9
Total	89	130

Table 2. Religion of Radical M.P.'s, 1874–85

DENOMINATION	1874–80	1880–85
Church of England	9	18
Church of Scotland	4	5
Baptist	4	8
Congregationalist	7	20
Methodist (including Calvinistic)	9	12
Primitive Methodist	1	1
Quaker	9	9
Unitarian	7	11
Scottish Dissenting Presbyterian (Free or United Church)	3	6
Presbyterian, undetermined type	5	2
Nonconformist, undetermined type	11	13
Roman Catholic	1	1
Jew	2	1
No religion	4	7
Unknown	13	16
Total	89	130

Table 3. Social and Civic Achievements of Radical M.P.'s, 1874–85

TYPE OF ACHIEVEMENT	1874–80	1880–85
Oxford & Cambridge graduates	19	29
Other university graduates	18	28
Public school only	2	3
Large landowners	17	31
Magistrates and D.L.'s	36	62
Aldermen, mayors	15	22
Chamber of Commerce officers	5	12
Whigs (member of Whig family)	4	5
Patrons of livings	1	3

Table 4. Types of Constituencies of Radical M.P.'s, 1874–85

KIND OF CONSTITUENCY	1874–80	1880–85
Small borough (0–1,999 electors)	12	7
Provincial towns (2,000–9,999 electors)	33	48
Large cities (more than 10,000 electors)	40	60
Rural counties	3	6
Industrial counties	1	5
Part rural, part industrial counties	0	4
Total	89	130

Table 5. Constituencies of Radical M.P.'s, by Region, 1874–85

REGION	1874–80	1880–85
England	66	97
Wales	8	13
Scotland	15	20
Total	89	130

Radicals and Radicalism, 1886

The following divisions were used in the voting analysis to select the Radical M.P.'s in the 1886 parliament (all citations from *Hansard*):

1. Bill to extend the franchise to women. 302 (February 18, 1886), 689–702.
2. Motion for money to administer areas in South Africa. 302 (March 1, 1886), 1614–31.
3. Resolution to abolish the hereditary principle of the House of Lords. 303 (March 5, 1886), 20–53.
4. Resolution to disestablish the Church in Wales. 303 (March 9, 1886), 305–61.
5. Motion to reduce money for maintaining Royal palaces. 303 (March 11, 1886), 479–87.
6. Resolution to establish parliamentary control over foreign and imperial policy. 303 (March 19, 1886), 1386–1423.
7. Resolution to disestablish the Church of Scotland. 304 (March 30, 1886), 293–355.
8. Resolution to abolish capital punishment. 305 (May 11, 1886), 767–90.

Of these, the EIDISC program utilized, in order of their power to discriminate Radicals from non-Radicals, numbers 5, 3, and 7.

RADICAL MEMBERS OF PARLIAMENT, 1886

England

1. W. S. Allen*
2. R. A. Allison
3. J. Arch*
4. B. Armitage
5. T. G. Ashton
6. L. A. Atherley-Jones*
7. J. H. Blades*
8. T. Blake*
9. T. H. Bolton*

* Denotes those referred to as Radicals in reliable contemporary sources.
† Denotes those from Whig families.

10. W. C. Borlase
11. C. Bradlaugh*
12. John Bright*
13. W. L. Bright*
14. H. Broadhurst*
15. A. H. Brown
16. J. T. Brunner
17. A. Buckley
18. T. Burt*
19. E. N. Buxton
20. W. S. Caine*
21. J. Chamberlain*
22. R. Chamberlain*
23. F. A. Channing*
24. H. P. Cobb*
25. F. T. Cobbold
26. B. J. S. Coleridge*
27. J. Collings*
28. J. J. Colman*
29. C. A. V. Conybeare*
30. E. R. Cook*
31. W. T. R. Cook*
32. H. Cossham*
33. L. H. Courtney*
34. J. Cowen*
35. J. Craven
36. W. Crawford*
37. W. R. Cremer*
38. C. Crompton
39. Sir W. Crossman
40. Sir C. Dilke*
41. G. Dixon*
42. J. C. Durant*
43. J. E. Ellis*
44. R. L. Everett
45. C. Fenwick*
46. R. Ferguson
47. Dr. B. Foster
48. L. Fry
49. T. Fry

50. G. P. Fuller
51. Sir J. Goldsmid
52. E. T. Gourley
53. Sir E. Grey*
54. Sir H. Havelock-Allan*
55. J. T. Hibbert
56. B. Hingley
57. A. Holden*
58. I. Holden
59. G. Howell*
60. A. Illingworth*
61. W. J. Ingram
62. J. A. Jacoby
63. W. H. James†
64. J. W. Johns
65. J. Joicey*
66. W. Kenrick*
67. A. G. Kitching
68. H. Labouchere*
69. H. L. W. Lawson*
70. R. Leake
71. E. A. Leatham*
72. J. Leicester*
73. A. McArthur
74. C. B. B. McLaren*
75. W. Mather
76. S. Montagu*
77. O. V. Morgan
78. A. Morley*
79. J. Morley*
80. J. F. Moulton*
81. A. J. Mundella*
82. G. Newnes
83. F. Otter
84. J. M. Paulton
85. R. Peacock*
86. B. Pickard*
87. E. H. Pickersgill*
88. J. A. Picton*
89. T. B. Potter*

90. B. Priestley
91. H. G. Reid*
92. T. Robinson
93. W. S. Robson*
94. T. Roe
95. J. E. T. Rogers*
96. J. Ruston*
97. P. Rylands*
98. Col. G. Salis-Schwabe
99. W. Saunders*
100. C. Seale-Hayne
101. T. Shaw*
102. G. J. Shaw Lefevre
103. H. B. Sheridan
104. W. S. Shirley*
105. J. Simon
106. H. Spensley*
107. J. Stansfeld*
108. F. S. Stevenson
109. S. Storey*
110. Prof. J. Stuart*
111. Sir J. Swinburne
112. P. Vanderbyl
113. H. Wardle
114. T. Watson*
115. T. Wayman
116. J. Westlake
117. J. C. Williams*
118. J. Powell Williams
119. H. J. Wilson*
120. J. Wilson*
121. J. Woodhead
122. C. Wright

Scottish
123. W. B. Barbour*
124. J. W. Barclay*
125. G. Beith*
126. J. C. Bolton
127. J. Boyd-Kinnear*

128. J. Bryce*
129. T. R. Buchanan
130. C. Cameron*
131. J. M. Cameron*
132. Sir G. Campbell*
133. H. Campbell-Bannerman*
134. Dr. G. B. Clarke
135. A. C. Corbett
136. P. Esslemont*
137. R. B. Haldane
138. W. A. Hunter*
139. W. Jacks*
140. J. McCulloch*
141. Dr. R. McDonald*
142. D. H. Macfarlane*
143. S. Mason
144. E. R. Russell*
145. A. Craig Sellar
146. G. O. Trevelyan*†
147. H. Watt
148. J. S. Will

Welsh
149. W. Abrahams*
150. R. Davies
151. L. L. Dillwyn*
152. G. O. Morgan*
153. J. L. Morgan
154. W. R. H. Powell
155. T. P. Price*
156. S. Rendel*
157. H. Richard*
158. J. Roberts*
159. J. Bryn Roberts*
160. S. Smith
161. A. Spicer
162. Alfred Thomas
163. C. M. Warmington
164. A. J. Williams*
165. F. A. Yeo*

The following M.P.'s possibly were Radical, but the evidence is ambiguous:

1. M. H. Beaufroy
2. H. F. Beaumont
3. R. B. Bruce
4. D. Crawford
5. E. Crossley
6. W. Davies
7. J. Ellis
8. Sir C. Forster
9. C. H. James
10. J. E. Johnson-Ferguson
11. C. Fraser Macintosh
12. G. A. Pilkington
13. J. Ramsey
14. W. Rathbone
15. R. Strong
16. C. Seely
17. E. Wason
18. J. D. Weston
19. I. Wilson
20. A. B. Winterbotham

Table 6. Occupations of Radical M.P.'s, 1886

OCCUPATIONS	NUMBER
Commerce and industry	75
Law	31
Professions	5
Writing and journalism	13
Teaching	7
Civil service	2
Workers	11
Armed forces	2
Land	8
Others	4
Unknown	7
Total	165

Table 7. Social and Civic Achievements of Radical M.P.'s, 1886

TYPE OF ACHIEVEMENT	NUMBER
Oxford and Cambridge graduates	40
Other university graduates	31
Public school only	2
Large landowners	25
Magistrates and D.L.'s	56
Aldermen, mayors	29
Chamber of Commerce officers	7
Whigs (members of Whig families)	2
Patrons of livings	3

Table 8. Religion of Radical M.P.'s, 1886

DENOMINATION	NUMBER
Church of England	14
Church of Scotland	4
Baptist	10
Congregationalist	17
Methodist	17
Primitive Methodist	5
Quaker	7
Unitarian	19
Scottish Dissenting Presbyterian (Free or United Church)	5
Presbyterian (undetermined type)	2
Nonconformist (undetermined type)	22
Roman Catholic	2
Jew	4
No religion	7
Not known	30
Total	165

Table 9. Types of Constituencies Represented by Radical M.P.'s, 1886

TYPE OF CONSTITUENCY	NUMBER HELD BY RADICALS
Small borough (0–5,500 electors)	4
Provincial towns (5,501–9,000 electors)	11
Large cities (9,000+ electors, including all borough constituencies that are part of a large city)	71
Rural counties	25
Industrial counties	42
Part rural, part industrial counties	12
Total	165

Table 10. Regional Basis of Constituencies Represented by Radical M.P.'s, 1886

REGION	NUMBER HELD BY RADICALS
England	122
Scotland	26
Wales	17

Table 11. Proportion of Seats Available in Each Region
Held by Radical M.P.'s, 1886

REGION	NUMBER OF SEATS IN REGION	PERCENT HELD BY RADICALS
England	461	26
Scotland	72	33
Wales	34	50

Radical M.P.'s and the Home Rule Division, 1886

Note: All of the following tables include as opposing Home Rule four M.P.'s who abstained on the division; all four are known to have opposed Home Rule. The tables do not include J. Lloyd Morgan and Jesse Collings, who held seats at one time in the parliament but not at the moment the division was taken; Morgan was for Home Rule, and Collings against.

Table 12. Radical M.P.'s and the Home Rule Division by Region

	FOR HOME RULE	AGAINST HOME RULE
Radicals, total	131 (80% of all Radicals)	32 (20% of all Radical M.P.'s)
English	97 (80% of English Radicals)	24 (20% of English Radicals)
Scottish	19 (73% of Scottish Radicals)	7 (27% of Scottish Radicals)
Welsh	15 (94% of Welsh Radicals)	1 (6% of Welsh Radicals)

Table 13. Radical M.P.'s and the Home Rule Division, by Religion

DENOMINATION	FOR HOME RULE	AGAINST HOME RULE
Church of England	12	2
Church of Scotland	3	1
Baptist	8	2
Congregationalist	13	4
Methodist	14	3
Primitive Methodist	5	0
Quaker	4	3
Unitarian	16	3
Scottish Dissenting Presbyterian (Free and United Church)	4	1
Presbyterian (undetermined type)	0	2
Nonconformist (undetermined type)	17	3

Table 13 (Cont.)		FOR HOME RULE	AGAINST HOME RULE
Roman Catholic		2	0
Jew		3	1
No religion		6	1
Not known		24	6
	Totals	131	32

Table 14. Radical M.P.'s and the Home Rule Division, by Occupation

OCCUPATION		FOR HOME RULE	AGAINST HOME RULE
Commerce and industry		57	17
Law		24	7
Professions		5	0
Writers and journalists		11	1
Teaching		7	0
Civil service		1	1
Workers		11	0
Armed services		0	2
Land		7	1
Others		4	0
Unknown		4	3
	Totals	131	32

Table 15. Constituencies of Radical M.P.'s Having Large Irish Populations in 1886

REGION		FOR HOME RULE	AGAINST HOME RULE
England		11	1
Scotland		7	1
Wales		1	0
	Totals	19	2

Radical Unionist M.P.'s, 1886–95

1886–92

1. A. H. Brown
2. John Bright
3. John Albert Bright
4. W. S. Caine
5. J. Chamberlain
6. R. Chamberlain
7. J. Collings
8. L. H. Courtney
9. Sir W. Crossman
10. G. Dixon
11. L. Fry
12. Sir J. Goldsmid
13. Sir H. Havelock-Allan
14. B. Hingley
15. W. Kenrick
16. J. Powell Williams

Scotland
17. J. W. Barclay
18. T. R. Buchanan
19. A. C. Corbett
20. G. O. Trevelyan

1892–95

1. John Albert Bright
2. J. Chamberlain
3. J. Austen Chamberlain
4. J. Collings
5. L. H. Courtney
6. G. Dixon
7. Sir J. Goldsmid
8. B. Hingley
9. J. Powell Williams

Scotland
10. T. H. Cochrane
11. A. Cross

Radicals and Radicalism, 1886–95

METHODS OF SELECTING RADICAL M.P.'S, 1886–95

The method of selecting the Radical M.P.'s for the 1886–95 period was essentially that outlined in Appendix A, with some modification for the 1892–95 parliament. The problems regarding the latter parliament arose from the fact that analysis of voting in the House of Commons by use of the EIDISC program gives much less clear-cut distinctions of Radicals from non-Radical Liberals than in any of the earlier parliaments. This is a reflection of the adoption by practically all of the Liberal candidates in the campaign of 1892 of the Newcastle Programme, which was a Radical platform. In other words, the increasing Radicalization of the party was shown in the voting patterns in the House of Commons from 1892 to 1895. Whereas an analysis of voting in earlier parliaments fairly clearly separates the Radicals from the conservative and moderate Liberals, leaving an unclassifiable group in between, such an analysis in the 1892–95 parliament shows nearly all of the Liberal M.P.'s to be at least generally Radical, and some of them very Radical. For the sake of symmetry in the study as a whole, the distinction between Radicals and non-Radicals has been treated as viable even for this last parliament; only the "very Radical" M.P.'s have been listed. In the final selection, more emphasis was placed on usage of the label "Radical" and on declared platforms of candidates, especially in borderline cases, than with the earlier parliaments.

DIVISIONS USED IN SELECTING RADICAL M.P.'S, 1886–92
(All references to *Hansard*)

1. Resolution to aid the Scottish crofters. 308 (August 31, 1886), 898–989.

2. Protest to annexations in Zululand. 315 (May 19, 1887), 525–39.
3. Bill to give local authorities the power to take land for the construction of chapels. 315 (June 13, 1887), 1846–54.
4. Resolution to abolish the hereditary principle of the House of Lords. 323 (March 9, 1888), 763–816.
5. Motion to establish parish councils. 326 (June 7, 1888), 1441–93.
6. Motion to disestablish the Church of Scotland. 327 (June 22, 1888), 1060–1107.
7. Resolution to begin payment of members. 328 (July 6, 1888), 631–80.
8. Motion to disestablish the Church in Wales. 336 (May 14, 1889), 70–120.
9. Motion to abolish the hereditary principle of the House of Lords. 336 (May 17, 1889), 430–84.
10. Motion to reduce Royal grants. 338 (July 26, 1889), 1436–1534.
11. Motion to abolish the hereditary principle of the House of Lords. 342 (March 21, 1890), 1519–47.
12. Motion to disestablish the Church of Scotland. 344 (May 2, 1890), 62–120.

Of the above, the EIDISC program utilized, in order of their power to discriminate between Radicals and non-Radicals, numbers 10, 7, and 6.

DIVISIONS USED IN SELECTING RADICAL M.P.'s, 1892–95
(All references to *Hansard*, 4th ser.)

1. Motion to begin payment of members. 10 (March 24, 1893), 1086–1125.
2. Motion for leave to introduce a bill for disestablishing the Church of Scotland. 12 (May 9, 1892), 462–63.
3. Motion to abolish the power of the House of Lords. 22 (March 13, 1894), 194–208.
4. Motion to begin payment of members. 31 (March 22, 1895), 1749–88.

The EIDISC program used, in order of discriminating power, numbers 3, 2, and 4.

British Radical M.P.'s, 1886–92

English

1. A. Acland
2. R. A. Allison
3. L. A. Atherley-Jones*
4. J. S. Balfour*
5. W. H. W. Ballantine*
6. J. Barran*
7. T. Blake*
8. T. D. Bolton
9. T. H. Bolton*
10. W. C. Borlase
11. C. Bradlaugh*
12. Jacob Bright*
13. W. L. Bright*
14. H. Broadhurst*
15. J. T. Brunner
16. T. Burt*
17. S. C. Buxton*
18. R. K. Causton*
19. F. A. Channing*
20. H. P. Cobb
21. B. J. S. Coleridge*
22. J. J. Colman*
23. C. A. V. Conybeare*
24. H. Cossham*
25. J. Craig
26. J. Craven
27. W. Crawford*
28. W. R. Cremer*
29. E. Crossley
30. J. E. Ellis*
31. F. H. Evans
32. S. Evershed
33. C. Fenwick*
34. C. Flower
35. Sir W. B. Foster*

36. T. Fry
37. G. P. Fuller
38. L. Gane
39. E. T. Gourley*
40. Sir E. Grey
41. W. C. Gully
42. E. T. Holden*
43. I. Holden
44. G. Howell*
45. A. Illingworth*
46. J. A. Jacoby*
47. W. H. James†
48. J. Joicey*
49. H. Labouchere*
50. G. Lambert
51. H. L. W. Lawson*
52. Sir W. Lawson*
53. R. Leake
54. H. S. Leon
55. A. McArthur
56. W. A. McArthur*
57. M. MacInnes
58. W. S. B. McLaren*
59. M. P. Manfield*
60. W. Mather
61. S. Montagu*
62. O. V. Morgan
63. A. Morley*
64. J. Morley*
65. A. Morton*
66. A. J. Mundella*
67. R. Neville
68. G. Newnes
69. M. Oldroyd
70. J. M. Paulton
71. R. Peacock*

* Denotes those referred to as Radicals in reliable contemporary sources.
† Denotes those from Whig families.

72. B. Pickard*
73. E. H. Pickersgill*
74. J. A. Picton*
75. Sir W. C. Plowden
76. T. B. Potter*
77. B. Priestley
78. T. Robinson
79. T. Roe
80. J. Rowlands*
81. J. Rowntree
82. C. E. Schwann*
83. C. Seale-Hayne
84. T. Shaw*
85. G. J. Shaw Lefevre*
86. W. S. Shirley*
87. P. J. Stanhope*†
88. J. Stansfeld*
89. S. J. Stern*
90. F. S. Stevenson
91. H. Stewart*
92. S. Storey*
93. Professor J. Stuart*
94. W. Summers
95. Sir J. Swinburne
96. H. Wardle
97. T. Watson*
98. T. Wayman
99. C. H. Wilson
100. H. J. Wilson*
101. J. Wilson*
102. J. Woodhead
103. C. Wright

Scotland
104. C. H. Anderson*
105. H. H. Asquith*
106. J. B. Balfour
107. W. B. Balfour*
108. A. Birrell*
109. J. C. Bolton

110. A. L. Brown*
111. J. Bryce*
112. T. R. Buchanan (former Unionist)
113. C. Cameron*
114. J. M. Cameron*
115. Sir G. Campbell
116. H. Campbell-Bannerman*
117. G. B. Clark*
118. D. Crawford
119. W. Dunn
120. P. Esslemont*
121. J. F. B. Firth*
122. R. B. Haldane*
123. W. A. Hunter*
124. J. S. Keay*
125. Sir J. Kinloch*
126. J. Leng*
127. Dr. R. Macdonald*
128. W. McEwan
129. A. D. Provand
130. R. T. Reid*
131. E. R. Russell*
132. A. Sutherland*
133. G. O. Trevelyan*† (former Unionist)
134. R. Wallace
135. H. Watt
136. J. S. Wills
137. S. Williamson
138. J. Wilson* (Lanarkshire)

Wales
139. W. Abraham*
140. W. Davies
141. L. L. Dillwyn*
142. T. E. Ellis*
143. D. Lloyd George*
144. G. O. Morgan*
145. J. L. Morgan

146. W. R. H. Powell*
147. T. P. Price*
148. D. Randell*
149. S. Rendel*
150. H. Richard*
151. J. Roberts*
152. J. B. Roberts*

153. S. Smith
154. Abel Thomas
155. Alfred Thomas
156. D. A. Thomas*
157. C. M. Warmington
158. A. J. Williams
159. F. A. Yeo*

BRITISH RADICAL M.P.'S, 1892–95

England

1. A. Acland*
2. D. Ainsworth
3. W. Allan*
4. W. Allen*
5. R. A. Allison
6. J. Arch*
7. L. A. Atherley-Jones
8. J. Baker
9. W. H. W. Ballantine*
10. J. Barran*
11. R. V. Barrow*
12. G. R. Benson
13. A. Billson
14. T. D. Bolton
15. T. H. Bolton*
16. A. G. Brand
17. Jacob Bright*
18. H. E. Broad*
19. H. Broadhurst*
20. J. T. Brunner
21. J. Burns*
22. T. Burt*
23. S. C. Buxton*
24. W. P. Byles
25. W. S. Caine*
26. R. K. Causton*
27. F. A. Channing*
28. H. P. Cobb*
29. F. M. Coldwells*

30. B. J. S. Coleridge*
31. J. J. Colman*
32. C. A. V. Conybeare*
33. J. Craven
34. W. R. Cremer*
35. W. Crosfield
36. Sir C. Dilke*
37. C. Dodd
38. J. E. Ellis*
39. F. H. Evans
40. R. L. Everett
41. S. Evershed
42. C. Fenwick*
43. H. T. Fenwick
44. C. J. Fleming*
45. Sir W. B. Foster*
46. M. Fowler
47. T. Fry
48. L. Gane
49. E. T. Gourley*
50. Sir E. Grey*
51. T. N. A. Grove*
52. W. C. Gully
53. D. C. Guthrie
54. W. Hazell*
55. Sir J. T. Hibbert
56. C. Higgins
57. H. E. Hoare*
58. C. E. B. Hobhouse
59. A. Holden*

60. T. Holden
61. W. H. Holland
62. C. H. Hopwood*
63. G. Howell*
64. C. P. Huntington
65. J. Husband*
66. A. Illingworth*
67. W. J. Ingram
68. J. A. Jacoby*
69. J. Joicey*
70. D. B. Jones*
71. H. E. Kearley
72. Sir J. Kitson*
73. H. Labouchere*
74. G. Lambert
75. B. Langley*
76. H. L. W. Lawson*
77. Sir W. Lawson*
78. R. Leake
79. J. F. Leese*
80. J. Leigh
81. H. S. Leon
82. T. Lough*
83. H. C. F. Luttrell*
84. W. A. McArthur*
85. J. A. M. Macdonald
86. M. MacInnes
87. C. B. B. McLaren*
88. W. S. B. McLaren*
89. J. H. Maden*
90. M. P. Manfield*
91. W. Mather
92. S. Montagu*
93. A. Morley*
94. J. Morley*
95. A. C. Morton*
96. E. J. C. Morton*
97. J. F. Moulton*
98. A. J. Mundella*
99. D. Naoroji*

100. R. Neville
101. T. W. Nussey*
102. C. W. Norton*
103. M. Oldroyd
104. J. M. Paulton
105. J. A. Pease
106. R. W. Perks*
107. B. Pickard*
108. E. H. Pickersgill*
109. J. A. Picton*
110. T. B. Potter*
111. R. J. Price
112. B. Priestley
113. H. J. Reckitt*
114. J. Richardson
115. T. Robinson
116. T. Roe
117. J. Rowlands*
118. G. W. E. Russell*†
119. W. Saunders*
120. C. E. Schwann*
121. C. Seale-Hayne
122. C. E. Shaw
123. G. J. Shaw Lefevre*
124. W. Smith*
125. T. Snape*
126. P. J. Stanhope*†
127. J. Stansfeld*
128. S. J. Stern*
129. F. S. Stevenson
130. H. Stewart*
131. S. Storey*
132. Professor J. Stuart*
133. J. S. Wallace*
134. T. C. T. Warner
135. T. Wayman
136. Sir J. Whitehead*
137. T. P. Whittaker
138. J. C. Williams*
139. H. J. Wilson

140. J. Wilson* (Durham)
141. C. Wright

Scotland
142. H. H. Asquith*
143. J. B. Balfour
144. G. Beith*
145. W. Birkmyre
146. A. Birrell*
147. J. Bryce*
148. T. R. Buchanan
149. C. Cameron*
150. H. Campbell-Bannerman*
151. Sir J. M. Carmichael
152. Dr. G. B. Clark*
153. D. Crawford
154. J. W. Crombie
155. J. H. Dalziel
156. W. Dunn
157. R. B. Haldane*
158. W. A. Hunter*
159. W. Jacks* (former Unionist)
160. J. S. Keay*
161. Sir J. Kinloch*
162. J. Leng*
163. W. McEwan
164. D. H. Macfarlane*
165. Dr. D. Macgregor*
166. J. Macleod*
167. H. Paul
168. A. D. Provand
169. R. T. Reid*
170. Sir J. Rigby*
171. T. Shaw*
172. H. Smith*
173. A. Sutherland*

174. Sir G. O. Trevelyan*†
175. R. Wallace
176. E. Wason
177. Sir W. Wedderburn*
178. J. G. Weir*
179. J. S. Will
180. S. Williamson
181. J. Wilson (Lanarkshire)

Wales
182. W. Abraham*
183. C. F. Allen
184. R. J. D. Burnie
185. W. R. Davies*
186. F. Edwards*
187. T. E. Ellis
188. S. T. Evans
189. A. C. Humphrey-Owen*
190. E. R. Jones*
191. H. J. Lewis
192. D. Lloyd George*
193. G. O. Morgan*
194. J. L. Morgan
195. T. P. Price*
196. D. Randell*
197. S. Rendel*
198. J. B. Roberts*
199. J. H. Roberts*
200. S. Smith
201. A. Spicer
202. Abel Thomas
203. Alfred Thomas
204. D. A. Thomas*
205. C. M. Warmington
206. A. J. Williams*
207. W. Williams*

(This list does not include two Labour M.P.'s who often were called Radicals, but actually stood to their left: J. Havelock Wilson and Sam Woods. Nor does it include B. Hingley, a Radical Unionist who finally supported the Home Rule bill of 1893.)

The following M.P.'s possibly were Radical, but the evidence is ambiguous:

1886–92

1. W. Davies	5. W. Bowen Rowlands
2. James Ellis	6. Sir J. D. Weston
3. W. P. Morgan	7. I. Wilson
4. W. Rathbone	8. A. B. Winterbotham

1892–95

1. A. Asher	7. L. Lyall
2. J. Austin	8. W. P. Morgan
3. T. Bayley	9. Sir C. M. Palmer
4. M. H. Beaufroy	10. W. Rathbone
5. J. Bennett	11. E. Wason
6. C. Furness	12. Sir J. D. Weston

Table 16. Average Number of Radical M.P.'s, 1874–95

	1874–80	1880–85	1886	1886–92	1892–95
Average number of Radical M.P.'s	80	120	160	145	200
Percent increase over previous parliament	—	+50	+33	−9	+38

Table 17. Occupations of Radical M.P.'s, 1886–95

OCCUPATION	1886–92	1892–95
Commerce and industry	71	89
Law	35	53
Professions	4	4
Writing and journalism	13	19
Teaching	5	7
Civil service	3	3
Workingmen	10	11
Armed forces	0	1
Land	9	6
Others	2	3
Unknown	7	11
Totals	159	207

Table 18. Religion of Radical M.P.'s, 1886–95

DENOMINATION	1886–92	1892–95
Church of England	19	20
Church of Scotland	4	3
Baptist	7	10
Congregationalist	18	24
Methodist	13	24
Primitive Methodist	3	3
Quaker	7	5
Unitarian	16	15
Scottish Dissenting Presbyterian	3	2
Presbyterian (undetermined type)	3	5
Nonconformist (undetermined type)	25	29
Roman Catholic	0	1
Jew	3	3
No religion	6	6
Not known	32	57
Totals	159	207

Table 19. Social and Civic Achievements of Radical M.P.'s, 1886–95

TYPE OF ACHIEVEMENT	1886–92	1892–95
Oxford and Cambridge graduates	42	63
Other university graduates	25	37
Public school only	5	8
Large landowners	13	14
Magistrates and D.L.'s	50	58
Aldermen, mayors	29	43
Chamber of Commerce officers	11	12
Members of Whig families	3	3
Patrons of livings	2	0

Table 20. Regional Basis of Constituencies
Represented by Radical M.P.'s, 1886–95

REGION	1886	1886–92	1892–95
England	122	103	141
Scotland	26	35	40
Wales	17	21	26
Totals	165	159	207

Table 21. *Types of Constituencies Represented by Radical M.P.'s, 1886–95*

TYPE OF CONSTITUENCY	1886–92	1892–95
Small borough (0–5,500 electors)	9	14
Provincial towns (5,501–9,000 electors)	7	14
Large cities (9,000+ electors, including all borough constituencies that are part of a large city)	62	67
Rural counties	25	47
Industrial counties	41	49
Part rural, part industrial counties	15	16
Totals	159	207

Bibliography

I. Manuscripts

John Bright Papers, British Museum.

Henry Broadhurst Papers, British Library of Political and Economic Science.

John Burns Papers, British Museum.

Henry Campbell-Bannerman Papers, British Museum.

Joseph Chamberlain Papers, University of Birmingham.

James Bryce Papers, Bodleian Library, Oxford University.

Leonard Courtney Collection, British Library of Political and Economic Science.

Sir Charles Dilke Papers, British Museum (includes Dilke's memoir and diaries).

J. L. Garvin Papers, University of Texas (useful for letters from Joseph Chamberlain to W. T. Stead).

Viscount [H. J.] Gladstone Papers, British Museum.

W. E. Gladstone Papers, British Museum.

R. B. Haldane Papers, National Library of Scotland.

Sir Edward Hamilton Papers, British Museum (includes the Hamilton diaries).

Frederic Harrison Papers, British Library of Political and Economic Science.

George Howell Collection, Bishopsgate Institute, London.

A. J. Mundella Papers, Sheffield University Library (includes the Mundella-Leader letters).

Earl of Rosebery's Papers, National Library of Scotland.

H. J. Wilson Papers, Sheffield Central Library.

H. J. Wilson Papers, Sheffield University Library.

II. Newspapers

The Baptist
Bee-Hive (London, 1874–78)
Birmingham Daily Post
The Congregationalist (*The Congregationalist Review* in 1887–88)
Daily News (London)
The Democrat
The Echo
Freeman's Journal
The Inquirer (Unitarian)
Labour Leader (1895)
Liberal Home Ruler
Manchester Guardian
Methodist Times
The Nonconformist (after 1879, *The Nonconformist and Independent*)
Pall Mall Gazette
The Radical
Reynolds's Newspaper
The Star (London)
The Times
United Ireland

III. Magazines and Reviews

British Quarterly Review
Contemporary Review
Edinburgh Review
Fortnightly Review
The Liberal Magazine

Macmillans
Nineteenth Century
The Speaker
Truth
Quarterly Review

IV. Contemporary Pamphlets, Books, etc.

Arthur, William. *Shall the Loyal Be Deserted and the Disloyal Set over Them? An Appeal to Liberals and Nonconformists.* London: Bemrose, 1886.

Beesley, Edward Spencer. *Home Rule.* London: Reeves & Turner, 1886.

———. *Mind Your Own Business. Some Plain Words to the Gladstonians about Mr. Parnell.* London: Reeves & Turner, 1890.

———. *Socialists against the Grain: The Price of Holding Ireland.* London: Reeves & Turner, 1887.

Bradlaugh, Charles. *The Irish Question: What It Has Been, What It Is, and How to Deal with It.* London: Austin, 1868.

Bryce, James. *England and Ireland: An Introductory Statement.* London: The Committee on Irish Affairs, 1884.

————, ed. *Handbook of Home Rule.* 2nd ed. London: Kegan Paul, Trench, 1887.

————, ed. *Two Centuries of Irish History, 1691–1870.* London: Kegan Paul, Trench, 1888.

Buxton, Sydney. *The Irish Government Bill: What It Is and the Arguments for It.* London: The National Press Agency, n.d.

Cassius. *A Letter to the Right Hon. A. J. Balfour, M.P., Dictator, Evictor-General, and Champion Coercionist of Ireland.* London: The Liberal and Radical Publishing Association, n.d.

Chamberlain, Joseph, ed. *The Radical Programme.* London: Chapman and Hall, 1885.

Craigen, Jesse. *Report on a Visit to Ireland in the Summer of 1881.* Dublin: R. D. Webb, 1882.

Crompton, Henry. *The Irish State Trial.* London: Bennett Brothers, 1881.

Dicey, A. V. *England's Case against Home Rule.* London: John Murray, 1886.

Evans, Frederick W. *A Workman's Views of the Irish Question.* London: The National Press Agency, n.d. (probably 1887).

George, Henry. *The Irish Land Question. What It Involves, and How Alone It Can Be Settled. An Appeal to the Land Leagues.* New York: D. Appleton, 1881.

Harrison, Frederic. *Mr. Gladstone!—Or Anarchy!* London: The National Press Agency, n.d. (probably 1886).

Holyoake, George Jacob. *The Opportunity of Ireland.* London: The National Liberal Printing and Publishing Association, 1886.

Home Rule Union. *The Lecture Scheme of the Home Rule Union.* London: Home Rule Union, n.d. (probably 1888).

————. *Report of the Deputation to Ireland, 1887.* London: Home Rule Union, 1887.

————. *Report of the Home Rule Union, 1886.* London: Home Rule Union, 1887.

Irish Loyal and Patriotic Union. *The Latest Invasion of Ireland.* London: The Irish Loyal and Patriotic Union, 1888.

Leake, Robert, ed. *The Conquest of Ireland.* Manchester: A. Ireland, 1886.

Massingham, H. W. *The Gweedore Hunt: A Story of English Justice in Ireland*. London: T. Fisher Unwin, 1889.

Mill, John Stuart. *England and Ireland*. London: Longmans, Green, Reader, and Dyer, 1868.

Potter, George. *Home Rule: The Truth about Ireland*. London: George Potter, n.d.

Reid, Andrew, ed. *The New Liberal Programme*. London: Swan, Sonnenschein, Lowrey, 1886.

Rogers, J. Guinness. *The Ulster Problem. Addressed to Nonconformists and Liberals in Reply to Rev. Mr. Arthur*. London: James Clarke, 1886.

Shaw Lefevre, G. *Combination and Coercion*. London: Kegan Paul, Trench, Trübner, 1890.

―――. *English and Irish Land Questions*. 2nd ed. London: Cassell, Petter, Galpin, 1881.

―――. *Incidents of Coercion: A Journal of Visits to Ireland in 1882 and 1888*. 3rd ed. London: Kegan Paul, Trench, 1889.

Watson, Spence. *England's Dealing with Ireland*. London: National Liberal Federation, 1887.

Working Men's Club & Institute Union. *Twenty-fifth Annual Report, 1886–87*. London: H. Vickers, n.d.

V. MEMOIRS, AUTOBIOGRAPHIES, LETTERS, ETC.

Arch, Joseph. *Joseph Arch: The Story of His Life, Told by Himself*. Ed. with a preface by the Countess of Warwick. London: Hutchinson, 1895.

Broadhurst, Henry. *Henry Broadhurst, M.P. The Story of His Life from a Stonemason's Bench to the Treasury Bench, Told by Himself*. London: Hutchinson, 1901.

Chamberlain, Joseph. *A Political Memoir, 1880–92*. Ed. C. H. D. Howard. London: Batchworth Press, 1953.

Channing, Francis A. *Memoirs of Midland Politics, 1885–1910*. London: Constable, 1918.

Evans, Howard. *Radical Fights of Forty Years*. London: Daily News and Reader, n.d.

Gladstone, Viscount [H. J.]. *After Thirty Years*. London: Macmillan, 1928.

Haldane, Richard Burdon. *An Autobiography*. London: Hodder and Stoughton, 1929.

Healy, T. M. *Letters and Leaders of My Day*. 2 vols. New York: Frederick M. Stokes, 1929.

Lucy, Henry W. *A Diary of the Home Rule Parliament, 1892–95*. London: Cassell, 1896.

———. *A Diary of the Salisbury Parliaments, 1886–92*. London: Cassell, 1892.

Morley, John. *Recollections*. 2 vols. New York: Macmillan, 1917.

O'Brien, William. *Evening Memories*. London: Maunsel, 1920.

O'Connor, T. P. *Recollections*. London: Macmillan, 1905.

———. *Memoirs of an Old Parliamentarian*. 2 vols. London: Ernest Benn, 1929.

Oxford and Asquith, Earl of. *Memories and Reflections, 1852–1927*. 2 vols. Boston: Little, Brown, 1928.

Ramm, Agatha. *The Political Correspondence of Mr. Gladstone and Lord Granville, 1876–86*. 2 vols. Oxford: The Clarendon Press, 1962.

Rogers, J. Guinness. *An Autobiography*. London: James Clarke, 1903.

Rosebery, Fifth Earl of. "Mr. Gladstone's Last Cabinet." *History Today* (January 1952), 1–17.

Soutter, Francis William. *Recollections of a Labour Pioneer*. London: T. Fisher Unwin, 1923.

West, Algernon. *Private Diaries of the Rt. Hon. Sir Algernon West, G.C.B.* Ed. Horace G. Hutchinson. London: John Murray, 1922.

VI. OFFICIAL GOVERNMENT AND PARTY PUBLICATIONS

Hansard, *Parliamentary Debates*.

Report of the Select Committee on the Irish Land Act (1870). Sessional Papers, 1878, no. 249, vol. 15, pp. 1–424.

Report of the Evicted Tenants Commission (1893). Sessional Papers, 1893–94, C. 6935, vol. 31, pp. 13–806.

Return by Provinces of Agrarian Offenses throughout Ireland Reported to the Inspector-General of the Royal Irish Constabulary, between 1 January 1892 and 31 December 1892. Sessional Papers, 1893–94, C. 7014, vol. 74, pt. 2, pp. 415–26.

Return by Provinces of Agrarian Offenses throughout Ireland Reported to the Inspector-General of the Royal Irish Constabulary, between 1 January 1893 and 31 December 1893. Sessional Papers, 1894, C. 7332, vol. 72, pp. 43–54.

Return by Provinces of Agrarian Offenses throughout Ireland Reported to the Inspector-General of the Royal Irish Constabulary, between 1

January 1894 and 31 December 1894. Sessional Papers, 1895, C. 7689, vol. 82, pp. 101–12.

Return of the Number of Agrarian Outrages Which Were Reported to the Inspector General of the Royal Irish Constabulary. Quarter Ending 31 March 1895, Sessional Papers, 1895, C. 7716, vol. 82, pp. 121–23. Quarter Ending 30 June 1895, Sessional Papers, 1895, C. 7849, vol. 82, pp. 125–27.

Liberal Party. *The Liberal and Radical Year Book and Statesman's Encyclopedia.* London, 1887–95.

Liberal Publication Department. *Pamphlets and Leaflets, 1887–1895.* London, 1887–95.

National Liberal Federation. *Proceedings of the Annual Conferences, 1877–1895.* London and Birmingham, 1877–95.

VII. BIOGRAPHICAL DICTIONARIES AND ALMANACS

Annual Register, 1874–95.

Whitaker's Almanack, 1874–95.

Bateman, John. *The Great Landowners of Great Britain and Ireland.* London: Harrison, 1878, 1883.

Boase, Frederic. *Modern English Biography.* New York: Barnes & Noble, 1965.

Burke's Landed Gentry.

Dictionary of National Biography.

Dod's Parliamentary Companion, 1874–95.

Foster, Joseph. *Members of Parliament, Scotland.* London: Hazell, Watson, and Viney, 1881.

———. *Men at the Bar.* London: Hazell, Watson, and Viney, 1885.

Kelley's Handbook of the Upper Ten Thousand, 1874–95.

Men of the Times.

The Parliamentary Directory of the Professional, Commercial, and Mercantile Members of the House of Commons. London: W. Kent, 1874.

Who Was Who.

VIII. SECONDARY SOURCES: RADICALS AND IRELAND TO 1874, A SELECT LIST

Bamford, Samuel. *Passages in the Life of a Radical.* 2 vols. London: Simpkin, Marshall, 1859.

Beer, Samuel H. *British Politics in the Collectivist Age.* New York: Alfred A. Knopf, 1965.

Black, R. D. Collison. *Economic Thought and the Irish Question, 1817–70*. Cambridge: Cambridge University Press, 1960.

Bowring, John, ed. *The Works of Jeremy Bentham*. 11 vols. London: Simpkin, Marshall, 1843.

Briggs, Asa. *The Age of Improvement, 1783–1867*. New York: David McKay, 1959.

Bulmer-Thomas, Ivor. *The Growth of the British Party System*. 2 vols. London: John Baker, 1965.

Christie, Ian. *Wilkes, Wyvill, and Reform: The Parliamentary Reform Movement in British Politics, 1760–85*. London: Macmillan, 1963.

Clark, Henry W. *History of English Nonconformity*. 2 vols. London: Chapman and Hall, 1913.

Clarke, Martin L. *George Grote: A Biography*. London: London University Press, 1962.

Cole, G. D. H., and Postgate, Raymond. *The British Common People, 1746–1946*. New York: Barnes & Noble, 1961.

———. *British Working Class Politics, 1832–1914*. London: George Routledge, 1941.

———. *The Life of William Cobbett*. London: Home & Van Thal, 1947.

Cowherd, Raymond G. *The Politics of English Dissent*. New York: New York University Press, 1956.

Curtis, Louis P., Jr. *Anglo-Saxons and Celts*. Bridgeport, Conn.: Conference on British Studies, 1968.

Davidson, John Morrison. *Eminent Radicals in Parliament*. London: E. J. Francis, 1879.

Derry, John W. *The Radical Tradition, Tom Paine to Lloyd George*. London: Macmillan, 1967.

Finlayson, Geoffrey. *Decade of Reform: England in the Eighteen Thirties*. New York: W. W. Norton, 1970.

Gash, Norman. *Reaction and Reconstruction in English Politics, 1832–52*. Oxford: Oxford University Press, 1965.

Gillespie, Frances E. *Labour and Politics in England, 1850–67*. Durham: Duke University Press, 1927.

Halevy, Elie. *A History of the English People in the Nineteenth Century*. 6 vols. New York: Barnes & Noble, 1961.

———. *The Growth of Philosophic Radicalism*. Boston: Beacon Press, 1955.

Hamburger, Joseph. *Intellectuals in Politics: John Stuart Mill and the Philosophic Radicals*. New Haven: Yale University Press, 1965.

————. *James Mill and the Art of Revolution.* New Haven: Yale University Press, 1963.

Harris, William. *The History of the Radical Party in Parliament.* London: Kegan Paul, Trench, 1885.

Harrison, Wilfrid. *Conflict and Compromise: History of British Political Thought, 1593–1900.* London: Collier-Macmillan, 1965.

Hinton, Richard J. *English Radical Leaders.* New York: G. P. Putnam's Sons, 1875.

Hobsbawm, E. J. *Labouring Men: Studies in the History of Labour.* London: Weidenfeld and Nicolson, 1964.

Hovell, Mark. *The Chartist Movement.* London: Longmans, Green, 1918.

Kent, C. B. Roylance. *The English Radicals: An Historical Sketch.* London: Longmans, Green, 1899.

Lecky, W. E. H. *A History of England in the Eighteenth Century.* 4 vols. New York: Appleton, 1883.

Lincoln, Anthony. *Some Political and Social Ideas of English Dissent.* Cambridge: Cambridge University Press, 1938.

Maccoby, Simon. *English Radicalism, 1762–85.* London: Allen & Unwin, 1955.

————. *English Radicalism, 1786–1832.* London: Allen & Unwin, 1955.

————. *English Radicalism, 1832–52.* London: Allen & Unwin, 1935.

————. *English Radicalism, 1852–86.* London: Allen & Unwin, 1938.

————. *English Radicalism, 1886–1914.* London: Allen & Unwin, 1953.

————. *English Radicalism, the End?* London: Allen & Unwin, 1961.

————, ed. *The English Radical Tradition, 1763–1914.* London: Nicholas Raye, 1952.

McCord, Norman. *The Anti-Corn Law League.* London: Allen & Unwin, 1958.

Machin, G. I. T. *The Catholic Question in English Politics, 1820 to 1830.* Oxford: The Clarendon Press, 1964.

MacIntyre, Angus. *The Liberator.* London: Hamish Hamilton, 1965.

Mack, Mary P. *Jeremy Bentham: An Odyssey of Ideas.* New York: Columbia University Press, 1963.

Maitland, Frederick William. *The Life and Times of Leslie Stephen.* London: Duckworth, 1906.

Marshall, Dorothy. *Eighteenth Century England.* New York: David McKay, 1962.

Nowlan, Kevin. *The Politics of Repeal, 1841–50.* London: Routledge & Kegan Paul, 1965.

Osborne, John W. *William Cobbett: His Thought and His Times.* New Brunswick, N.J.: Rutgers University Press, 1966.

Packe, Michael St. John. *The Life of John Stuart Mill.* London: Secker and Warburg, 1954.

Patterson, M. W. *Sir Francis Burdett and His Times (1770–1844).* 2 vols. London: Macmillan, 1931.

Perkin, Harold. *The Origins of Modern English Society, 1780–1880.* Toronto: University of Toronto Press, 1969.

Rudé, George. *Wilkes and Liberty.* Oxford: The Clarendon Press, 1962.

Ruggiero, Guido de. *The History of European Liberalism.* Trans. R. G. Collingwood. Boston: Beacon Press, 1959.

Skeats, Herbert S., and Miall, Charles S. *History of the Free Churches of England, 1688–1891.* London: James Clarke, 1891.

Thompson, E. P. *Making of the English Working Class.* New York: Vintage Books, 1964.

Vincent, John. *The Formation of the Liberal Party, 1857–68.* London: Constable, 1966.

Wallas, Graham. *The Life of Francis Place, 1771–1854.* London: Longmans, Green, 1898.

Walpole, Spencer. *A History of England.* 4 vols. 2nd ed. London: Longmans, Green, 1879.

Webb, R. K. *Harriet Martineau: A Radical Victorian.* New York: Columbia University Press, 1960.

White, R. J. *Waterloo to Peterloo.* London: William Heineman, 1957.

Wiener, Joel H. *The War of the Unstamped: The Movement to Repeal the British Newspaper Tax, 1830–1836.* Ithaca: Cornell University Press, 1969.

IX. Radicals and Ireland, 1874–95

Abels, Jules. *The Parnell Tragedy.* London: Bodley Head, 1966.

Adorno, T. W., *et al. The Authoritarian Personality.* New York: Harper, 1950.

Armytage, W. H. G. *A. J. Mundella, 1825–97: The Liberal Background to the Labour Movement.* London: Ernest Benn, 1951.

Arnstein, Walter L. *The Bradlaugh Case: A Study in Late Victorian Opinion and Politics.* Oxford: The Clarendon Press, 1965.

———. "Victorian Prejudice Reexamined." *Victorian Studies* 12 (June 1969), 452–57.

Ausubel, Herman. *John Bright: Victorian Reformer.* New York: John Wiley, 1966.

Bassett, Arthur Tilney. *The Life of the Rt. Hon. John Edward Ellis, M.P.* London: Macmillan, 1914.

Beales, A. C. F. *The History of Peace.* New York: Dial Press, 1931.

Beckett, J. C. *The Making of Modern Ireland, 1603–1923.* London: Faber and Faber, 1966.

Berrington, Hugh. "Partisanship and Dissidence in the Nineteenth Century House of Commons." *Parliamentary Affairs* 21 (Autumn 1968), 338–74.

Bonner, Hypatia Bradlaugh, and Robertson, John M. *Charles Bradlaugh: A Record of His Life and Work.* 2 vols. London: T. Fisher Unwin, 1894.

Booth, Charles. *Life and Labour of the People in London.* Final volume. London: Macmillan, 1903.

Buckley, Kenneth D. *Trade Unionism in Aberdeen, 1878 to 1900.* Edinburgh: Oliver & Boyd, 1955.

Chilston, Viscount. *Chief Whip: The Political Life and Times of Aretas Akers-Douglas, 1st Viscount Chilston.* London: Routledge & Kegan Paul, 1961.

Churchill, Winston. *Lord Randolph Churchill.* New ed. London: Odhams Press, 1952.

Clegg, H. A.; Fox, Alan; and Thompson, J. F. *A History of British Trade Unions since 1889.* Vol. I, *1889–1910.* Oxford: The Clarendon Press, 1964.

Corder, Percy. *The Life of Robert Spence Watson.* London: Headley, 1914.

Corfe, Tom. *The Phoenix Park Murders: Conflict, Compromise and Tragedy in Ireland, 1879–82.* London: Hodder and Stoughton, 1968.

Cornford, James P. "The Transformation of Conservatism in the Late Nineteenth Century." *Victorian Studies* 7 (September 1963), 35–66.

Curtis, L. P., Jr. *Coercion and Conciliation in Ireland, 1880–92: A Study in Conservative Unionism.* Princeton: Princeton University Press, 1963.

Dale, A. W. W. *The Life of R. W. Dale.* London: Hodder and Stoughton, 1898.

Davitt, Michael. *The Fall of Feudalism in Ireland.* New York: Harper, 1904.

Duncan, William. *Life of Joseph Cowen.* London: Walter Scott Publishing, 1904.

Ensor, Robert. *England, 1870–1914.* Oxford: The Clarendon Press, 1936.
————. "Some Political and Economic Interactions in Later Victorian England." *Transactions of the Royal Historical Society*, 4th ser., 31 (London, 1949), 17–28.

Evans, Howard. *Sir Randal Cremer: His Life and Work.* London: T. Fisher Unwin, 1909.

Eversley, Lord. *Gladstone and Ireland: The Irish Policy of Parliament from 1850–1894.* London: Methuen, 1912.

Fisher, H. A. L. *James Bryce (Viscount Bryce of Dechmont, O.M.).* 2 vols. London: Macmillan, 1927.

Fowler, W. S. *A Study in Radicalism and Dissent: The Life and Times of Henry Joseph Wilson, 1833–1914.* London: Epworth Press, 1961.

Fraser, Peter. *Joseph Chamberlain: Radicalism and Empire, 1868–1914.* London: Cassell, 1966.

Fyfe, Henry Hamilton. *T. P. O'Connor.* London: George Allen & Unwin, 1934.

Gardiner, A. G. *The Life of Sir William Harcourt.* 2 vols. London: Constable, 1923.

Garvin, J. L., and Amery, Julian. *The Life of Joseph Chamberlain.* 6 vols. London: Macmillan, 1932–69.

Glaser, John F. "English Nonconformity and the Decline of Liberalism." *American Historical Review* 63 (January 1958), 353–63.
————. "Parnell's Fall and the Non-conformist Conscience." *Irish Historical Studies* 2 (September 1960), 119–38.

Gooch, G. P. *Life of Lord Courtney.* London: Macmillan, 1920.

Guttsman, William L. *The British Political Elite.* New York: MacGibbon & Kee, 1965.

Gwynn, Stephen, and Tuckwell, Gertrude M. *The Life of the Rt. Hon. Sir Charles Dilke.* 2 vols. London: John Murray, 1918.

Hamer, D. A. *John Morley: Liberal Intellectual in Politics.* Oxford: Oxford University Press, 1968.
————. "The Irish Question and Liberal Politics, 1886–94." *Historical Journal* 12 (1969), 511–32.
————. *Liberal Politics in the Age of Gladstone and Rosebery.* Oxford: Oxford University Press, 1972.

Hammond, J. L. *C. P. Scott of the Manchester Guardian.* London: G. Bell, 1934.
————. *Gladstone and the Irish Nation.* London: Longmans, Green, 1938.

————, and Hammond, Barbara. *James Stansfeld: A Victorian Champion of Sex Equality.* London: Longmans, Green, 1932.

Hanham, H. J. *Elections and Party Management: Politics in the Time of Disraeli and Gladstone.* London: Longmans, Green, 1959.

————. *Scottish Nationalism.* Cambridge, Mass.: Harvard University Press, 1969.

Harris, S. Hutchinson. *Auberon Herbert: Crusader for Liberty.* London: Williams & Norgate, 1943.

Harrison, Brian. *Drink and the Victorians.* London: Faber and Faber, 1971.

Harrison, Henry. *Parnell, Joseph Chamberlain and Mr. Garvin.* London: Robert Hale, 1938.

————. *Parnell, Joseph Chamberlain and "The Times."* Belfast: Irish News, 1953.

Harrison, Royden. *Before the Socialists: Studies in Labour and Politics, 1861–81.* London: Routledge & Kegan Paul, 1965.

Hawkins, Richard. "Gladstone, Forster, and the Release of Parnell, 1882–88." *Irish Historical Studies* 16 (September 1969), 417–45.

Herrick, Francis H. "The Origins of the National Liberal Federation." *Journal of Modern History* 17 (June 1945), 116–29.

Heyck, T. W. "British Radicals and Radicalism, 1874–95: A Social Analysis." In *Modern European Social History*, ed. R. J. Bezucha. Lexington, Mass.: D. C. Heath, 1972.

————, and Klecka, William. "British Radical M.P.'s, 1874–95: New Evidence from Discriminant Analysis." *Journal of Interdisciplinary History* 4 (Autumn 1973), 161–84.

Hirst, F. W. *Early Life and Letters of John Morley.* 2 vols. London: Macmillan, 1927.

Hodder, Edwin. *The Life of Samuel Morley.* 2nd ed. London: Hodder and Stoughton, 1887.

Holland, Bernard. *The Life of Spencer Compton Eighth Duke of Devonshire.* 2 vols. London: Longmans, Green, 1911.

Howard, C. H. D. "Documents Relating to the Irish 'Central Board' Scheme, 1884–85." *Irish Historical Studies* 8 (March 1953), 237–63.

————. "Joseph Chamberlain and the 'Unauthorized Programme.'" *English Historical Review* 65 (October 1950), 477–91.

————. "Joseph Chamberlain, Parnell and the Irish 'Central Board' Scheme, 1884–85." *Irish Historical Studies* 8 (September 1953), 324–61.

————. "Joseph Chamberlain, W. H. O'Shea, and Parnell, 1884, 1891–92." *Irish Historical Studies* 13 (March 1962), 33–37.

————. "The Parnell Manifesto of 21 November, 1885, and the Schools Question." *English Historical Review* 62 (January 1947), 42–51.

Howarth, Janet. "The Liberal Revival in Northamptonshire, 1880–95: A Case Study in Late-Nineteenth Century Elections." *Historical Journal* 12 (1969), 78–118.

Humphrey, A. W. *Robert Applegarth: Trade Unionist, Educationist, Reformer*. Manchester: National Labour Press, 1913.

Hurst, Michael. *Joseph Chamberlain and Liberal Reunion: The Round Table Conference of 1887*. Toronto: University of Toronto Press, 1967.

————. *Joseph Chamberlain and West Midland Politics, 1886–95*. Stratford-on-Avon: Dugdale Society, 1962.

————. *Parnell and Irish Nationalism*. London: Routledge & Kegan Paul, 1968.

James, Robert Rhodes. *Rosebery: A Biography of Archibald Philip, Fifth Earl of Rosebery*. New York: Macmillan, 1963.

Jenkins, Roy. *Asquith*. London: Collins, 1964.

————. *Victorian Scandal: A Biography of the Right Honourable Gentleman Sir Charles Dilke*. Rev. ed. New York: Chilmark Press, 1965.

Jennings, Ivor. *Party Politics*. Volume II: *The Growth of Parties*. Cambridge: The University Press, 1961.

Jones, Evan Rowland. *The Life and Speeches of Joseph Cowen, M.P.* London: Sampson Law, Marston, Searle and Rivington, 1885.

Kellas, James G. "The Liberal Party and the Scottish Church Disestablishment Crisis." *English Historical Review* 79 (January 1964), 31–46.

————. "The Liberal Party in Scotland 1876–95." *The Scottish Historical Review* 64 (April 1965), 1–16.

Kinnear, Michael. *The British Voter: An Atlas and Survey since 1885*. London: Batsford, 1968.

Koss, Stephen G. "Morley in the Middle." *English Historical Review* 82 (July 1967), 553–61.

————. *Sir John Brunner: Radical Plutocrat, 1842–1919*. Cambridge: Cambridge University Press, 1970.

Larkin, Emmet. "The Roman Catholic Hierarchy and the Fall of Parnell." *Victorian Studies* 4 (June 1961), 315–36.

Leslie, Shane. *Henry Edward Manning: His Life and Labours*. London: Macmillan, 1921.

Leventhal, F. M. *Respectable Radical: George Howell and Victorian Working Class Politics*. Cambridge, Mass.: Harvard University Press, 1971.

Lloyd, Trevor. *The General Election of 1880*. London: Oxford University Press, 1968.

Lynd, Helen Merrell. *England in the 1880's: Toward a Social Basis for Freedom*. London: Oxford University Press, 1945.

Lyons, F. S. L. *John Dillon: A Biography*. Chicago: University of Chicago Press, 1968.

———. *The Fall of Parnell, 1890–91*. Toronto: University of Toronto Press, 1960.

———. *The Irish Parliamentary Party, 1890–1910*. London: Faber and Faber, 1951.

McBriar, A. M. *Fabian Socialism and English Politics, 1884–1918*. Cambridge: Cambridge University Press, 1966.

McCaffrey, Lawrence J. *Irish Federalism in the 1870's: A Study in Conservative Nationalism*. Philadelphia: Transactions of the American Philosophical Society, 1962.

———. *The Irish Question, 1800–1922*. Lexington: University of Kentucky Press, 1968.

McCready, H. W. "Home Rule and the Liberal Party, 1880–1901." *Irish Historical Studies* 13 (September 1963), 316–48.

McDowell, R. B. *The Irish Administration, 1801–1914*. Toronto: University of Toronto Press, 1964.

McGill, Barry. "Francis Schnadhorst and Liberal Party Organization." *Journal of Modern History* 34 (March 1962), 19–39.

Mackie, J. B. *The Life and Work of Duncan McLaren*. 2 vols. Edinburgh: Thomas Nelson, 1888.

Magnus, Philip. *Gladstone: A Biography*. New York: E. P. Dutton, 1964.

Mansergh, Nicholas. *Ireland in the Age of Reform and Revolution*. London: George Allen & Unwin, 1940.

Miall, Charles S. *Henry Richard, M.P.* London: Cassell, 1889.

Moody, T. W. "The New Departure in Irish Politics, 1878–79." In *Essays in British and Irish History in Honour of James Eadie Todd*, ed. H. A. Cronne, T. W. Moody, and D. B. Quinn. London: Frederick Muller, 1949.

Morgan, Kenneth O. *Wales in British Politics*. Cardiff: University of Wales Press, 1963.

Morley, John. *The Life of William Ewart Gladstone*. 3 vols. New York: Macmillan, 1903.

Newton, John. *W. S. Caine, M.P.: A Biography*. London: James Nisbet, 1907.

Nieburg, H. L. *Political Violence: The Behavioral Process.* New York: St. Martin's Press, 1969.

O'Brien, Conor Cruise. *Parnell and His Party, 1880–90.* Oxford: The Clarendon Press, 1957.

O'Brien, R. Barry. *The Life of Charles Stewart Parnell.* 2 vols. London: Smith, Elder, 1899.

O'Connor, T. P. *The Parnell Movement.* London: Kegan Paul, Trench, 1886.

O'Donnell, F. Hugh. *A History of the Irish Parliamentary Party.* 2 vols. London: Longmans, Green, 1910.

O'Shea, Katherine. *Charles Stewart Parnell: His Love Story and Political Life.* 2 vols. London: Cassell, 1914.

Ostrogorsky, M. *Democracy and the Organization of Political Parties.* 2 vols. London: Macmillan, 1902.

Palmer, Norman. *The Irish Land League Crisis.* New Haven: Yale University Press, 1940.

Pearson, Hesketh. *Labby (The Life and Character of Henry Labouchere).* London: Harper, 1937.

Pelling, Henry. *A History of British Trade Unionism.* Harmondsworth: Penguin Books, 1963.

———. *The Origins of the Labour Party, 1880–1900.* Oxford: The Clarendon Press, 1965.

———. *Popular Politics and Society in Late Victorian Britain.* New York: St. Martin's Press, 1968.

———. *Social Geography of British Elections, 1885–1910.* New York: St. Martin's Press, 1967.

Pomfret, John E. *The Struggle for Land in Ireland.* Princeton: Princeton University Press, 1930.

Reid, T. Wemyss. *Life of the Right Honourable William Edward Forster.* 2 vols. 4th ed. London: Chapman and Hall, 1888.

Roberts, B. C. *The Trades Union Congress, 1868–1921.* London: George Allen & Unwin, 1958.

Russell, G. W. E., ed. *Sir Wilfrid Lawson: A Memoir.* London: Smith Elder, 1909.

Rylands, L. Gordon. *Correspondence and Speeches of Mr. Peter Rylands, M.P.* 2 vols. London: Simpkin, Marshall, Hamilton, Kent, 1890.

Sanford, Nevitt. "The Approach of the Authoritarian Personality." In *Psychology of Personality: Six Modern Approaches,* ed. J. L. McCary. New York: Grove Press, 1956.

Savage, Donald C. "Scottish Politics, 1885–86." *Scottish Historical Review* 40 (October 1961), 118–35.

Shannon, R. T. *Gladstone and the Bulgarian Agitation, 1876*. London: Thomas Nelson, 1963.

Sommer, Dudley. *Haldane of Cloan: His Life and Times, 1856–1928*. London: George Allen & Unwin, 1960.

Southgate, Donald. *The Passing of the Whigs, 1832–86*. London: Macmillan, 1962.

Spender, J. A. *The Life of the Rt. Hon. Sir Henry Campbell-Bannerman, G.C.B.* 2 vols. London: Hodder and Stoughton, 1923.

————. *Sir Robert Hudson: A Memoir*. London: Cassell, 1930.

Stansky, Peter. *Ambitions and Strategies: The Struggle for Leadership of the Liberal Party in the 1890's*. Oxford: The Clarendon Press, 1964.

Steele, E. D. "Gladstone and Ireland." *Irish Historical Studies* 17 (March 1970), 58–88.

Stephen, Leslie. *Life of Henry Fawcett*. London: Smith, Elder, 1885.

Strauss, Eric. *Irish Nationalism and British Democracy*. London: Methuen, 1951.

Strauss, William L. *Joseph Chamberlain and the Theory of Imperialism*. Washington, D.C.: American Council on Public Affairs, 1942.

Tholfsen, Trygve. "The Transition to Democracy in Victorian England." *International Review of Social History* 6 (1961), 226–48.

Thomas, J. A. *The House of Commons, 1832–1901: A Study of Its Economic and Functional Character*. Cardiff: University of Wales Press Board, 1939.

Thompson, F. M. L. "Land and Politics in England in the Nineteenth Century." *Transactions of the Royal Historical Society*, 5th ser., 15 (London, 1965), 23–44.

Thompson, Paul. "Liberals, Radicals and Labour in London, 1880–1900." *Past and Present* 27 (April 1964), 73–101.

————. *Socialists, Liberals and Labour: The Struggle for London, 1885–1914*. Toronto: University of Toronto Press, 1967.

Thornley, David. *Isaac Butt and Home Rule*. London: MacGibbon & Kee, 1964.

Thorold, Algar. *Labouchere: The Life of Henry Labouchere*. London: Constable, 1913.

Tremlett, George. *The First Century of the Working Men's Club and Institute Union*. London: The Working Men's Club and Institute Union, 1962.

Trevelyan, George Macaulay. *Grey of Falloden*. Boston: Houghton Mifflin, 1937.

————. *The Life of John Bright*. London: Constable, 1913.

————. *Sir George Otto Trevelyan: A Memoir.* London: Longmans, Green, 1932.

Tsuzuki, Chushichi. *H. M. Hyndman and British Socialism.* London: Oxford University Press, 1961.

Watson, Robert Spence. *The National Liberal Federation: From Its Commencement to the General Election of 1906.* London: T. Fisher Unwin, 1907.

Webb, Sidney, and Webb, Beatice. *The History of Trade Unionism.* London: Longmans, Green, 1894.

White, Terence de Vere. *The Road of Excess.* Dublin: Browne and Nolan, 1946.

Index